UND

HU

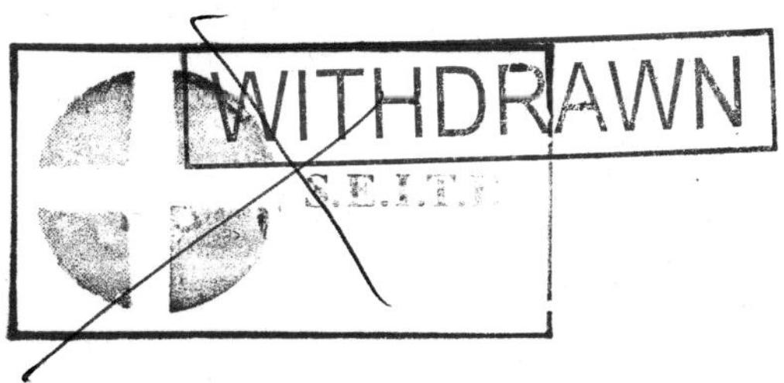

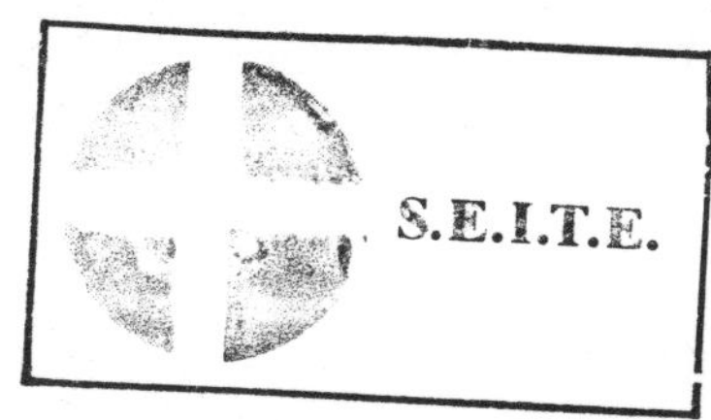

UNDERSTANDING HUMAN RIGHTS

An Interdisciplinary and Interfaith Study

The Proceedings of the International Consultation
held in Dublin 1978

Edited by Alan D. Falconer

Preface by Michael Hurley S.J.

Irish School of Ecumenics
Dublin

ISBN 0 9506842 0 1

Cover design Dermot McGuinne
Origination by Joe Healy Typesetting, Dublin 2
Printed and bound in the Republic of Ireland by
Cahills (Printers), Dublin

CONTENTS

THE CONTRIBUTORS

Garrett Barden: Lecturer in Philosophy, University College Cork.

José Míguez Bonino: Methodist Minister, Professor of Theology in Instituto Superior Evangelico de Estudios Teologicos, Buenos Aires. Currently one of the Presidents of the World Council of Churches.

Declan Costello: Judge of the High Court of Ireland, formerly Attorney General for Ireland.

Gabriel Daly O.S.A.: Lecturer in Theology at the Irish School of Ecumenics and the Milltown Institute.

Alan D. Falconer: James of Kildare and Leighlin Lecturer in Systematic Theology at the Irish School of Ecumenics.

Rosemary Haughton: Theologian and Writer, Scotland.

Michael Hurley S.J.: Director of the Irish School of Ecumenics from its inception in 1970 until 1980.

David Jenkins: Professor of Theology at the University of Leeds, England; formerly in charge of the World Council of Churches' Study on Humanum.

Rashid Ahmad Jullundhri: lately Director of the Islamic Research Institute, Islamabad, Pakistan.

Martti Lindqvist: Lecturer in Christian Social Ethics and Ecumenical Theology at Helsinki University, Finland.

Seán MacBride: Nobel and Lenin Peace Laureate and recipient of the American Medal of Justice; former Minister for Foreign Affairs, Ireland.

Richard A. McCormick S.J.: Rose F. Kennedy Professor of Christian Ethics, the Center for Bioethics, Georgetown University, Washington D.C.

Frederick R. McManus: Vice Provost and Dean of Graduate Studies, The Catholic University of America, Washington D.C.

István Mészáros: Professor of Philosophy, School of European Studies, University of Sussex. A Hungarian by nationality.

Jürgen Moltmann: Professor of Systematic Theology, Evangelisch – Theologisches Seminar, Tübingen University.

Michael O'Boyle: Member of the Legal Secretariat of the European Human Rights Commission, Strasbourg.

PREFACE

Michael Hurley

The papers collected in this volume were prepared for presentation to the plenary sessions of a Consultation organized by the Irish School of Ecumenics and held in Dublin from 30 November to 4 December 1978, in celebration of the 30th anniversary of the UN Declaration of Human Rights.

This Consultation brought together representatives from various countries, disciplines, churches and religions. It was an international, interdisciplinary, interdenominational and interfaith event, the ethos of which cannot be conveyed in these pages. The aim, however, remains the same: to promote study and action on issues of human rights in a world still largely insensitive to the demands of justice.

The Irish School of Ecumenics which commissioned these papers would hold that ecumenics is an interdisciplinary science, including in its scope not only topics of Interchurch and Interfaith Dialogue, but also Religion and Society topics such as Human Rights. If the ecumenical ideal is a unity of believing communities in the service of the world, there is an urgent need for a new emphasis on faith working through justice.

It seems altogether appropriate that the editor of these pages should occupy a post called after the famous nineteenth century Irish Roman Catholic bishop, Dr. James Doyle, who wrote under the initials, JKL, James of Kildare and Leighlin. Dr. Doyle was the author in 1824 of a quite remarkable *Letter on the Union of Churches.* It caused considerable stir at the time. In particular, it startled two exiled Frenchmen teaching at Maynooth and provoked the shocked comment: *'Mon Dieu! Est-ce possible qu'il prêche la Révolution?'.*[1] The reference, it is true, was to the Bishop's political asides, but the *Letter's* central thesis was no less revolutionary. 'If Doyle's proposals had been heeded', a modern ecumenist has written, 'the ecumenical movement would be a hundred years in advance of its actual condition, at least as far as Catholics are concerned'.[2]

More significantly perhaps JKL belonged to that shortlived generation in which 'Irish Catholicism stood out as the most advanced, the most liberal, the most relevant to the times'.[3] It stood out because it succeeded in reconciling Christianity and liberty: it recognized the right of every man to freedom of conscience. JKL claimed this right, not only for Catholics, but also – like Daniel O'Connell, his great contemporary – for Protestants. He held that 'every man is at liberty to choose what religion he pleases, and to follow it in peace'[4] and that 'whoever is baptized . . . if he retain the grace of that first adoption pure and unsullied until death, he enters heaven – no matter to what sect or denomination of Christians while on earth he may have belonged'.[5]

In his concern for the freedom of human beings, JKL went beyond O'Connell by emphasizing 'economic rights'. He defended 'the just, the natural, the indefeasible rights of the poor to the necessaries of life in the land which gave them birth'.[6] He advocated legal provision for the poor and clashed on the point in the 1830s with the Liberator. O'Connell then would only affirm the moral duty of every man to support the needy; he denied the legal right of the poor to relief.[7]

This Catholic liberalism of JKL and O'Connell aroused much interest at the time on the continent of Europe, especially in France, and it had considerable influence on Lacordaire and Montalembert. Unfortunately, it was to be 'scrubbed from the race-memory of the Irish by an ultramontane clergy, a parochial nationalism and a bigoted unionism'.[8] It had to wait until Vatican II to become acceptable generally in Roman Catholic circles.

In addition to the papers printed here, shorter essays on a variety of more specialized topics (such as 'The Right to Work', 'Human Rights within the Churches' etc.) were also commissioned by the Irish School of Ecumenics for discussion in workshop sessions during the 1978 Consultation. These, however, are not included in the present volume. Omitted also for reasons of space are the opening address given by the exiled Bishop of Umtali, Most Rev. Donal Lamont, the closing address given by the General Secretary of the World Council of Churches, Rev. Dr. Philip Potter, and the contributions made by Rev. Professor Enda McDonagh, Rev.

Canon E. P. M. Elliott, Very Rev. Dr. A. J. Weir, Right Rev. Francisco Claver, Rev. Dr. José Míguez Bonino and Right Rev. Colin Winter to two public symposia on 'The Irish Churches and Human Rights' and 'The Churches and Human Rights: A World View'.

It remains only to express my thanks to the editor and to our contributors, and to express my hope that this publication will forward the aims and expectations of the Consultation as formulated in its final Statement which is printed here as the Appendix.

1. W. J. Fitz-Patrick, F.S.A., *The Life, Times and Correspondence of the Right Rev. Dr. Doyle, Bishop of Kildare and Leighlin,* 2 vols. Dublin 1890, I, p. 351.
2. G. H. Tavard, *Two Centuries of Ecumenism,* London 1961, p. 57.
3. Louis McRedmond, 'Northern Ireland: A Challenge to the Churches in Ireland?', *One in Christ* 12 (1976) p. 92.
4. Fitz-Patrick, op.cit. II, p. 389.
5. *Ibid.* I, p. 216.
6. *Ibid.* II, p. 363.
7. *Ibid.* II, p. 368.
8. Louis McRedmond, 'Not to be Coerced' *Studies* 67 (1978), p. 33.

INTRODUCTION

Alan Falconer

> Justice impels us to desire and to insist that everyone receives what we all have a right to. The Christian is a witness and an apostle of justice in the world. He cannot bear any form of inequality, oppression or tyranny.

These words are taken from a contemporary exposition of the Christian faith and its implications by Max Thurian of the Taizé Community.[1] Such a perspective as this finds expression in the writings of theologians of all denominations, and in the contemporary confessions of faith of churches of all traditions. Unfortunately, the history of the involvement by Christians and churches in the creation and maintenance of structures of 'injustice' demonstrates that often 'word' has not been matched by 'action'. The churches have been as much a part of the problem of injustice as of its solution.

Throughout this century, however, individual Christians and groups have helped the churches to see the importance of their playing a greater role in the promotion of 'justice'. One sign of the Churches' increasing awareness of this dimension to their witness has been the increasing attention paid to the problem of human rights, both in the sphere of theological reflection, and in that of the study and implementation of strategies for their promotion.

In the area of theological reflection, important studies have emerged from the various World Confessional Families and from the World Council of Churches. The reports of these studies have stimulated further thought and action by individual churches throughout the world. Such studies have tended to be conducted as a dialogue between theologians in an attempt to come to a common theological position. The motive behind them has been that once a common theological stance has been enunciated then the churches would be able to engage in human rights concerns with a renewed sense of commitment.

In the history of human rights, however, the churches and Christian theology have not played a central part. In his analysis of the American *Declaration of Independence* (1776) and the *Déclaration des Droits de l'Homme et du Citoyen* (1789), Karl Barth has pointed to the many influences which contributed to the formulation of human rights in these fundamental documents. One influence, and by no means the predominant one, was that of Christian theology.[2] In trying to understand human rights, then, it is particularly appropriate to conduct the examination from the perspectives of a number of different disciplines, some of which have been more prominent in relation to human rights than has theology. In the context of an interdisciplinary study, theologians are invited to reflect on the concrete reality and rhetoric of human rights. This can have the effect of sharpening the theological perspectives which emerge.

This present volume, then, is an attempt to engage in an interdisciplinary conversation. What is quite remarkable is that despite the various disciplines and perspectives presented here, there is evident a number of common strands which appear to be prominent for the authors. I shall note some of these after outlining the structure of the volume.

Alongside the importance of the interdisciplinary nature of this volume, lies its interfaith dimension. It is not only Christians, and Christian theology, who have been awakened to the importance of human rights. Other religions and ideologies have also been engaged in reflection on human rights. In facing up to the implications of human rights then it is helpful also that reflection takes place with those of other traditions of thought. Indeed the recent World Conference: Religious Workers for Lasting Peace, Disarmament and Just Relations among Nations, held in Moscow (1977), discovered that their interfaith discussions were:

> a stimulating and vigorous experience, broadening our horizons and deepening our insights . . . Proceeding from our differing spiritual foundations, we found it possible to agree together on the ways of truth and love, of justice and peace.[3]

In the search for the unity of humankind, then, this volume is also an attempt to engage in an interfaith conversation.

As the occasion for this volume is the celebration of the thirtieth anniversary of the *Universal Declaration of Human Rights,* the opening contribution is an examination of the content of the Declaration and its impact since its enunciation in 1948, by the Nobel and Lenin Peace Laureate and world statesman, Mr Seán MacBride, who has himself done so much to make the Declaration a reality for peoples throughout the world.

After this, the question is raised as to why religions and ideologies are concerned with human rights at all, and thus why any conversation on human rights from a faith perspective can take place. Dr José Míguez Bonino examines the relationship between Christianity and human rights and demonstrates why Christians are impelled to be involved with those who cry for their humanity. Dr Rashid Jullundhri explores the foundations for human rights which are explicit and implicit in Islam, and in his exposition emphasises the importance of treating minority groups within society with humanity and respect. The Marxist theory of human rights is analysed by Professor István Mészáros in a way which demonstrates remarkable points of convergence with perspectives from Christian theology.

Despite this commitment to human rights in the broad sense, however, there is great confusion abroad as to what precisely human rights are. Dr Garret Barden therefore in his contribution examines this question through a philosophical analysis. The same question is then addressed from two quite different spheres. Fr Richard McCormick takes a very specific area, namely, the decision to treat or not to treat medically defective newborn babies, and explores the human rights issues which arise in the taking of such a decision. Then Professor Martti Lindqvist approaches the nature of human rights through an examination of the needs of the 'developing world', and an examination of the concept, 'distributive justice'.

One of the fundamental problems in human rights is the way in which Institutions both violate and promote human rights within themselves. In this volume two 'institutions' are examined.[4] The first is that of Industry. Professor David Jenkins outlines the history of the steps which have had to be taken within British industry for the protection of the exploited and for the promotion of the human, and poses pertinent questions to contemporary industrial society. Secondly, the Church itself has a very mixed record in the field of promoting liberty. Each denomination has created structures to protect those who feel oppressed. Dr Frederick McManus examines the structure that the Roman Catholic Church has had to create, in the medium of Canon Law, to protect those who are not in a position to assert themselves, and to promote human freedom within its bounds. Through this examination of specific institutions and types of institutions fundamental questions are raised to other institutions as to their own human rights mechanisms. The implicit question being raised here is that of the way in which a particular society relates to the questions of humanity posed within it.

Arising from this treatment of institutions, the problem of the particular mechanism associated with the protection of those people who are unable to assert themselves is examined, viz. the role of Law in the sphere of human rights. There are three main treatments of this theme, each with a different emphasis. The first, by Mr Michael O'Boyle examines the *European Convention of Human Rights* and its protocols, and the way in which this instrument is made effective. This is an important area of political and legal controversy. The European Convention was the first, and until 1978 the only, International Human Rights Declaration enforceable by agreed international mechanisms. What effect does such a situation as this, have on the signatory States?Does it expand their vision of human rights? The second approach is an examination of a Constitution in relation to human rights. This is undertaken by the Hon. Mr Justice Declan Costello. Human rights are concretized in the particular, and ultimately discussion of them must be localized. In this paper, Mr Justice Costello, by examining the Consititution of Ireland, raises questions about the importance of a Constitution or Bill of Rights for the protection and promotion of human rights within a nation. The third contribution here examines the problem of Church-State relations. Fr Gabriel Daly, once again because this question has to be approached in a particular situation,[5] discusses it in relation to the Roman Catholic Church in Ireland. Implicitly two related questions are raised: the relation of majorities to minorities, and the right of groups in society apart from the legislature to press for change, or to dissent.

It is on the basis of such perspectives and considerations as these which have appeared thus far in the book that theological reflection must take place. Professor Jürgen Moltmann examines the recent theological studies on human rights undertaken by the individual World Confessional Families, and points to the areas of agreement and divergence in these. Further questions are then proposed for a deeper theological approach to human rights. The present writer attempts to discover the fundamental problem which is being appealed to in the phenomena of human rights, and on the basis of this seeks to reflect theologically on what this tells us about the nature of God and humankind. Finally Mrs Rosemary Haughton, through an exegesis of Psalm 72 (73) explores these same perspectives in the context of the 'oppressed' and the 'oppressor' and recalls us to 'the way of exchange'.

These then are the papers presented in this volume. At first sight one may be struck by the diversity of themes treated and opinions expressed. In fact, the over-riding impression left by the papers is their unity. There are a number of central themes in the volume.

The first theme is that of the *particularity* of human rights. Most contemporary studies on the theory of human rights, and the perspectives of the recent theological studies, stress the universality of human rights. The emphasis by the contributors to this volume lies on particularity. There is a strong stress by the various authors that however one may want to define human rights, they are primarily concerned with *right relations.* Such human relationships cannot be defined or regulated, either at the individual level or that of the institution, once for all. What has to be taken into account always is the fact that relationships grow, and that circumstances change in such a way that a relationship which was previously 'right' is no longer so and cannot be contained within the previous categories of thought or modes of operation. The definition of human rights is therefore dependent on the particularity of the situation. The importance of this is further seen in the theological reflection which stresses the understanding of history and the self-emptying of Jesus for those in specific situations. This does not deny the universality of human rights, but it does point to the necessity for their continual redefinition in the light of the concrete struggle of those who cannot assert their own humanity.

The second major theme which emerges from the papers revolves round the problematic of human rights. Despite the lack of clarity in the literature of human rights movements on the definition of human rights there seems to be widespread agreement as to where the problem is to be located in the experience of human beings. Human rights arise because of the need to *protect* individuals and groups who are unable to protect themselves. For one reason or another, and either consciously or unconsciously, individuals or groups find themselves rendered powerless because of the actions or attitudes of other groups. Out of specific conflicts there emerges a widening of the understanding of what it means to be human. Thus human rights are concerned also with the *promotion* of the human within societies and institutions.

These then are the central themes which appear throughout these very diverse contributions in this volume. They provided at the Consultation itself a helpful starting point for our discussions. They enabled a fruitful discussion on human rights and the theology of human rights to take place. The publication of this volume it is hoped will enlarge the participation in that discussion, so that a greater involvement in human rights movements will ensue.

Notes

1. Max Thurian *Our Faith:* Basic Christian Belief trans. Emily Chisolm Taisé, Les Presses de Taizé 1978 p. 208.
2. Karl Barth *Protestant Theology in the Nineteenth Century* trans. Brian Cozens London, SCM 1972 pp. 49-54.
3. World Conference: Religious Workers for Lasting Peace, Disarmament and Just Relations Among Nations (Moscow, June 1977) 'Final Documents: Appeal' in *Journal of the Moscow Patriarchate* 1977 no. 8 p. 18.
4. It was intended to have a contribution on the subject of The State and human rights at the Consultation but this finally proved impossible due to circumstances outwith the control of the organizers.
5. On the topicality of the theme and the approach cf Lukas Vischer (ed) *Church and State:* Opening a new ecumenical discussion Faith and Order Paper no. 85 Geneva, WCC 1978.

CHAPTER 1

"THE UNIVERSAL DECLARATION – 30 YEARS AFTER"

SEÁN MacBRIDE

It is most opportune and appropriate that the Irish School of Ecumenics should have taken the iniatiative of convening this International Consultation on Human Rights at this juncture of world history. The *Universal Declaration of Human Rights* (10 December 1948) is undoubtedly the most important instrument ever produced in the history of the endless struggle for the assertion of human liberties.[1] When it was adopted in 1948, it marked an important landmark; a landmark which everyone hoped would be a turning point that could give a new sense of direction to governments and to those exercising influence in the world. Our task, 30 years later, is to examine how far these hopes have been realised.

The new era in history which commenced with the end of World War II saw the beginning of a new and vast attempt to recreate a world in which man could live in peace, free from fear and want. At the heart of these endeavours lay a distinct inclination on the part of nations to construct a new world order subject to the Rule of Law; the hope was that governments would conduct themselves in accordance with the principles of justice and law. This inclination to recognise and abide by the supremacy of the rule of law is reflected in the Charter of the United Nations. Effect was given to this concept by the International Court of Justice, the adoption of international Conventions and Regional Agreements, the creation of many international organisations with particular competences, the establishment of the International Law Commission and the taking of other steps involving the acceptance by States of the principles of International Law.

A constant factor throughout all these achievements, and one of the ultimate aims of the statesmen responsible for them has been the need to provide for the protection of fundamental human rights and freedoms by international legal processes as well as by political and moral influences. This urgent need was recognised at an early stage of World War II, by the allied powers, and is reflected in the *Charter of the United Nations,* which recites the determination of the peoples of the United Nations "to reaffirm faith in fundamental human rights", and which provides that one of the purposes of the United Nations is:

> To achieve international cooperation in solving international problems of an economic, social, cultural, or humanitarian character, and in promoting and encouraging respect for human rights and for fundamental freedoms for all without distinction as to race, sex, language or religion.

The Charter incorporates a number of provisions relating to human rights, thus representing for the first time an attempt to create international legal standards for the protection of human rights. This feature distinguishes the *Charter of theUnited Nations* from the *Covenant of the League of Nations,* which did not mention human rights at all.

Therefore, the promotion and protection of human rights may be said to be one of the ultimate, if not the initial, aim of the Charter. Clearly, it is only in a world where peace prevails, and where reasonable economic and social standards have been realised, that man's fundamental rights and freedoms can be secured and can achieve full significance. These aims will be most readily achieved by the development of international law and by the acceptance of its precepts by governments.

Since the adoption of the *Charter of the United Nations* at San Francisco on the 26th June 1945, some 50 major international Conventions and Instruments for the Protection of Human Rights have been adopted.

Each of these instruments *stems* from the United Nations Charter, in which the peoples of the United Nations reaffirmed their faith in fundamental human rights, in the dignity and worth of the human person, and in the equal rights of men and women. Its declared objective was the promotion of social progress and better standards of life with greater freedom and security for the individual.

The question of human rights had first been adumbrated in a statement made by the "Allied Powers" on 1 January 1942, in which they claimed that "complete victory over their enemies is essential to defend life, liberty, independence and religious freedom and to preserve human rights and justice in their own lands as well as in other lands". Later, in the summer of 1944 at a meeting held in Dumbarton Oaks, proposals were formulated for the establishment of the United Nations, and it was then contemplated that the United Nations "should facilitate solutions of international, economic, social and other humanitarian problems, and should promote respect for human rights and Fundamental Freedoms". In the autumn of 1945 the preparatory Commission of the United Nations recommended that the first task of the Commission on Human Rights should be "the formulation of an international Bill of Rights". This recommendation was adopted by the General Assembly in January 1946. The first meeting of the newly created Commission on Human Rights took place at Lake Success on 27 January 1947. The President of the Commission on Human Rights chosen was Mrs. Eleanor Roosevelt. A drafting Committee was appointed to prepare the Universal Declaration of Human Rights, and finally, the *Universal Declaration of Human Rights* was adopted in Paris on 10 December 1948.

It is noteworthy that one of those who played an important part in the formulation of the draft Universal Declaration of Human Rights was Monsignor Roncalli, as he then was, subsequently Pope John XXIII. Monsignor Roncalli was then Papal Nuncio in Paris after having passed some years as Nuncio in Greece during the war and the famine there. He often, in conversations with me, expressed the hope that the Universal Declaration would save humanity from another war.

The eminent French jurist and Nobel Peace Laureate, the late René Cassin, has paid eloquent tribute to the assistance which Monsignor Roncalli then gave to the French Delegation.[2] This may also possibly explain the fact that some fifteen years later in his Encyclical *Pacem in Terris,* Pope John XXIII lays specific reference on the need for a Charter of Fundamental Human Rights. He urged:

> . . . In the juridicial organisation of States in our time, the first requisite is that a Charter of Fundamental Human Rights be drawn up in clear and precise terms, and that it be incorporated in its entirety in the Constitution.

Others who played an active role in the drafting of the Universal

Declaration were Lester Pearson, Canada, Robert Schuman from France, Herbert Evatt from Australia, and Peter Fraser, New Zealand.

In the course of history, usually at an important turning point, men have made important declarations of intent and of principles. Such declarations include; *Magna Carta* in England in the year 1215; the *Habeas Corpus* Act of 1679; the English *Bill of Rights,* 1688; the American *Declaration of Independence* of 1776; the French *Déclaration des Droits de l'Homme,* 1789; Karl Marx's *Das Kapital,* 1876; Lenin's *Manifesto* of 1917; and last, but not least, our own *Declaration of Independence* enacted by Dáil Éireann in 1919. These were all important historical documents but they were limited both in scope and in territorial application, even if they had an influence which reached out far beyond the national boundaries of the territories from which they emanated. The *Universal Declaration of Human Rights,* on the other hand, is both *universal* and *comprehensive.*

It is one of the most important instruments and landmarks in the history of mankind. It is the Charter of Liberty of the oppressed and the downtrodden. It defines the limits which the almighty State machine should not transgress in its dealings with those whom it rules. It was influenced by the determination of the world in 1948 to ensure that the world should never again witness the genocide, the destruction of human rights, and the brutality that engulfed humanity in the neo-barbarism that accompanied World War II.

One of the most distinguished members of the International Court of Justice, H. E. Sir Muhammed Zafrulla Khan of Pakistan who is also a leader of the Moslem Community in the World, has this tribute to pay to the Universal Declaration:

> It stands as a shining milestone along the long, and often difficult and weary, paths trodden by man down the corridors of history, through centuries of suffering and tribulations towards the goal of freedom, justice and equality. It is the first comprehensive formulation, based upon consensus, of the values which are designed to secure the dignities of man. Man's struggle for freedom, justice and equality has been waged in all ages and in many fields and theatres with varying fortunes. Each of these battles, and the ground won in each, have, in turn, forwarded

the cause of Man and have contributed towards the formulation and adoption of the Declaration which is entitled to rank with the great historical documents and Charters which were directed towards the same objectives

However, the *Universal Declaration of Human Rights* was merely an enumeration of principles and a declaration of intention. It was not, when it was adopted, a binding legal document, but it has now acquired the status of being enforceable as part of international customary law. It would certainly appear to fall well within the definition of international customary law defined in what is known as the "Marten's Clause", which is embodied in all the Hague and Geneva Conventions:[3]

> Until a more complete code of the laws of war can be drawn up, the High Contracting Parties deem it expedient to declare that, in cases not covered by the rules adopted by them, the inhabitants and the belligerents remain under the protection and governance of the principles of the law of nations, derived from the usages established among civilised peoples, from the laws of humanity and from the dictates of the public conscience.

In some countries the Universal Declaration has been specifically included in, or endorsed by, the existing constitutional enactments. In some other jurisdictions, it has been used by the courts as guidelines, or for purposes of judicial interpretation.

Certainly, by now most international lawyers of repute regard the *Universal Declaration of Human Rights* as forming part of international customary law.

It was agreed at the time of its adoption that the principles enshrined in the Universal Declaration would be given binding legal effect by two United Nations international conventions. One of the Conventions was intended to deal with the economic, social and cultural rights, and the other Convention intended to deal with civil and political rights. It was also agreed that there would be an optional protocol to the Convention dealing with civil and political rights which would contain effective provisions for the implementation of the civil and political rights guaranteed; this protocol was to enable an individual, or group of individuals, or an organisation, to formulate complaints in appropriate instances to be established by the United Nations, whenever the rights guaranteed were infringed by any of the parties to the Convention.

It took fifteen years to draft and elaborate these international treaties, which came to be known as "The International Covenants for the Protection of Human Rights", or more briefly, "The International Bill of Human Rights". Finally, these instruments were unanimously adopted by the General Assembly on 16 December 1966. This was an important landmark in the history of the implementation of the *Universal Declaration of Human Rights* and of the Charter of the United Nations.

However, their unanimous adoption by the General Assembly, was only a pyrrhic victory, as the Covenants could only come into operation when they had received a prescribed number of ratifications. In the case of the two major Covenants, they could only come into force once each had received thirty-five ratifications: the Optional Protocol to the International Covenant on Civil and Political Rights required a minimum of 10 ratifications. It took more then ten years to obtain the necessary ratifications but finally, the Covenants and the Protocol received the required number of ratifications and entered into force on the 3rd January 1976, the 23rd March, 1976, and the 23 March 1976 respectively.

Up to the end of June 1978, the position as to ratifications was as follows:

The International Covenant on Economic, Social and Cultural Rights – 51 ratifications
The International Covenant on Civil and Political Rights – 50 ratifications
The Optional Protocol – 19 ratifications

There are undoubtedly violations of human rights in many areas of the world today. They have been aggravated by a breakdown in the standards of morality throughout the world; this has led to an escalation in violence and brutality in the world. The world is more than ever in need of a clear lead in matters of public morality and human rights. The religious leaders of the world in particular have a special responsibility to discharge in these matters.[4]

Human rights have, in recent years, been used sometimes dishonestly, for propaganda purposes. In one sense this has been useful in that it has high-lighted the importance of human rights, but in another sense it has made them more controversial. The time has come to decide realistically how best human rights can be protected. Part 4, Article 28–47 of the Covenant on Political and Civil Rights, contains specific implementation mechanism to enable complaints and violations of human rights to be dealt with internationally. The Protocol recognises the rights of individual petition to the instances created by Part 4.

Instead of trying to use human rights issues as a form of international political football, may I suggest that Governments should ratify the Human Rights Covenants, and Protocol, and should use the machinery which has been specifically set up for the purpose. These Covenants and Protocol do represent the combined wisdom of the International Community, and set up acceptable machinery for their implementation. The time has come when the provisions created must be fully utilised. I am convinced that the Covenant and the Protocol when ratified can play an effective role in giving effect to the *Universal Declaration of Human Rights.* It took a long time to secure the recognition of human rights as a part of the rights enforceable under international law. The old concept that only States, as distinct from individuals, could invoke international law, took a long time to die.

The laws abolishing slavery which came to form part of international law, were possibly the first breach in this restrictive view of international law. Next came the Humanitarian Laws, the *Declaration of St. Petersburg* of 1868, the *Hague Conventions* of 1899 and 1907, and the *Geneva Conventions,* which created rights which could be enforced through the agency of States. The first specific major recognition of the rights of minorities and of individuals came with the post World War I treaties, dealing with Upper Silesia. These conventions invested minorities and individuals with direct rights which were enforceable under international law.

The next important developments were the *Universal Declaration of Human Rights,* the United Nations *Covenants for the Protection of Human Rights,* and particularly, the *European Convention for the Protection of Human Rights and Fundamental Freedoms,* 1950. The European Convention of 1950 not only created and declared rights enforceable by the individual, but it also established a supra-national authority with jurisdiction to protect the rights specified in the Convention, namely the European Commission of Human Rights, and the European Court of Human Rights, both of which function in Strasbourg. Thus, the old concept that the individual could not acquire or enforce rights under international law was finally demolished.

The Law of Human Rights, as embodied in the two International Covenants provide a fairly comprehensive statement of the rights that are protected under international law in normal times. The same can be said of the European Convention and of the much more recent Inter-American Convention. Thus, it can be said that in normal times of peace in a country the provisions of the Law of Human Rights should obtain in full.

However, in times of war or other public emergency threatening the life of a nation, the position becomes more complex. Three separate and distinct codes come into operation.

(a) The *Hague Conventions* and the *Geneva Protocol* of 1925
(b) The *Geneva Convention* of 1949
(c) Those portions of the Law of Human Rights that survive even in time of a public emergency which threatens the life of a nation.

In addition to making provisions for the protection of human rights in normal times, Article 4 of the International Covenant on Civil and Political Rights provides that in times "of public emergency, which threatens the life of the Nation", States may derogate from the provisions of the Covenant "to the extent strictly required by the exigencies of the situation, provided that such measures are not inconsistent with their obligations under International Law and do not involve discrimination . . ." Article 4 then goes on to provide that no derogation can be made in regard to seven specified Articles of the Covenant. These articles are:

Article 6 (Right to Life)
Article 7 (Provision against torture or degrading treatment)
Article 8 (Slavery and Servitude)
Article 11 (Freedom from Imprisonment for contractual Obligations)
Article 15 (Retro-Active Legislation or Penalties)
Article 16 (Recognition of Persons before the Law)
Article 18 (Freedom of Conscience)

Accordingly, we have a situation in which, even in time of war or "public emergency threatening the life of a nation," certain specified rights continue to be in full operation. The United Nations International Covenants contain certain basic minimum rights that are safeguarded under International Law even in times of war or grave emergencies. Similar provisions, with slight differences are contained in Article 15 of the European Convention on

Human Rights and have been applied by the European Commission and Court of Human Rights.

This introduces a new concept in the area of Human Rights Law and one which may be of considerable importance. Hitherto, the rule was that "silent enim leges inter arma" prevailed in time of war or emergency; this no longer applies.

The sole protection under international law in time of war or grave emergency was that provided by the Hague or the Geneva Conventions. Now, we have in addition, the protection offered by the seven Articles of the International Covenant on Civil and Political Rights referred to above, which subsist in times of war. This situation raises a number of new and important issues that will require careful consideration. The principal issues which arise are:

(a) Governments will be bound by the provisions of the Covenant on Civil and Political Rights in their entirety, unless it can be established that there is a war or a "public emergency threatening the life of the nation".

(b) Even if a Government does establish the existence of such an extreme degree of emergency, it will nevertheless be bound:

   1. by Articles 6, 7, 8, (1 & 2), 11, 15, 16 and 18 of the International Covenant.
   2. by its other obligations "under International Law". This obligation would include the obligations it has under the Hague and Geneva Conventions.
   3. not to discriminate on grounds of race, colour, sex, language, religion or social origin;

(c) Governments are not entitled to derogate from their obligations under the Covenant beyond "the extent strictly required by the exigency of the situation". In other words, even if they do derogate successfully, they do not have "carte blanche" to act as they wish.

(d) There is also an obligation on Governments to serve a notice of derogation, through the Secretary-General, on other States. This notice must specify the particular provisions from which it has derogated and the reasons for the derogation.

(e) Irrespective of any derogation in conflicts of an international nature, the Hague and Geneva Conventions apply. There cannot be a derogation from them. In addition of course, the seven Articles of the Covenant from which there can be no derogation, also apply.

(f) In conflicts "not of an international character" the provisions of Article 3 of the four Geneva Conventions continue to apply; but superimposed upon Article 3, the provisions of Articles 6, 7, 8, (1 & 2), 15, 16, and 18 of the Covenant also apply. This raises important questions.

(g) The implementation procedures and machinery provided by Part IV of the International Covenant would appear to apply also to a situation in which a State has derogated on grounds of grave emergency from its obligations under the Covenant. The provisions of the Optional Protocol to the Covenant also survive in time of grave emergency. For the purposes of the present note, the Human Rights Committee set up under the Covenant has jurisdiction to deal with, inter alia, the following matters:

I. The extent to which a State in a given situation is entitled to derogate from its obligations under the Covenant under the provisions of Article 4 of the Covenant.

II. The extent to which the measures taken in derogation were in excess of those strictly required by the exigencies of the situation.

III. The extent to which the measures taken are not inconsistent with their obligations under International Law (e.g. the Geneva or the Hague Conventions).

IV. The extent to which measures taken involve discrimination.

Of course, the very best safeguard for the protection and respect of personal liberty is an enlightened government, and democracy. A representative, democratically elected parliament, public discussion, free press, fair operation of the mass media and an educated public opinion are the very best guarantees for the protection of human rights.

But, even in the most enlightened democracy, abuse of power by the executive, by the administration or even by parliament, may and does occur. Such abuses may be incidental; they may not have been contemplated when a particular law was enacted. They may have been anticipated but disregarded because they only affected a small number of people. They may have been motivated by a good, but mistaken view of what was for the "common good". On the other hand, even in a well regulated democracy, abuses of power, for political or other improper purposes, do occur and have to be guarded against.

Accordingly, we have to recognise that, no matter how well intentioned or democratic a State may be, it is nevertheless necessary to provide effective machinery for the protection of the rights of the public or of individual members of the public.

In parts of the world, where democracy is new or is not solidly entrenched, the same problems exist, but to a much greater extent. They are much more difficult to resolve because there is no tradition for the protection of human rights under the law, and usually no informed public opinion capable of making itself felt.

In areas of the world which have suffered from colonial rule before reaching independence, the problem is particularly difficult. There is an inevitable tendency to turn towards the methods which the colonial powers used – arbitrary arrests, imprisonment without trial, unfair trials, suppression of freedom of expression, and so on. The rulers of such areas tend to copy far too easily the methods of their former rulers; the ordinary citizens still tend to regard themselves as "subjects" who have no individual rights against the omnipotent ruler. Such systems may provide a temporary advantage, but inevitably, they lead to disaster. The dictum of Lord Acton that "power tends to corrupt, and absolute power corrupts absolutely" is not an abstract proposition of the last century. It is just as true in our present day world.

Before dealing with the institutional methods for the protection of human rights, I should like to utter a word of warning against certain concepts which often creep into the legislative or executive process. Among such concepts I would include the doctrine of the "common good" or of the "public interest". As a reaction against a society in which the self interest of a privileged class prevails, rulers – even in democracies – often tend to elevate the doctrine of the "common good" or of the "public interest" to the status of a legal answer for any act which infringes the rights of a minority or of an individual. It should always be remembered that these were the very doctrines which were invoked to justify the extermination chambers of the last war, and the destruction of democracy in many areas of the world wherein democratic rule has been overthrown.

At national level, the most effective mechanisms are:

1. A watchful parliament with an effective and courageous opposition.
2. A free press which will not hesitate to expose injustice.
3. A constitution which spells out the rights guaranteed and delimits clearly the powers of the executive, the legislature and the judiciary.
4. An independent judiciary, not subject to direct or indirect pressures by the Executive or by parliament, charged with the function of upholding the constitution and enforcing its provisions.
5. An "ombudsman" directly responsible to parliament and/or administrative tribunals with full power of investigation of complaints of maladministration.

These are, broadly speaking, the desirable institutions which are necessary to safeguard human rights. They may vary in particular functions, jurisdiction and emphasis in different countries; but in our increasingly complex society it is the combination of these institutions that will most effectively safeguard democratic rule and personal liberty.

A constitution, in itself, is only one element and may be valueless unless it can be invoked and enforced. Many highsounding constitutions are valuesless because they are ignored, misinterpreted, or because the constitutional safeguards are not judicially enforceable by an independent judiciary. Hence, the importance of a fearless independent judiciary charged with the task of enforcing compliance with the consititutional provisions. Not infrequently, high sounding constitutional guarantees become illusory unless there is adequate machinery to constrain the executive and even the legislature to conform with the provisions of the constitution.

Because English lawyers have not had a written constitution, they have relied on procedural remedies rather than on the proclamation of certain rights. Professor Dicey always insisted that:

> The legal remedies for the enforcement of the Rights of Man is more important than a formal declaration of the Rights.

Accordingly, English lawyers have concentrated on the remedial and procedural safeguards. *Magna Carta,* the *Habeas Corpus* Acts, Trial by Jury, the independence of the judiciary and often, "judge made laws", have been the principal safeguards of personal liberty in England. However, the English Constitutional system should not be regarded as a valid prototype in the present day world. Long usage and tradition have made it work and in England an enlightened public opinion and press have been its watchdogs. But, these safeguards were not always effective in the British colonies, or, indeed, in Ireland at times. The English system should be regarded as the exception that proves the rule.

However, the real problem is how to ensure the objectivity of a tribunal trying a case in which its own State is involved? In many cases the government controls the judiciary. It appoints them, and it can have them removed. Although Courts are able to judge objectively in most circumstances, a problem does arise where the conduct of the State itself is at issue. Where a government bureaucracy has embarked on a programme that infringes basic human rights and where the offending government dominates, or significantly influences the judiciary, it becomes difficult to ensure complete objectivity and justice.

Where the Courts have compromised in order to sanction or to cover up violations of human rights, the courts become impaired in a more general sense, lose credibility, and ultimately, they cease to be effective. Unless there are, in such cases, independent international tribunals to which recourse may be had, the administration of justice becomes precarious.

It is for all these reasons that it has long been accepted that in order to ensure objectivity and impartiality, it is necessary to have recourse to courts composed of judges from different areas who are as far removed as possible from the issues in dispute. Hence, the concept of an international court for the trial of issues between States has long been accepted. The Permanent Court of Arbitration created at the Hague Conference of 1899, the Permanent Court of International Justice set up by the League of Nations, and the present International Court of Justice were established to ensure a greater degree of objectivity.

When it came to the adoption of a *European Convention for the Protection of Human Rights,* all the nineteen member states of the Council of Europe agreed that for the protection of human rights, it was desirable and necessary to have an international commission and court composed of judges from the different member States of the Council of Europe. A similar system has now been adopted under the Inter-American Convention, which also contains very effective machinery for the enforcement of the rights embodied in the Inter-American Convention. It has just come into operation.

Notes

1. see Ian Brownlie (ed) *Basic Documents on Human Rights* London, O.U.P. 1971.
2. Philippe de le Chapelle *La Declaration Universelle des Droits de L'Homme et le Catholicisme* Paris, Librairie Generale de Droit et de Jurisprudence 1967.
3. International Committee of the Red Cross *The Geneva Convention* Geneva, International Committee of the Red Cross 1950 also *Protocols Additional to the Geneva Convention* Geneva 1977.
4. I would like to draw particular attention to Sodepax *Peace – the Desperate Imperative:* Consultation on Christian Concern for Peace held at Baden, Austria 1970 Geneva, Sodepax 1970.

CHAPTER TWO

RELIGIOUS COMMITMENT AND HUMAN RIGHTS: A CHRISTIAN PERSPECTIVE

JOSÉ MÍGUEZ BONINO

Why should a Christian be concerned with human rights? What are the elements in Christianity which provide a basis for being concerned about human rights?

The first approach to these questions that comes to mind is the attempt to articulate a doctrinal platform, a Christian philosophy that would make the concern for human rights a 'logically necessary' corollary of the Christian faith. I will, nevertheless, avoid such an approach, because I think it would be historically inaccurate and, perhaps, not quite honest intellectually. What we call today 'human rights' – for instance as defined in the *Charter of the United Nations* – is the result of a long process, developed mainly in the West, in the course of which a number of forces have operated – economic, political, cultural, ideological – the Christian faith being one of them. We will not attempt to determine now what is the precise correlation of those forces or whether any one of them is ultimately determinative. But, whatever our view of the dynamics of history, I think we will have to admit that they have mutually stimulated, checked and shaped each other. We cannot, therefore, speak of a Christian understanding of human rights as something which would have developed autonomously nor in isolation.

It would be equally misleading to try to distinguish a Christian doctrine in itself from its historical embodiments. Religious doctrines, attitudes, norms of conduct, forms of worship are born in response to historical circumstances – and, in turn, they influence that history. At each point in that history, a religion is a 'synthetic' historical phenomenon. Its permanent elements cannot, in any case, be found beyond or above that history but in and through it.[1]

We must, therefore, choose a different path, a historical one. Our attempt will be to follow the historical process in which the Christian faith has attained a consciousness of itself in relation to the question of human rights. Only then will it be possible to try and abstract the 'motifs' which have become visible in that movement and which may point to the peculiar Christian understanding or the specific Christian roots of a conception of human rights. For this purpose we must follow the movement of what has been called 'the history of freedom' in the Western world, in relation to which – at times supportively, at times in conflict – Christian theology and praxis have developed.[2]

THE CHRISTIAN CONSCIENCE AND THE HISTORY OF FREEDOM

1. Freedom to believe

The first form in which Christians faced the problem of human rights on a practical, existential way was the matter of religious freedom. The Roman Empire knew a type of religious tolerance as long as it did not conflict with the 'religion of the state'. When it become clear that Christians could not be subsumed – either religiously or ethnically – under the rights granted to the Jewish people, the problem of the 'legality' of the Christian faith could not be avoided. Two Christian claims made it particularly acute: the claim of universality – Christians would not accept ethnic, geographic or any other limitations to the extent of their mission – and the claim of exclusiveness – Christians would not accept any other 'supreme loyalty' alongside their obedience to the 'Lord'. The conflict was unavoidable.

In the process of defending their right, the early Christian Church resorted to two basic arguments. The first is the inherently free character of religious faith. "For see that you do not give a further ground for the charge of irreligion (*irreligionitatis*)" – claims Tertullian in his Apology – by taking away religious liberty (*libertatem religionis*) and forbidding free choice of deity".[3] "That is not worship (sacrifice) which is extorted from a person against his will", adds Lactantius.[4] Although the argument is advanced in favour of the Christian religion, the principle has universal validity and left a permanent imprint on Christian doctrine. The other argument was a consequence: if the religious preference was exclusively a right of the human conscience, the state could have no competence on the matter. Peter and John's declaration according to *Acts* 4:19 is a first and terse affirmation of that principle: "Whether it is right in the sight of God to listen to you rather than to God". It was not a rebellion against civil authority; quite to the contrary, even under very severe conditions, Christians were directed by their leaders to obey them. But there was a clear limitation of the sphere of competence of political power; it had no right to interfere in the realm of conscience. The autonomy of the religious sphere was thus vigorously affirmed over against the predominant 'political theologies'.

The attitude of Christians concerning religious freedom was to change quite substantially in the course of time, when the Christian faith itself became the religion of the Empire. Religious compulsion was justified, the power of the state was enlisted in the service of Christianity and a new type of 'Christian' political theology was articulated. The process is clearly reflected in the shifts that we can document between Augustine's early and late writings. Nevertheless, the earlier principle is attested by the very contradiction in which Christian thought becomes entangled. On the one hand, Christian theologians continue to assert 'the free character of the act of faith': faith cannot be imposed; even if a person would confess the true faith against his conscience, his act would be sin. How could this be reconciled with the invitation to civil power to forbid any religious practice other than the Christian? The only solution that medieval thought is able to find is the concept of tolerance as defined, for instance, by Thomas Aquinas.

In spite of the contradictions and ambiguities, we must register these two basic contributions to the history of freedom: the freedom of the act of faith and the limitation of the competence of the state in religious matters.

2. The freedom of the 'citizen'

In the XVI to XIX centuries the initiative in the struggle for freedom changed hands. A great transformation in the social fabric of the European population found dramatic expression in France towards the end of the XVIII century. People on the lower sector of the economy, largely emancipated from the cruder forms of feudalism, grown in numbers in a sort of population explosion, had begun to press for better conditions, and those in the new middle sectors – the bourgeoisie – aware of their increasing significance, took the lead of 'the people', claiming for the 'third estate' an amount of power equivalent to their importance in relation to the traditional power factors: the nobility and the

Church. The result, as we know, was the French Revolution and, as its initial document, the 'Declaration of the Rights of Man' *(Déclaration des droits le l'homme et du citoyen,* August 27, 1789). But thirteen years earlier, a new nation, the United States of America, led by the same social group, had constituted itself around a very similar platform.

Both statements were intended to embody what was believed to be an eternal and universal truth: states and political bodies do not create or grant such rights: they can only 'recognize' and 'proclaim' them. In fact, their very justification as states rests on this recognition. What is the source of these rights? In the American *Declaration of Independence,* the divine origin is explicit. The French Declaration substitutes nature for the Creator. But the religious background is here also unmistakeable: these rights are pronounced 'sacred'.

The *Déclaration des droits de l'homme* appeared originally in Paris in a pamphlet bearing above its title the picture of an eye within a triangle. The symbolism of the triune God is evident. At the bottom of the page, however, the symbol is explained otherwise: 'the supreme eye of reason that rises to dispel the clouds that darkened it'. When we put together the two kindred documents, one thing becomes clear: we have the mutual interpenetration of two ideological interpretations, that had run at times a parallel, at times a common, course at least since the second century: an idealistic humanism of Greek origin and the Hebrew-Christian prophetic tradition. Creation and nature, human brotherhood with a common reason and a common father, the dignity of a rational self and of an object of God's love in creation and redemption – these two had together become the basis for a new self-understanding of man. The Christian motif had the upper hand in the US document, the humanistic in the French: but both were legitimate children of this marriage. *Equality and universality* are the distinctive marks of these proclamations, understood under severe limitations. The French *Déclaration,* for instance, gives to 'property rights', which it proclaims 'sacred and inviolable' (Art. 17), a prominent place which becomes, at the hour of determining who enjoys 'the rights of citizen', one of the decisive criteria. In fact, in a population of some 27 million, only 4,300,000 qualified. In the USA it was clear that the Indians, and later the Blacks, were in practice not included among the 'men' (not to mention 'women') who had been 'created equal'. The proclamation of human rights was, towards the end of the XVIII century, the embodiment of the concerns and aspirations of a social group, a sector of society.

Human rights are defined in this stage in the perspective of the individualism that characterises modern thought. There is, no doubt, a primacy of the economic dimension of this individualism. 'Every man is free to employ his arms, his industry and his capital as he deems fit and useful for himself; he can produce what pleases him as he likes' establishes the French *Déclaration.* But it is not limited to that area. The individual is also conceived as a 'citizen': a social order cannot be imposed from above or outside the will of the individuals: it must be 'contracted' or 'convenanted' by the free will of free individuals. As both expression of and foundation for these freedoms we find a philosophical conception which Hegel summarises in this way:

> Against the faith in authority is established the sovereignty of the subject by itself and the laws of Nature are seen as the only connecting link between external phenomena . . . Thought is also directed to the spiritual realm: right and morality are based on the basis of the actual man, which previously were considered as commandment of God, given from outside . . .
>
> These general considerations grounded on the present consciousness, the laws of nature and the content of that which is right and good, has been called Reason.[5]

I have said that modern freedoms were 'legitimate offspring' of the marriage of the Christian faith and the classical hellenic humanism. But it was not easy for the churches to recognise or acknowledge this fact. This is understandable in view of the anti-religious attitude that characterised the movement. By locating religion also exclusively in the individual's free conscience and rejecting all revelation and authority, modernity seemed to do away entirely with dogma and Church authority. There was, nevertheless, a certain continuity between the early Christian claim for freedom in the act of faith and the modern claim for freedom of conscience. For reasons that are historically clear, this similarity was more easily visible for Protestantism. Hegel saw it in this way:

> This is the essential content of the Reformation: man is self-

> determined for freedom . . . Luther had done away with this authority [of the Church] and placed in its stead the Bible and the testimony of the human spirit. The fact that now the Bible itself becomes the foundation of the Christian Church is of the greatest importance: each individual should now enlighten himself through it, each individual can now guide his conscience by it. This is the paramount change in principle.[6]

This interpretation of Protestantism is certainly open to debate. But it can hardly be disputed that, objectively, the Reformation participated in the historical process that gave birth to modern society with its characteristic freedoms.

Again, for historical reasons which are not difficult to perceive, Roman Catholicism found it much more difficult to come to terms with modern freedoms. Its strenuous opposition throughout the XIX century is partly a legitimate rejection of a purely immanentistic form of humanistic philosophy, partly a fear that men would drift away from religious truth and endanger both the peace of the earthly city and their eternal salvation. The new society, nevertheless, was here to stay, and the Catholic Church slowly came, first, to find practical arrangements and then to appreciate the values and significance of the modern world. Vatican II finally articulates the encounter of the Roman Catholic Church with modern freedoms and rights.[7]

When this 'joint origin' of modern freedoms is recognised, it becomes possible to explore the Christian element present in it – although it is impossible to isolate it from other moments in this dynamic. It is this Christian element that gives to Christians a strong basis to stand for human rights in the critical situations which are faced today in many areas of the world. The search for theological foundations has gravitated in the direction of securing a firm basis for the universality of human dignity and right. It is not necessary to rehearse here the vast amount of theological work that has been done in this respect. It has rested basically on the doctrine of creation and/or the doctrine of redemption. The human being as God's creation and image, his/her dignity as God's steward and representative, the unity of the human race constitute a strong basis for asserting the rights of all. On the other hand, the Incarnation, the universal love of God attested by and operative in Christ's death and resurrection, the dignity of a humanity which in Christ has been exalted at the right hand of God, indicate an ultimate and unwavering commitment of God himself to the human being which underlines the value of each human being.[8]

3. The freedom of 'the poor'

At the end of World War II, when the *Universal Declaration of Human Rights* was proclaimed by the United Nations, a new chapter was added to the classic formulations of human rights of the XVIII century: 'social rights'. It was a timid and minimal recognition of a social and political reality which has been looming larger and larger in history for the last century and a quarter: the growing masses excluded from the 'citizen's rights' defined by the bourgeois world – the industrial proletariat of the 'central countries' in the northern hemisphere and, the hungering, exploited, culturally violated and deprived, repressed masses of the so called 'Third World'.

The voice of those who, in the words of G. Gutiérrez, had been 'absent from history' made itself heard in the struggle of the workers for better labour conditions, a just salary, the right to work and the right to shape a society in which they would be actual subjects of their own history. For the peoples of the 'Third World', in turn, this does not only mean a change in the internal conditions of their own societies but the 'rights' of the underprivileged nations in international trade, the transformation of the conditions of the 'division of labour' among the nations of the world; in sum, nothing less than 'a new world economic order'. Thus, to the 'social, economic, political and cultural rights' (Art. 22) of the U.N. Charter, one would have to add 'the universal rights of the peoples'. The Preamble of the Algiers Conference of 1970 reads: 'The respect for human rights implies the respect for the rights of the peoples'.

The relation of Christians and the churches to this new phase of the human search for freedom is also varied and not without ambiguities. Given the fact that the claims for these rights are raised quite often over against the privileges and the domination of social classes and countries in which Christians have been conspicuously present, it is not surprising that there has been a resistance to the recognition of such rights in many Christian quarters. The struggle for the rights of the poor has been waged quite often under the impulse of ideologies that rejected and denounced religion as a means of social domination. On the other hand, many Christians in the oppressed sector of humankind – and with them not a few of their brothers in the affluent countries and classes – have discovered in their faith a basis and impulse for the struggle. Thus, the awareness of the question of 'the rights of the poor' has led to a rediscovery of the prophetic tradition of the Jewish Christian faith.

A new fact begins to emerge. The Bible, it would seem, discovers and underlines another dimension of human rights. The books of the law, for instance, do not say anything in general about the rights of the human person, but they speak quite frequently of the judge who, at the gate, 'gives the poor man his right', of right done to the widow, the orphan and the alien, *Deuteronomy* 10); The prophets are equally explicit. When Jeremiah wants to point out the good government – the god-like behaviour as king – of Josiah, he summarises: 'He judged (that is, established the right) the cause of the poor and the needy; then, it was well' (*Jer.* 22:16). And the wisdom literature does not hesitate in equating the 'rights of the poor' as 'right of God': 'He who oppresses a poor man insults his Maker' (*Prov.* 14:31).

The line of this reasoning is not difficult to follow. Everyone has somebody to protect and to uphold his/her right (interestingly, the Hebrew word that we translate 'redeemer' means also 'avenger'): the child has a father, the wife a husband, men have brothers, a tribe, a family. But the 'fatherless', the 'widow', the 'foreigner' have no avenger-redeemer when they are wronged. God, nevertheless, cares for them: he has protected their right in the Law, he has pledged that no human life will be lost without vindication. A good government, therefore, becomes particularly responsible for the rights of those who have no protection, no power to vindicate their rights. The condition of the weakest in the society gauges the quality of government. The rights of the poor measure the health of the nation. For this reason when God himself makes his 'good government' (his Kingdom) present among us in Jesus Christ, the 'rights of the poor' (women, children, the despised, the sick people, above all 'the poor of the land') mark the thrust of his ministry. The Jubilee, the great symbol of the restoration of all who had suffered dispossession, deprivation or oppression, becomes the paradigm of his mission (Luke 4). The universal scope and significance of the ministry, death and resurrection of Jesus, according to the Christian faith, is not restricted but defined and highlighted in the concrete priority of the poor that he taught and illustrated in his life. This is the heritage that the Church has received, and that it begins to rediscover and re-claim in this new phase of the historical search for freedom.[10]

THE DISCERNMENT OF A CHRISTIAN ETHOS

This brief and only suggestive sketch of the history of the relation between the human quest for freedom and the Christian faith makes clear that we cannot speak of a ready-made, immutable 'Christian doctrine of human rights'. Rather, we see a development in which the historical experience of mankind stimulates Christians to explore the resources of their faith and this, in turn, inspires them to commit themselves more vigorously to the struggle for human rights. This process is not independent from the social conditions of Christians and churches and consequently, it generates ambiguities, tensions and contradictions within the Christian communities both in terms of doctrine and practice. On the other hand, it seems to me that we can discern, within this process, an 'ethos', related to an understanding of God's relation to mankind and history. This 'ethos' drives in the direction of a search for a 'more human life', for the fulfilment, within the conditions of history, of the best material and spiritual possibilities available for the human person and society. As we look at this history, it seems that we can discern three such insights which can be considered a permanent achievement.

1. The universality of human rights

'There is only one God and Father of all': this conviction is the basic ground on which the Christian faith rests. It is the basic confession of the Old Testament: (*Deut.* 6:4). Far from retreating from it, the New Testament makes it even more explicit in terms of its trinitarian faith: (*Eph.* 4:4-6). The consequence cannot be avoided: there is only one mankind. Within the New Testament this consequence is first drawn in relation to the new Christian community: all are one body, in which all members have equal dignity and value: social, ethnic, cultural, even sexual distinctions cannot justify any discrimination. But this universality overflows the limits of the community. Every human being bears the image of God; it is therefore absurd and sacrilegious 'to bless the Lord and Father . . . and to curse men, who are made in the likeness of God' (*James* 3:11). There is no doubt that it was the encounter with Platonic and Stoic philosophy which first gave to Christian theologians the possibility of articulating this conviction in conceptual theological terms. When Christians used this conceptual framework, though, they were not merely borrowing a Greek idea: they were formulating something that was profoundly their own.[11]

2. 'Humanity as criterion

The American theologian Paul Lehmann has coined a felicitious expression when he said that what God has been and is presumably doing in the world is 'what it takes **to make and to keep human life human'**.[12]

It is a very modern formulation, but it expresses an insight which permeates the whole Biblical testimony. Only a full biblical theology developed in the perspective of 'life' as God's goal for his creation could do justice to this theme. But perhaps it is not superfluous to lift up briefly one of the very early and pregnant expressions of such insight: the priestly account of God's covenant with humankind in Noah (*Gen.* 9: 1-17). God voices and pledges his will concerning the 'fallen' human being, humanity 'as it is' – vitiated by wickedness, violence, sin. And he simply reiterates the promise and commandment of creation: 'Be fruitful, and multiply, and fill the earth'. Human life is still the key to creation. But three new provisions are added: (1) Man has a right to put all existing life . . . at the service of his life: (2) Human life is sacred: God himself will avenge violence done against man: (3) Man himself is made responsible for respecting and enforcing this provision.

It is impossible to exaggerate the importance of this Biblical motif. God's 'covenant' with man has 'life', particularly 'human life', as its fundamental content. He is unconditionally and absolutely the God of life. And consequently, he entrusts man with a mission: the perpetuation, enriching and protection of life. This is God's most precious treasure, so much so that not even his just and necessary wrath against man's sin is cause enough to annul the alliance. When the decisive time comes, the God-made-man will protect the human race with his own life. He will take upon himself the just punishment and the senseless violence of the fallen world so that men may live. The new covenant 'in his blood' eternally seals and affirms the early convenant with mankind.

Once again, it took the Church a long time to explore the content of its affirmation of human life: the inviolability of the human conscience, the freedom to develop one's own intellectual and spiritual possibilities, the instransferable value of each human person, the unity of spiritual and physical life, the social character of human existence, emerge slowly in the encounter of the Christian faith with different historical circumstances and philosophical conceptions as the ever enlarging implications of this 'Covenant'. But each new insight operates on the Christian conscience because Christians are faithful only when and to the extent that they do in the world 'whatever it takes to make and keep human life human'.

3. The 'poor' as the test

Universality and 'partiality' seem contradictory terms. But it is one of the deepest insights of the Biblical picture of God that his universality finds concrete expression in his 'partiality' in favour of the poor, the oppressed, the disadvantaged, the powerless, the marginal. In the strong words of one of the most important theologians of our century: 'God always takes his stand unconditionally and passionately on this side and on this side alone: against the lofty and on behalf of the lowly . . .'.[13] At this point, the biblical concept of justice parts company with the classical tradition. It is not the 'blind' rendering 'to each his own' – which presupposes a stable and basically unchangeable order – but the liberation of those who have been deprived of the conditions for an authentic human life. Such a vision does not mean a rejection of universality, but there are always historical tests for universality. In biblical terms, this test is the condition of the poor. Here we have the basis for a deeper understanding of the struggle for human rights. When the Brazilian bishops, for instance, refer at length to the condition of the Indians, they are not arbitratily selecting a special case: they are offering a witness which indicates the inhumanity of the whole society.

This relation between universal definition and a historical concrete focus is crucial for the understanding of human rights and the participation in support of them. As the slogan of 'human rights' becomes one of the rallying points today in the world, it is of paramount importance for us to bear this historico-theological test in mind. For the vast majority of the population of the world today the basic 'human right' is 'the right to a human life'. The deeper meaning of the violation of formal human rights is the struggle to vindicate these large masses who claim their right to the means of life. The defence of formal human rights is meaningful as a pointer to that deeper level. In that sense, the drive towards universality implicit in our Christian faith, which found partial expression in the quest of the American and French revolutions, the aspirations expressed in the *UN Declaration*, finds its historical focus today for us in the struggle of the poor, the economically and socially oppressed, for their liberation. At this point the biblical teaching and the historical junction coalesce to give the Christian churches a mission.

Notes

1. This paper presupposes a concept of the development of Christian doctrine in which the historical circumstances and the encounter with trends of human thought significantly play a role in 'activating' and helping to develop virtualities implicit in the Christian revelation.
2. The 'history of freedom' has been a predilect subject of Hegel and the Hegelian tradition. In recent theology J. B. Metz and J. Moltmass have developed this theme and assessed it from a theological point of view.
3. Apology XXIV, *Ante-Nicene Fathers* Grand Rapids, 1951, Vol. III, p. 38.
4. Divinarum Institutionum, V. 21, *The Ante-Nicene Fathers* (Grand Rapids, 1951), Vol. VII, p. 158.
5. Lectures on the Philosophy of History, in G. W. F. Hegel, *Sämtliche Werke,* ed. H. Glockner (Jubiläusausgabe), Vol. II, pp. 550, 551. (Translation is ours).
6. *Ibid.,* p. 525 (translation and underlining is ours).
7. I have interpreted the Council in this sense in *Concilio Abierto* (Buenos Aires, La Aurora, 1968), although rather uncritically in the evaluation of 'the modern world'.
8. In the preceding section and parts of what follows I have quoted freely from my article "Whose Human Rights", *International Review of Mission,* Vol. LXVI, No. 263, July 1977, pp. 220-224.
9. cf. the interesting study of this theme in Wisdom literature by Hugo Etchegaray, S.J., "Direitos do pobre-direitos de Deus", CEI, *Biblia Hoje-*47, Agosto 1978.
10. cf. *La Iglesia en la actual transformación de América Latina a la luz del Concilio* Buenos Aires, Bonum, 1968, Doc. "Paz", III/22. (E. T. *The Church in the Present Day Transformation of Latin America in the*

Light of the Council. Vol. 2. Conclusions. Bogota, Celam 1970. Doc. 'Peace').

11. cf. the formulation of Col. Rainborough centuries later, quoted by A.S.P. Woodhouse (ed.), *Puritanism and Liberty* London, Dent, 1951, p. 5.
12. *Ethics in a Christian Context* New York, Harper and Row, 1963, p. 101.
13. Karl Barth, *Church Dogmatics* Edinburgh, T. and T. Clark, Vol. II/I, p. 186.

CHAPTER 3

HUMAN RIGHTS AND ISLAM

RASHID AHMAD JULLUNDHRI

Every age has its own ills from which man has suffered, but he has never gone through such spiritual perplexity and agony of soul as he is experiencing nowadays. Because he is fully aware of the fact that the total destruction of the human race will be the ultimate fate if he fails to overcome his present crisis, he, therefore, is longing for unity and peace among mankind. At the same time he has become very conscious of his rights, the further denial of which will lead human society to disaster.

Islam wishes to see man happy both in this world and in the life to come. To achieve this goal, Islam calls man to restore his broken relations with heaven, since, if he does not do so, human life loses its significance. The main object of the Quran is to make man conscious of his place in the universe as well as of his relations with God.[1] In addition, Islam wants to create a society based on a deep sense of moral responsibility and justice in order to preserve human dignity accorded to man by God. Any system, therefore, which brings disgrace to man's honour, is denounced by Islam. Needless to say, without the practical recognition of the basic rights of man, all talk of human dignity will remain empty verbiage.

The question of human rights is not a phenomenon of our age. In fact, the State is supposed, as Abu Bakr, one of the close companions of the Prophet, said, to protect the rights of those who cannot protect themselves. In his first official speech, Abu Bakr said:

> O, People! I have been appointed ruler over you, while I am not the best of you. If you see me with truth, help me, and if with falseness set me right. The strong among you, in my opinion, is the weak unless I redress his wrong, and the weaker among you, in my view, is the strong, until I snatch at the right from him.[2]

His policy was continued by his successor Umar. In fact, Muslim law is described as the knowledge of one's rights and duties.[3]

Muslim theologians have divided rights into two categories; God's rights and human rights. Divine rights, in the Ulama's view, stand second to man's rights. For example, if a man wants to make a pilgrimage to Mecca but owes something to his fellowmen, he has to fulfil first his duties towards his fellowmen. If he acts differently he will be responsible in the world to come. It is related that the Prophet never offered prayers for those who passed away without paying their debts. By doing so, he himself tried to make his followers realise their duties towards their fellow men. Later, he used to pay the debt of those who died without paying it.

The Arabic word *"huqūq"* is used for human rights. *Huqūq* is plural of *haqq*. In Arabic one says: *Hathihi haqqi,* this is my right. *Haqq* is also one of the divine names, which means the real. Opposed to *haqq* is *bātil,* un-real or false. In sufi language, *Haqq* means the Absolute.[4] This word has also been used in the traditions of the Prophet. The Prophet is quoted as saying: "O, God, you are the Truth." He also said: "Hand over to every beneficiary his right".[5] The Ulama regarded human rights as an integral part of faith. A man cannot be considered religious in the true sense of the word if he does not grant the rights of his fellowmen.[6] The measure of judging a man's religiosity is how he deals with people, not how much he prays.

Muslim jurists have made a detailed study of human rights. Even the rights of animals did not escape their attention. In addition to the rights of parents, neighbours, children, wives, they also discussed civil rights. Every citizen of a Muslim state has the right to a decent living and to hold property. In addition, he has freedom of opinion, profession and movement. No one can deprive him of these rights. Life is a divine gift, whose sanctity must be observed.

To put a life to death without justice means to put all humanity, as the Quran says, to death.[7] A Muslim himself is not allowed to commit suicide. He also has the right to own property as long as it does not harm the public interest. It may be noted that under the guise of public interest one cannot be deprived of one's basic requirements of life. For example, if a person has a piece of land which he himself cultivates or a house in which he lives, he will remain master of his personal property. It is related that in his last pilgrimage the Prophet said: "Your blood and your property are sacred until you meet your Lord . . . and He will ask you of your work".[8] The State or society, according to Islamic teachings, is bound to provide man with the basic requirements of life; i.e. *food, housing, clothing.*[9]

As regards the individual's freedom, no restriction would be imposed on it by a government, and no one will be put in prison without a legal order from a court. Both the Prophet and his successors made it clear that a person would not be arrested only on the ground of an accusation made by someone.[10]

It is also related that Umar was informed of false testimonies taking place in the court. "By God! a man would not be arrested without justice",[11] he said. According to Muslim jurists, there are two kinds of detention; first, the detention sanctioned by a court, second, the detention for investigation.[12] Needless to say the second kind of detention would be for a short period. The present law in some Muslim countries is to put a man under custody without trial for 3 to 6 months which is absolutely against Islamic law. Instead this law is one of the colonial legacies handed over to their true local successors.

FUNDAMENTAL RIGHTS

Freedom

Muslim thinkers consider freedom as the most essential value in human life, while slavery is an evil opposed to human dignity. The idea of the free man is very clear in the Quran, but it also says that a free man who determines his affairs as he likes is he who frees himself from the bondage of evil. The free man of the Quran is a man of virtue and generosity, and one who has liberated himself from the coils of evil. Once some women came to the Prophet for conversion to Islam. The Prophet advised them not to commit certain sins, of which adultery was one. "Would a free woman commit adultery, O apostle of God?", the women answered the Prophet.[13] A man of evil character may label himself as free in profane society, but Islamic traditions do not consider him free in the true sense of the term.

Before we discuss various aspects of freedom, I wish to say a few words about slavery. Islam did not abolish at once the centuries old institution of slavery which had already existed in the Arab society at the time of the Prophet, but it determined to wipe it out gradually and systematically. It adopted the same method about other social evils.

The Quran undertook the task in its own way. On the intellectual plane, both the Quran and the Prophet's actions reminded people that all human beings are brothers in the family of God. Division among men on the basis of race, colour, language and wealth has no place in Islam, because 'all men are sons of Adam'. Piety alone makes a man noble in the eyes of God. On the practical level, the Quran urge Muslims to set their slave brothers free. In addition, the Quran made certain laws to the effect that a Muslim should pay atonement for his mistakes or errors. Setting slaves free is one form of atonement. It also ordained upon the State to spend a portion of *Zakat* on the freedom of slaves.[14] It is to be noted that it was a common custom to distribute prisoners of war as slaves among victorious armies. But the Quran abolished this custom by declaring that the prisoners of war should be set free.[15] The Prophet himself set his bitter opponents free when he entered into Mecca as a visitor.

Since freedom is as Muslim jurists say, an essential aspect of human life[16] and slavery is a temporary phase, they tried their best to find out ways leading to freedom. Once a band of slaves joined the Prophet when he besieged the fort of Tāif. The Prophet freed them all. Later, their masters came to the Prophet and spoke of their slaves. "They are free", the Prophet answered. Later, Muslim Jurists made a law to the effect that any slave, regardless of his faith, who entered into the land of Islam, was a free man.[17] Muslim thinkers also made another law which shows their deep sense of commitment to history. It says that if Muslims dispute with non-Muslims over the social status of some people who, according to the non-Muslim claim are free, their point of view will be accepted against those Muslims who regarded them as slaves.[18] These few examples bear witness to the fact that Islam introduced reforms and laws in order to give a new life to the unfortunate men of society. The Prophet and his close companions set examples by freeing their own slaves. Had the Quranic message been carried out by Muslim rulers[19] as it was carried out by the Prophet's early successors, slavery would have vanished from Muslim society centuries ago.

Freedom of Religion

According to Quranic teachings, religion is a personal affair between man and God, so everyone is completely free in his choice of faith. No one has the right to impose his faith on others. There is, as the Quran says, no compulsion in religion. The Prophet's duty, as described by the Quran, is to convey his message to people who on their part have the right to accept or reject it. The reason for the conflict between the Prophet and the Meccans was not the denial of Islam by the Meccans; on the contrary, it was the denial of freedom of thought and expression. The Meccans refused, for one reason or another, to recognise the Prophet's right to have his own faith and practice, although he told them: "To you your religion and to me my religion."[20] Further, he offered co-operation to the people of the Book to work for the glory of God, the Meccans paid no heed to the Prophet's appeal. They tried to bring him back to paganism by force. Consequently, the Prophet and his followers underwent a great deal of suffering. Thus the denial of freedom of conscience to the Muslims on the part of Meccans led to conflict.

It is to be noted that a Muslim's relations with his non-Muslim fellowmen are based on peace and not on war. War is a temporary phase which is allowed if Muslims have become victim of an aggression, otherwise, they are not permitted to wage a war against peaceful peoples, whatever their faith may be. The majority of Muslim jurists, such as Imam Abu Hanīfa, Mālik, Ibn Hanble and others held the view that the cause of war is an aggression and not the denial of Islamic faith, secondly, the aim of war is to bring the persecution to an end, thirdly, Muslims are allowed to enter into a temporary or permanent no war pact with those who believe in peaceful co-existence.[21]

The Quran enjoined upon them the defence of the right to religious freedom. This not only secured religious freedom for Muslims but also for all those who worshipped God in their own temples. On this point, the Quran made a statement to the effect that it is the divine will which brings people face to face with aggressors who ultimately fall. By doing so, he saves the synagogue, the church and the mosque from destruction.[22] The Quranic statement concerning various places of worship reveals the fact that whether believers be Jews, Christians, Muslims, Hindus, or Buddhist they should work for the freedom of conscience and for the better understanding of faiths. In fact, a devotee of God alone appreciates another lover of God and freedom, because religion makes him revere the great traditions of freedom, truth, and generosity.

It may be noted that in ancient times, the Roman empire in the West[23] and Asoka's in the East,[24] recognised freedom of faith and practice. But with the passing of time, this noble tradition was abandoned and the impression was created that persecution, stagnation and ignorance go hand in hand with religion. Islam restored this noble tradition and made a notable contribution to the history of religious freedom and tolerance.

The concept of religious freedom, also requires that one should not attack the teachers of other faiths while preaching one's religion. Thus, in accordance with Quranic teachings and the Prophet's pact that he made with the Christians,[25] non-Muslim citizens of a Muslim majority country have complete freedom of faith and practice. Muslims are bound by their faith to observe the sanctity of non-Muslim temples.[26]

Political Rights

Every citizen of a Muslim state has the right to participate in the State's affairs. To play a positive and active role, one can criticise the administration and the government for which he would not be penalised. Islam did not introduce a specific form of government, but it explained with clarity the final goal of the State and its nature. Government, according to the Quran, must be based on *Shūra,* i.e. Consultation. The concept of Shūra led early Muslims to believe rightly that the community is the master of its political destiny. People can depose a head of state whom they have elected by free will. The head of the state is bound to consult and Advisory Council, and to work for the establishment of justice and law which grants no special privilege to anyone. It was the misfortune of the Muslim nations that the remarkable early experiments made by Muslims were not allowed to mature. Consequently, Shūra could not develop into an effective institution. Political and military adventurers managed to seize power, and "consequently failed to do anything for the political improvement of Asia".[27] In spite of all the political blunders, Muslim thinkers remained faithful to the early noble traditions set by Abu Bakr and Umar that government must be democratic and that polity must be based on principles of brotherhood and equality.

A few words should be said about the rights of non-Muslims living in a country where Muslims form the majority. It is evident from classical literature that Muslim jurists hold non-Muslims to be equal to Muslims, regarding their political rights. They can take part in government and have access to the public services. The only post confined to a Muslim is the office of the Caliph, i.e. the head of State. This classical view is based on a Quranic verse which says: "O believers, obey God, and obey the Messenger and those in authority among you." (4:59). The Ulama interpreted the word (s'yiygl) as rulers. Some jurists did not agree with this interpretation. To them it applied to the men of Quranic knowledge and of religion.[28] In support of this second opinion, one can say that Muslims are not supposed to obey corrupt rulers even if they claim to be Muslims.

Secondly, early Muslims migrated to Abyssinia, a Christian state which granted them political asylum. They, of course, acknowledged the political sovereignty of the non-Muslim king. They did so with the full permission of the Prophet. Third, there are authentic classical texts which reveal that Muslim citizens of a non-Muslim state have always remained faithful subjects of non-Muslim rulers under whose protection they enjoyed freedom of faith and practice.[29] These examples would suffice to refute the opinion that Muslims in their political and secular affairs should obey none save a Muslim ruler. Today, this opinion seems to be insignificant since political authority and sovereignty rest with parliament and the constitution. We have witnessed that a Muslim head of State in India could do no harm to Hinduism, which is the main force in Indian social life. In fact, if a constitution guarantees that no law would be introduced in a Muslim majority country repugnant to Islam, then the question of a constitutional head of State, whether or not a Muslim, becomes immaterial. However, according to classical authorities, the Caliph can nominate a non-Muslim as a minister,[30] a governor or a secretary. Consequently, many Christians and Jews occupied high positions in Muslim governments, including the post of prime minister.[31]

Needless to say non-Muslims have the right to vote and take part in elections for National Assemblies. In other words, they, together with their Muslim countrymen, can elect their head of state.

Mention must be made of certain constitutional restrictions

imposed by some Muslim countries on their non-Muslim citizens. According to these restrictions certain administrative posts of importance, like those of prime minister, are confined to Muslims alone. These restrictions have no authority from the classical age of Muslim polity as we have already seen. The joint ruling system, in which every community participates in government on an equal footing, at least in theory, is a common custom of modern times and is a product of secularism, but it by no means goes against the early traditions of Muslim polity. The Madina agreement between the Prophet and the Jews recognised the equal political rights of both parties.[32] Because, as Muslim thinkers say, both Muslim and non-Muslims are equal so far as material and worldly suffering is concerned.[33] To deliver them from such suffering is the basic requirement of justice for which Islam stands. Such restrictions, therefore, contradict the claim of equal rights for everyone. It is surprising to note that some Ulama[34] have recommended these restrictions, while knowing the fact that some Muslim states had joined the British Commonweath and other International bodies whose heads were non-Muslims. None of the Ulama raised an objection against this decision on the basis of religion.

Freedom of Financial Life

Political freedom is indeed important, but it remains a myth and illusion without the emancipation of man from exploitation. It is difficult for a Western citizen to realise to what extent the common people and peasants have suffered at the hands of landlords in the East. The landlords, together with the ruling class, denied the right of decent life to their own countrymen.[35] To make man free of material anxiety, Islam does not allow a man to live at the cost of other men. True, Capitalism is a product of modern times and the term does not strictly apply to the systems of medieval ages. Nevertheless, the Prophet and his early successors introduced land reforms with a view to bringing to an end humiliation, repression and exploitations which prevent man from gaining happiness. Land, which remained the main source of wealth in those days, was given to those who cultivated it. Once the Prophet gave a piece of land to Bilāl al-Muzani, but Umar took it back from him and said: "The Messenger of God has not granted it to you so that you should prevent other people from holding it: he granted it to you in order to work. Take whatever you can cultivate and return the rest."[36] It is also related that the Prophet asked some of his companions to give up their lands which they themselves did not cultivate.[37] In Madina, people used to give their lands to the peasants on the condition that they would receive a portion from the harvest. The Prophet absolutely prohibited it and advised people to surrender their surplus land to their brethren. Thus the custom of *muzara'a* was abolished by the Prophet. The social policy adopted by the Prophet and Umar shows that a man should not live at the cost of his fellowmen. Secondly, they recognised the right of a limited ownership for an individual as long as it does not harm the interest of society. In fact, Islam does not allow an individual to impose his will on society. At the same time, it does not permit a party to impose its will on society. It seeks harmony between both; individual and society. It is, therefore, opposed to feudalism and capitalism in which man becomes a slave. It is the duty of the State to liberate its citizens from such exploitation. To do so, the means of production must be made public.[38]

It is a pleasure to note that some Muslim revolutionaries are trying their best to bring the centuries old corrupt economic system to an end. Speaking on the subject of social justice,, Qadhāfī says:

> Islam protects the rights and dues of every people, irrespective of their religion, colour and nationality. Socialism is, from the economic point of view, the only solution for man's economic problems. It is neither communism nor is it capitalism.[39]

In the end I wish to say that responsibility for the denial of human rights in a Muslim country lies with the ruling class and not with Islam. It is hoped that Muslim peoples will be able to put their ideals into practice, because application is the measure of all ideals. To believe in truth is, no doubt, good, but to live with truth is the true and the most difficult task in the life of man. Faith in human rights alone cannot make man free of fear and spiritual anxiety.

> "To speak of a person's liberty, life and security as his or her right is in fact a curious legalistic formation. What we really want to protect is not the person's right but the person himself."[40]

Notes

1. Quran. 17:70 "We have honoured the Children of Adam, and preferred them greatly over many of those We created." (Arberry's translation).
2. This speech is also attributed to 'Umar. See Mubarrad *al-Kamil* (ed. Ali al-Mirsafi), Cairo 1927, v. I. p. 82.
3. *"ma'rifa al-nafs ma Iaha wa ma* 'alaiha", see Bahr-al-ra'iq. p. 6. See also H. A. R. Gibb, *Modern Trends in Islam,* London, 1946 p. 87. "The science of Law", says Gibb, in the words of one of the famous Muslim definitions, "is the knowledge of the rights and duties whereby man is enabled to observe right conduct in this life, and to prepare himself for the world to come".
4. Muhammad al-Thānawī, *Kashshaf instilahat al-Funun,* Calcutta 1864, pp. 329-30 (ar. haqq); Sarskhsi, *Usul,* Cairo 1954 V. 2. pp. 332-40.
5. In fact, these words were spoken by Salman to his companion. Later he informed the Prophet who endorsed Salman's saying. see Bukhari *Al-Jam'i al-Sahih* (ed.) Ludolph Krehl Leiden 1862, v. I. p. 490. (ch. Fasting).
6. Writing on this point, Ashraf Alī Thānawī says: Those who consider themselves men of religion by virtue of mere prayers are wrong because a true man of religion pays to both God and man their dues. There is, Thānawī says, no distinction between Muslim and non-Muslin, so far as the question of man's rights is concerned. See. *Huquq-o- Fara'id,* Karachi (Urdu) pp. 426-27. In fact, the concept of prayer or divine service is often misunderstood. What is meant by prayer today is to observe certain rituals in the mosque. The Quran does not support this notion. A true believer seeks welfare of man because he is the external manifestation of Divine Will.
7. Quran. 5:32.
8. Ibn Hisham, *Sirat Rasul Allah,* Cairo 1955 v. 2. p. 603.
9. Ibn Hazm, *al-Muhalla,* Cairo v. 6. pp. 156-58. "Rich people of society are bound, says Ibn Hazm, "to look after their needy fellowmen. If they fail to do so, the ruler can force them to do so". This view, that society or the State is bound to care for its members, is based on Quranic verse; 17:26; 4:36.
10. Abu Yusuf, *Kitab al-Kharaj,* Cairo (H. Bulag.), 1302, p. 107.
11. Malik *Muwatta'.* Cairo 1951, ch. Witnesses.
12. Abu Sulaiman al-Khattābī, *Maa'lim al-Sunan,* Halab 1933, v. 4, p. 179. (It is related that the Prophet detained a man (for investigation) for one hour during the day, then he released him. p. 179).
13. al-Qurtubi, *Ahkam al-Quran* Cairo 1949 vol. 8, p. 72 (*Quran* 60:12).
14. *Quran* 9:60.
15. *Quran* 47:4

16. "al-asl fi al-nasi al-hurriya", see, Sarakhsi, *Sharh al-Siyar al-Kabir* Deccan n.d. v. 4, p. 71.
17. Ibid., v. 4, p. 380.
18. *Sharh al-Siyar al-Kabir,* v. 4, p. 71.
19. It is a matter of deep regret that despite Quranic teaching on the subject of human freedom and dignity, the Ulama of the court supported the corrupt rulers and utterly failed to lead Islamic law to the path of the abolition of slavery.
20. *Quran,* 109:6.
21. Ibn Taimiya, *Risala al-Qital,* p. 116, quoted by Abu Zahra, Ibn Taimiya, Cairo, p. 317, Abu al kalam Azad, *Tarjuman al–Quran,* Lahore, v. 2, p. 145-146., see also Rashid Ahmad "Rights of non-Muslims in an Islamic State".
22. The Quran 22:44 says: Had God not driven back the people, some by the means of others, there had been destroyed cloisters and churches, oratories and Mosques wherein God's Name is much mentioned.
23. J. B. Bury, *A History of Freedom Thought,* London 1957, p. 33. The decree is as follows: "We are disposed to extend to those unhappy men the effects of our wonted clemency. We permit them, therefore, freely to profess their private opinions, and to assemble in their conventicles without fear or molestation, provided always that they preserve a due respect to the established laws and government."
24. See Radhakrishnan, *The Hindu View of Life* London 1961, p. 41.
25. Abu Ubaid *Kitab al-Amwal,* Cairo, p. 188. See also *Al-Kharaj* of Abu Yusaf, Cairo 1302, p. 41.
26. *Speeches, Writings and Statements of Iqbal,* Lahore, p. 9.
27. Ibid., p. 120.
28. This view is attributed to Mujahid and Malik, see, Qurtubi, *Ahkam al-Quran,* Cairo 1949, v. 5, –. 259. The Ulama hold, says Qurtubi, that guidance of honest and sincere non-Muslim (in secular affairs) can be accepted. v. 8. p. 145.
29. Mas'udi, *Muruh al-Dhahab,* Cairo 1949, pp. 170, 210 ed. by Muhammad b. Abd al-Hamid. See, also, M. Hamid Allah. *The Muslim Conduct of State,* Lahore 1964, pp. 122-125.
30. According to al-Mawardi and Abu Yala, a non-Muslim can be appointed as minister with limited powers. It seems that the concept of 'limited powers' held by both classical jurists was a reaction against the powerful non-Muslim ministers of the Caliph.
31. T. W. Arnold, *The Preaching of Islam,* Lahore 1961, p. 64.; Salahuddin Khuda Bakhsh & Margovouth, *The Renaissance of Islam,* Lahore 1961, p. 51.
32. According to the Agreement, both Muslims and the Jews were asked (a) to consult each other, (b) to bear the expenses of war, (c) to defend

Madina, (d) the Jews are one community with the Muslims, (Umma Wahida) (e) both are free in their religion. This Agreement shows the political wisdom of the Prophet who considered political unity among various parties to be essential for the solidarity, and stability of state. See Ibn Hisham, *Sirat Rasul Allah,* Cairo 1955, vol. 1, p. 503, 504, R. B. Serjeant; The Constitution of Madina, *Islamic Quarterly* London: June 1964, pp. 7-16. Abu Ubaid *Kitab al-Amwal,* p. 125.

33. See M. Hamid Ulich, *Muslim Conduct of State* Lahore 1964, p. 72.
34. Maududi *A. Islami Riyasat,* Lahore 1962, pp. 365, 366. Maududi is of the view that non-Muslims have no right to be members of Parliament. But under the pressure of modern life, it appears, he has not stuck to his view. Ibid., p. 363.
35. Speaking in the Punjab Assembly, once Iqbal said: "I think it was Charles Lamb who said that mankind are really divided into two classes, creditors and debtors. In so far as this Province is concerned, if we drop the religious labels – Hindu and Muslim – and substitute the economic labels, lenders and borrowers", Lamb's remark is perfectly true. On another occasion, he said: "The future of Islam in India largely depends, in my opinion, on the freedom of Muslim peasants in the Punjab." See *Statements,* pp. 41, 61.
36. Abu Ubaid. *Kitab al-Amwal,* Cairo, p. 290; see also Yahya b Adam's Kharaj, p. 110.
37. *Sahih* of Bukhari op. cit. v. 2. p. 72, 73 (book of muzara'a). On the basis of traditions related on the authority of Raf'ib Khadij, a majority of distinguished jurists and scholars of the early days, rejected the custom of *muzari'a.* Abu Hanifa whose followers form a majority in the non-Arab Muslim countries like Pakistan, Afghanistan, Turkey, was one of those who regarded *musari'a* as unlawful. It is surprising to note that Hanafi Ulama have tolerated landlordism. Instead of Abu Hanifa, they followed Abu Yusuf (Abu Hanifa's pupil) who allowed muzari'a. See for details, Ibn Hazm, *al-Mulhalla* v. 8, p. 212, 213. Sarakshi, Mabsut cf. v. 23, p. 11, 12.

    In modern times, Manazer Hasan is perhaps the only outstanding scholar of the sub-continent of India who denounced landlordism and considered it un-Islamic. Writing on the subject, he says: I do not know whether there is anyone in the history who held like the Prophet that land is a divine gift like air and light. Those who do not work on land have no right to take benefit of it. See *Islam awr Jagirdari Zimindari* Lahore 1975, p. 30.
38. In fact, the collective will of Muslim community has rejected the feudal system long ago. Furthermore, it forced the pro-feudal system Ulama to reconsider their views. For example Maudūdī opposed land reforms and said: since there are no legal restrictions on the ownership of money,

animal, things for personal use, houses, transport, why is it claimed that the Shari'a is inclined to limit rights of ownership for the cultivated land. On the same point, he further says: This prohibition of muzar'a, condition of self-cultivation, limitations on land's ownership, all these restrictions do not fit in the whole system of Islam. (*Masala Milkiyyat Zamin,* Lahore, 1950 pp. 53, 54). But in the Elections of 1970 in Pakistan, Maudūdī accepted the idea of limited ownership of land. (*Manshur of Jama at Islami*). It is to be noted that in 1970 the majority of Pakistani Ulama denounced socialism as a heresy, but their opponents who raised the slogan of Islamic socialism were able to win the election with an absolute majority. This shows that the common people are fully aware of their decadent social system. Thus to set people free from economic slavery the state can take the means of production under its control.

39. See *Nadwa Bris* (Discourses of Paris), Beruit, p. 70. In 1970, Quadafi paid a short visit to Paris where he arranged a meeting with French intellectuals and discussed in detail several social, political and religious problems of Arab society; see also *The Green Book,* London, part 2. In the second part of his Green Book, Quadafi describes his 'new socialist society', in which everyone will be entitled to have a limited personal property, necessary for his material and spiritual happiness. It is said that Qudafi held a meeting with some divines who raised objections against his economic policies. In their argument, they quoted some traditions of the Prophet. In answering, Quadafi cited Quranic verses and said that the Quran is the main source for Muslims. (see *New Statesman,* Sep. 22, 1978).

    This approach is indeed similar to that of Umar who was in the words of Iqbal, "the first critical and independent mind in Islam who, at the last moment of the Prophet had the moral courage to utter these remarkable words: The Book of God is sufficient for us."

40. *The Times,* April, 6, 1977. Quoted by P. J. O'Mahoney *The Fantasy of Human Rights,* London, Mayhew-McCrimmon, 1978.

CHAPTER 4

MARXISM AND HUMAN RIGHTS

ISTVÁN MÉSZÁROS

In this paper I intend to survey those aspects of Marx's theory of law which carry the most important implications for human rights.

The wide-spread idea that Marxism is a crude economic reductionism according to which the functioning of the legal system is directly and mechanically determined by the economic structures of society, represents a Liberal interpretation of Marx's radical rejection of the Liberal conception of Law. To be sure, no one could deny that Marx had no use for the 'juridical illusion' which treats the sphere of rights as independent and self-regulating. However, the rejection of an illusion does not mean in the slightest that the legal sphere as a whole is considered to be illusory. Far from it, as we shall see in a moment. But first we must glance briefly at Marx's critique of Liberal theory in the context of human rights.

Marx's principal objection concerns the fundamental contradiction between the 'Rights of Man' and the reality of capitalist society in which these rights are supposed to be implemented. Marx makes it clear in his *Economic and Philosophic Manuscripts* of 1844 that 'The political economist reduces everything (just as does politics in its 'rights of man') to man, i.e. to the individual whom he strips of all determinateness so as to class him as capitalist or worker.'[1] He contrasts this tendency with the conditions of feudal landed property. Under feudalism the ties between land and its proprietor are not yet reduced to the status of mere material wealth:

> The estate is individualised with its lord: it has his rank, is baronial or ducal with him, has his privileges, his jurisdiction, his political position etc. It appears as the inorganic body of its lord. Hence the proverb *nulle terre sans maitre* which expresses

> the fusion of nobility and landed property. Similarly the rule of landed property does not appear directly as the rule of mere capital. For those belonging to it, the estate is more like their fatherland. It is a constricted sort of nationality.[2]

Thus Marx pinpoints the illusory element in the various theories concerned with the 'rights of man' in their *abstraction* from the material conditions of a radical social transformation which sees a shift from *nulle terre sans maitre* to *l'argent n'a pas le maitre;* the latter corresponding to conditions in which alienation predominates in all walks and over all facets of life, from the functioning of the fundamental economic structures to the most intimate personal relations of the individuals who constitute society.

We cannot go into the details of why the bourgeois opposition to feudal ideology had to champion the rights of 'Man' in its insistence on the alienability of land and with it on the equality of the right to possession and acquistion.[3] The point that directly concerns us here is that this insistence on the 'rights of man' could not be more than a formal-legalistic postulate ultimately devoid of content. It is precisely the latter characteristic which meets with Marx's sarcastic disapproval. For the application of the claimed equal right to possession culminated in a radical contradiction in that it necessarily implied the *exclusion* of everybody else from one's effective possession. Thus the only form in which land could be alienated in accordance with the 'rights of man' was one that transferred the *rights of possession* – through not in principle, as in feudal ideology, but *de facto* – to a limited number of people, excluding at the same time the rest of the population from the possession of land while maintaining the legal fiction of equality at the level of abstract rights.

As we can see, Marx's point is that the 'abstractness' we witness is not just a feature of legal theory which could be in principle remedied through an adequate theoretical solution, but an insoluble contradiction of the social structure itself. Bourgeois theories which abstractly champion the 'rights of man' are inherently suspect because they also champion the rights of universal alienability and exclusive possession, and thus they necessarily contradict and effectively nullify the selfsame 'rights of man' which they claim to establish. According to Marx the solution to this contradiction can only be envisaged at the level of social practice, where it originates. And he identifies this solution as the necessary abolition of the right to exclusive possession: the right which serves as the ultimate legal buttress to the whole network of exploitative relations which turn the 'rights of man' into an obscene mockery of its own rhetorics.

The irony is that somewhere at the beginning of the developments which produce the universal diffusion of 'contractual' relations, Hobbes can still assert with a somewhat naive openness that

> 'Riches, are Honourable; Poverty, Dishonourable'; 'The Value, or Worth of a man, is as of other things, his Price; that is to say, so much as would be given for the use of his Power: and therefore is not absolute; but a thing dependant on the need and judgment of another . . . 'And as in other things, so in men, not the seller, but the buyer determines the Price'.[4]

By the time we reach Locke: the idol of modern Liberalism, the main concern is the rationalisation of the prevailing inequality – no matter how grotesque are the devices employed, such as the blatantly self-serving concept of a 'tacit consent' – while maintaining the fiction of an 'original compact'. The real meaning of the 'rights of man' inherent in such an attitude becomes transparent when we remind ourselves of the unequal standard which Locke wants to apply on the one hand to the strictly controlled poor (requiring special passes even for the 'privilege' of begging, with dire consequences for the infringement of the rules: 'whoever shall counterfeit a pass shall lose his ears for the forgery for the first time that he is found guilty thereof'[5] and on the other to those who are in charge of the poor ('if any person *die* for want of due relief in any parish in which he ought to be relieved, the said parish be *fined* according to the circumstances of the fact and the heinousness of the crime.'[6]) – not to mention the top of the social hierarchy which assumes the right to enact such 'enlightened' measures.

Even Rousseau, the most radical of Marx's predecessors, fails to resolve the contradiction mentioned above. While he insists on the essential requirement of a genuine equality and condemns the ways in which legal systems perpetuate inequality,[7] he can only oppose an abstract moral ideal to the prevailing conditions. The reason for this deficiency in his theory is that he cannot imagine civilised life without private property as its ultimate foundation and regulatory force:

> Must *meum* and *tuum* be annihilated, and must we return again to the forests to live among bears? This is a deduction in the manner of my adversaries, which I would as soon anticipate as let them have the shame of drawing.[8] It is certain that the right of property is the most sacred of all the rights of citizenship, and even more important in some respects than liberty itself; . . . property is the true foundation of civil society, and the real guarantee of the undertakings of citizens: for if property were not answerable for personal actions, nothing would be easier than to evade duties and to laugh at the laws.[9]

We wonder therefore, that in the end even Rousseau must content himself with an abstract advocacy of the idealised circumstances 'when all have something and none too much', without being able to define what would amount to being 'too much' and what would constitute the necessary and sufficient 'something' to the advantage of all. Nor does he show whether or not the possession of just 'something' by some and the vaguely undefined 'not too much' by others are compatible, indeed permanently tenable. He simply assumes the feasibility of his idealised Social Contract without seriously questioning its necessary implications for the rule of private property.

The human rights of 'Liberty' 'Fraternity' and 'Equality' are therefore problematical, according to Marx, not in and by themselves, but in the context in which they originate as abstract and unrealisable ideal postulates, set against the disconcerting reality of the society of self-seeking individuals. A society ruled by the inhuman forces of antagonistic competition and ruthless acquisition coupled with the concentration of wealth and power in fewer and fewer hands. There can be no aprioristic opposition between Marxism and human rights. Quite the contrary. In point of fact, Marx never ceases to advocate 'the *free development of individualities*'[10] in a society of *associated,* and not antagonistically opposed, individuals (the necessary condition of both 'Liberty' and 'Fraternity') simultaneously anticipating 'the artistic, scientific, etc. development of individuals in the time set free, and with the means created, for all of them'[11] (the necessary condition of a true equality). The object of Marx's criticism is not human rights as such but the use of the alleged 'rights of man' as prefabricated rationalisations of the prevailing structures of inequality and domination. He insists that the values of any given system of rights must be assessed in terms of the concrete determinations to which the individuals of the society in question are subjected, otherwise they become supporting pillars of partiality and exploitation which they are in principle supposed to oppose in the name of the interest of all. The sore point for Liberal theory is, of course, that Marx emphatically rejects the view that the right to private property (exclusive possession) constitutes the foundation of all human rights. For self-serving Liberal theory the equation is astonishingly simple; since Marx wants to abolish the 'sacred rights' to private property, he is the enemy of all human rights. But then we happen to know the necessary implications of the axiomatic assumption of private property for human rights in general. We know that the 'rights of man' in their application to possession are destined to mean for the overwhelming majority of individuals nothing more than the mere possession of rights to possess the 'rights of man'. Thus we know only too well – and not simply as a matter of theoretical consistency but also as a matter of bitterly dehumanising and ever-worsening historical fact in our divided world of 'haves' and 'have-nots' – that private property as the ultimate foundation of human rights deprives them of any meaningful content and transforms them, whether in the name of a 'tacit consent' or of its more sophisticated later versions, into a blatant justification of the crude reality of power, hierarchy and privilege.

Marx's rejection of the 'juridical illusion' according to which 'law is based on the will, and indeed on the will divorced from its real basis – on free will,'[12] services the purpose of identifying the real nature of the legal system precisely in order to grasp, and ultimately to gain control over, the actual determinations which arise from the legal system itself and affect the life-activities of all individuals. There can be no question of an economic reductionism, since the various legal factors are not one-sidedly determined by the material base but simultaneously also act as powerful determinants in the overall system of complex interchanges. Thus while it is nothing more than a 'juridical illusion' to assume that the contractual relations of capitalist society simply emanate from the 'individual (free) will of the contracting parties',[13] seen that in fact they correspond to the objective needs of functioning of the existing socio-economic structures, it would be completely foolish to deny the vitally important active role of the legal framework in the development and stablilisation as well as continued reproduction of the society in question under changing circumstances and in the face of both internal and external pressures. Consequently, the radical social transformation advocated by Marx becomes feasible only if the full weight of the legal sphere is duly acknowledged, with a view to facing up to the challenge represented by the specific legal structures themselves in the overall process.

The difficulty is that 'all elements exist in *duplicate form,* as *civic* elements and those of the *State'.*[14] Hence nothing is resolved by the proclamation of rights alone, not even by the most solemn proclamation of the rights of man. The legal sphere becomes effective to the very extent to which it succeeds in penetrating deep into the body of 'civil society'. By the same token, while in principle even the totality of legal statutes could be abolished through some generic proclamation to this effect, such an act would accomplish absolutely nothing without the corresponding real transformation of 'civil society', without which the abolished legal devices would be reproduced in some other form. When Marx refers to the 'fight for the abolition of the State and of bourgeois society'[15] in this necessary coupling of the two, he acknowledges not only the 'duplicate form' in which the civic elements and those of the State exist and co-exist in a reciprocal interpenetration, but simultaneously also the immense power which the legal structures continue to exercise until the radical transformation of civil society is really accomplished.

This acknowledgment of the determining power of the legal forms and structures is totally unintelligible in terms of the traditional (mechanistic) view of Marxism which stipulates a relationship of direct correspondence between the 'material base' and the 'ideological superstructure'. Such a view would be not only crudely simplistic, in its direct reduction of ideas to material processes, but would become also self-contradictory the moment it tried to assert the active role of the ideological forms in the overall process of social metabolism, having condemned them to passivity in the first place through the mechanistic reduction. Thus either the interpretation of Marx as an economic reductionist is untenable or his constant references to the active role of the ideological forms are totally devoid of meaning.

There is no space here to explore this problem in detail. Let it suffice to say that the necessary condition of an active intervention of ideas in the fundamental material processes is their mediation through the agency of individuals and institutions which occupy the required intermediary position between the two in virtue of being simultaneously both material and idea. Man is both *homo faber* and *homo sapiens,* and inseparably so. At the same time, the ideas which are not mediated to the material base of social life through the life-activities of the individuals who constitute society are in no sense active; on the contrary, they are lifeless relics of a bygone age. And since the individuals operate in determinate social contexts, they have to mediate their ideas in an insititutional form appropriate to the nature of the problems involved. Kierkegaard may well be right in saying that the question of 'faith' concerns the relationship between the individual and God; but the moment the idea of faith is generalised in a human context and enters the world as a 'religion' in the form of values and actions, the institution of the church is born as the concrete (and historically changing) framework of the religious 'idea in action' in the totality of social interchanges. The same goes, *mutatis mutandis,* for the intricate network of legal forms. The 'juridical illusion' is an illusion not because it predicates the impact of legal ideas on material processes but because it does so while ignoring the necessary *material mediations* which make such an impact possible at all. Laws do not simply emanate from 'the individuals' free will' but from the total life-processes and institutional realities of a dynamic social development of which the individuals' volitional determinations are an integral part.

In his attempt at locating with precision the legal and political structures in the total framework of social interaction, Marx first asserts that 'the anatomy of civil society has to be sought in political economy'[16] in that the analysis of the material conditions of life makes possible the solution of problems which remained a mystery to the 'ideologists' who tried to explain the development of juridical, political, philosophical, etc. ideas as self-developing entities. In oppostion to such views this is how Marx summarises what he calls his own 'guiding principle':

> In the social production of their existence, men inevitably enter into definite relations which are *independent of their will*, namely *relations of production* appropriate to a given stage in the development of their material forces of production. The totality of these relations of production constitutes the *economic structure* of society, the real foundation, on which arises a *legal and political superstructure* and to which correspond definite forms of social consciousness.[17]

As we can see, Marx's terms of reference are incomparably more complex than traditionally assumed. His primary concern is how to change the dehumanising conditions which make men enter into relations which are 'independent of their will' so as to able to oppose to them a social interchange in accordance with a 'general plan of freely combined individuals.'[18] Thus his dismissal of the juridical illusion is coupled with a search for the conditions under which the exercise of one's will is not nullified by the rectifying power of the prevailing material and institutional conditions of existence. Far from being a 'crude determinist' and an 'enemy of human rights', Marx is very much concerned here with the conditions of personal freedom, defined as a meaningful control by the individuals themselves of the relations into which they enter, as sharply opposed to their given conditions of existence which escape their will. This analysis of 1859 is conceived in the same spirit as his earlier discussion of freedom in another context where Marx writes:

> in imagination, individuals seem freer under the dominance of the bourgeoisie than before, because their conditions of life seem accidental; in reality, of course, they are less free, because they are more subjected to the violence of things.[19]

At the same time, it is important to notice that even Marx's concept of the 'economic structure of society' is very different from the distorting technological-reductionist interpretation. The economic structure of society for Marx is not a brute material existent but a set of determinate *human relations* which precisely as such are subject to change, and indeed even to the most radical change arising out of a socially conscious (socialist) human deliberation. Furthermore, we should also notice that Marx's set of concepts does not define the forms of social consciousness (let alone the individuals' ideas) in a direct relationship to the economic structure or material base but through the *intermediary link* of the 'legal and political superstructure' to which they 'correspond' at the level of ideas, without, however, being *identical* with it. Asserting the simple identity of the legal and political superstructure and the forms of social consciousness would in fact undermine the whole conception and make a mockery out of the idea of the active role of the superstructure. For the autonomy of ideas vis-a-vis the legal and political superstructure is a necessary precondition of the latter. The production of ideas beyond the immediate institutional constraints of the legal and political superstructure acts as a powerful propellent on this superstructure which in its turn dynamically affects the material functions of social life. Without it, the class realities would automatically assert themselves as an iron determination, destroying the very concepts of law and politics in any meaningful sense of these terms. Their place would be taken by the crudest form of legal dictates – which would be in fact identical with the determination of the most elementary production functions – devoid not only of any system of justification, appeal and adjustment (with dire implications for the destruction of this framework of 'Law') but also of the possibility of a proper Legislature whose function would be taken over by the frightful mechanism of the totally dehumanised material dictates. And since this sham 'Law' as strictly determined by the immediate material dictates could not possibly regulate itself, nor indeed the vital material functions of the given economic structure, the contradictions of the latter would run riot and totally disrupt the social metabolism in no time at all. Similarly with a 'Politics' of direct material determinations, it would exhibit the same structure and contradictions as its legal counterpart, with the most devastating implications for social life as a whole.

Accordingly, the elementary condition of a successful functioning of the social metabolism in a society in which the economic structure is not free from contradictions is the active role of the legal and political superstructure made possible by its relative autonomy from the material base – which in its turn necessarily implies the relative autonomy of ideas and forms of social consciousness from the legal and political superstructure itself, as we have seen. It is in this framework of complex dialectical interactions that the idea of human rights becomes intelligible and truly meaningful. For whatever the material determinations of a class society, its contradictions are tolerable only up to the point when they start endangering the fundamental social metabolism itself. When this happens, the self-legitimation of this society is radically undermined and its class character is sharply pushed into relief through its failure to sustain itself as a system corresponding to the requirements of elementary human rights. Thus, paradoxically, the conditions of its erstwhile legitimation – the ideologically successful appeal to human rights – turn against it, in that at the time of a devastating crisis of the social metabolism itself it is no longer able to claim to represent the most adequate realisation of human aspirations.

The point is that the 'interest of the social metabolism' is not an arbitrary or rhetorical notion, but a most vital reality, since it refers to the ultimate conditions of human existence itself. In this sense, the legitimation of a socialist alternative to the capitalist mode of social interchange cannot bypass the issue of human rights. Socialism must prove its superiority to capitalism precisely in overcoming the contradictions of partiality by releasing the suppressed energies of human fulfilment for *all* individuals. This is why Marx – 'young' and 'old' alike – insists on the 'free development of individualities'[20] anticipating a framework of social interaction in which men live 'under conditions most favourable to, and worthy of, their human nature.'[21] Equally, his way of pointing to the dramatic alternative of 'socialism or barbarism' indicates the same appeal to the higher interest of human self-realisation, as opposed to the threatening perspectives of self-destruction: this ultimate, categorical, and final negation of all human rights.

Admittedly, human rights – i.e. the most comprehensive category in which legal relations can be articulated – concerns the whole of humanity. Yet, the idea of human rights would be meaningless if they did not apply directly to the individuals. Offenders against human rights are individuals or groups of individuals, and their offence does not affect some impersonal collective entity but the conditions of existence of particular individuals, including in the last analysis the offenders themselves. Socio-economic systems which ultimately threaten the destruction of mankind are operated by individuals who carry on their activities on a limited time scale and under determinations (e.g. the danger of bankruptcy) which make it difficult for them to see the destructive implications of their line of conduct in the longer run. The circumstance, however, does not alter the fact that what we see at work here is an objective contradiction between a sectional interest and the interest of humanity at large in which the offenders themselves participate.

Enforcing the conditions of a genuine exercise of human rights, therefore, necessarily involves the application of an equal standard to the totality of individuals. For 'right by its very nature can consist only in the application of an equal standard.'[22] If the application of this equal standard simultaneously requires the denial of another right – in that the destructive functioning of the partial interest must be restricted – this is not a contradiction of the system of human rights but of the given socio-economic structure which produces such contradictory determinations. And while there is no conceptual difficulty in suggesting that the right expressing the higher interest of humanity overrules the sectional interest, in reality the exercise of human rights remains a mere postulate and an ideological rhetoric so long as the sectional interests of a divided society prevail and paralyse the realisation of the interest of all. In such a society 'the interest of all' is defined as the undisturbed functioning of a social order which leaves the prevailing sectional interests intact and circumscribes the possibilities of an admissible social change from that perspective. Seeing how things work in such a society, it is tempting to conclude that 'the interest of all' is an empty ideological concept whose function is the legitimation and perpetuation of the given system of domination. However, to agree with this view would mean to be trapped by the contradiction which sets permanently one sectional interest against another and denies the possibility of escaping from the vicious circle of sectional determinations.

In sharp contrast to such views Marx forumulates his strategy of a socialist transformation as embracing the interest of the whole of society. He insists that the proletariat is fit to accomplish the task of 'universal emancipation' precisely because it constitutes the 'universal class'[23] which cannot impose itself on society as a new form of exploitative and parasitic sectional interest since it represents the condition of labour. Marx is, therefore, not concerned with establishing a social order simply on the basis of the *de facto* effective power of the majority to subdue the sectional interests of the formerly ruling minority, but with the superiority *de jure* of socialism over capitalism, defined as the ability to release the energies of self-realisation in all individuals, as against capitalism which must deny to them the possibility of self-realisation in the interest of the unhampered 'self-expansion of capital,'[24] no matter how destructive its consequences.

Marx describes the conditions of liberation as the emancipation of all individuals from the overpowering forces and determinations to which they are subjected. In this respect he repeatedly stresses not only that the exploited class must be emancipated from the domination of the ruling class but also that the individuals must be emancipated from their subjection to their own class and to the corresponding social division of labour:

> The class in its turn achieves an independent existence over against the individuals, so that the latter find their conditions of existence predestined, and hence have their position in life and their personal development assigned to them by their class, become subsumed under it. This is the same phenomenon as the subjection of the separate individuals to the division of labour and can only be removed by the abolition of private property and of labour itself.[25]

The defeat of the exploiting class is therefore a hollow triumph if it does not carry with it the emancipation of individuals as individuals. The real issue at stake is personal freedom, in the fullest sense of the term. It necessarily implies the abolition of the division of labour in that the latter sharply contradicts the conditions of self-realisation of individuals as individuals:

> The transformation, through the division of labour of *personal* powers (relationships) into *material* powers, cannot be dispelled by dismissing the general idea of it from one's mind, but can only be abolished by the *individuals* again subjecting these material powers to themselves and abolishing the division of labour. This is not possible without the community. Only in community with others has each individual the means of cultivating his gifts in all directions; only in the community, therefore, is *personal freedom* possible. In the previous substitutes for the community, in the State, etc., *personal freedom* has existed only for the individuals who developed within the relationships of the ruling class, and only insofar as they were

> individuals of this class. The illusory community, in which individuals have up till now combined, always took on an *independent* existence in relation to them, and was at the same time, since it was the combination of one class over against another, not only a completely illusory community, but a new fetter as well. In the real community the *individuals* obtain their *freedom* in and through their *association.*[26]

Marx lays great stress on the point that so long as the individuals are subsumed under a class they do not possess a true individuality: they can only assert themselves as '*average* individuals'[27], but not as unique individuals who realise to the full their potentialities. This is why in Marx's view the realisation of true individuality necessarily implies not only the abolition of the division of labour but simultaneously also the abolition of the State, which can only deal with average individuals,[28] and thus even in its most en lightened possible form it imprisons them in the conditions of abstract individuality.

Thus, Marx distinguishes three very different phases of social development to which human rights apply in significantly different form:

> (1) Under the conditions of a capitalist society the appeal to human rights involves the rejection of the ruling sectional interests and the advocacy of personal freedom and individual self-realisation, in opposition to the forces of dehumanisation and increasingly more destructive material domination or reification.
>
> (2) In a society of transition, human rights provide the standard which stipulates that in the interest of a true equality 'right instead of being equal would have to be unequal,'[29] so as to be able to discriminate positively in favour of needy individuals, in order to redress the inherited contradictions and inequalities.
>
> (3) In a 'higher phase of communist society', when – on the premise of the highest development commensurate with them – society gets 'from each according to his ability' and gives 'to each according to his needs,'[30] the need for the application of an equal standard is no longer present, since the full development of one individual in no way interferes with the self-realisation of others as true individuals. Under such circumstances – when both the division of labour and the State are effectively

superseded – the question of enforcing rights (be they human rights) cannot and need not arise in that the 'free development of individualities' (which in previous forms of social development, including the transitional society, could only be postulated in a more or less abstract form) is integral to the social metabolism and acts as its fundamental regulating principle.

But so long as we are where we are, and so long as the 'free development of individualites' lies as far ahead of us as it does, the realisation of human rights is and remains a concern of paramount importance for all socialists.

Notes

1. Marx, *Economic and Philosophic Manuscripts of 1844,* p. 129.
2. *Ibid.,* p. 61.
3. I discussed these problems in Chapters IV. and V. of my book on *Marx's Theory of Alienation,* London, 1970.
4. Hobbes, *Leviathan,* Chapter X.
5. Locke, *Project for the Reform of the Poor Law in England.*
6. *Ibid.,*
7. 'Under bad governments, this equality is only apparent and illusory; it serves only to keep the pauper in his povery and the rich man in the position he has usurped. In fact, laws are always of use to those who possess and harmful to those who have nothing: from which it follows that the social state is advantageous to men only *when all have something and none too much.'* Rousseau, *The Social Contract.*
8. Rousseau, *A Discourse on the Origin of Inequality: Appendix.*
9. Rousseau, *A Discourse on Political Economy.*
10. Marx, *Grundrisse,* Penguin ed., p. 706.
11. *Ibid.,*
12. Marx/Engels, *The German Ideology,* p. 80.
13. *Ibid.,* p; 81.
14. Marx, *Draft Plan for a Work on the Modern State* (1845).
15. *Ibid.,*
16. Marx, 'Preface' to *A Contribution to the Critique of Political Economy.*
17. *Ibid.,*
18. *The German Ideology,* p. 90.
19. *Ibid.,* p. 95.
20. *Grundrisse,* p. 706.
21. Marx, Capital, Vol. III., p. 800.
22. Marx, *Critique of the Gotha Programme.*
23. Marx, 'Introduction' to the *Critique of Hegel's Philosophy of Right.*
24. *Capital,* Vol. I., p. 621.

25. *The German Ideology*, pp. 69-70.
26. *Ibid.*, p. 93.
27. *Ibid.*, pp. 85 and 93.
28. *Ibid.*, p. 96.
29. *Critique of the Gotha Programme.*
30. *Ibid.*,

CHAPTER 5

A DIALECTIC OF RIGHT

GARRETT BARDEN

My intention is to indicate that all the major philosophical questions concerning human rights posed from the Hobbesian tradition emerge from the presupposition that a right is what one is to be permitted. I think that this presupposition is not so much incorrect as incomplete and I shall try to place rights in a wider context.

The Hobbesian notion of right comes from and coheres with a more general idea of society. In Hobbes a fundamental image is one of antagonism – human society is an association of antagonists who band together because of a greater fear of what solitary living would bring with it. The image may be softened so that instead of antagonists one thinks of fundamentally independent partners and society as the result of a contract between them. Rights within this context are a bundle of freedoms which are retained within the contract. The contract involves the abandonment of certain rights for what seems like a greater good and rights within the contract are those that are not abandoned, e.g. when a person lets his house he abandons certain rights which he had before the contract was signed. In fact, contract is the adjustment of rights.

However, to write of contract as the adjustment of rights is already to move away from the narrow context of what I am here calling the Hobbesian view into a broader context akin to that of Roman Law. Return to the narrower space. Rights tend to be conceived as at once absolute (in a special sense of being abandoned only by contract or, as perhaps in Spinoza, by force with some identification of right and might) and unlimited. It is not that Hobbes considered that it was unreasonable to abandon certain rights in favour of the social contract; on the contrary he considered it most reasonable to do so. But Hobbes did think that it was rights that one was reasonably abandoning. In other words, for Hobbes, there is a division between right and reason.

Although he does not make the identification the way is open for linking right and power or might.

This division between right and reason is crucial and shows how far the term had come in its development. Although the term 'right' is somewhat less ambivalent in modern English than in many other modern European languages it still retains some considerable ambiguity. First, it is the right hand with all it symbolises of honour, goodness, justice; then it is 'straight' (with its transferred images) and 'correct'; the 'right way' has the meaning of correctly using an implement, or properly doing a job and also the modern moral sense.[1] In middle High German the term 'recht' meant 'duty' and referred to the right way of performing one's work not only technically but socially.[2] In all of these senses right and reason are associated.

The division between right and reason finds an echo in the thinking of freedom. In the modern period freedom has come to mean absence of restraint and it has seemed dishonest and needlessly confusing to think of freedom in any other way. Once again it has not been thought that all restraints are unreasonable but, however reasonable, restraints are a restriction of a prior freedom.[3]

Thomas Hobbes is the great political thinker of this strand within European philosophy but the division has other and older sources. The dichotomy between body and soul as it was sometimes expressed by Plato and as it was systematically reconceived in the rationalist tradition is, on the individual level, what Hobbes is on the social. The soul is to the body what society is to the citizen. In different thinkers and at different periods different values may be given to either side of the dichotomy but the fundamental context remains the same.

Reason is by no means absent from this context but it is a contractual reason. The social contract is not arbitrary (that is, wilful, divorced utterly from considered reflections etc.) – quite the contrary. But the reasonableness involved is within the confines of the horizon set by the notion of society as a contract (in passing it is useful to recall that the idea of society as contracted did not emerge in the seventeenth century: it was known to, and rejected by, Plato. Aristotle, in the *Rhetoric* (I, xv, 1376b)[4] admits that the law is a kind of contract, Aquinas in the *De regimine principium* uses the image of contract.) Later Kant, while clearly stating that the social contract was not an historical event, still considered it an idea of reason without which it was impossible to correctly conceive society.

What, then, are the confines of contract? Contract is not arbitrary in the sense of being utterly divorced from considered reflection. It is possible to draw up what would normally be called a reasonable contract. It is even possible to imagine a situation where the only reasonable course seems to be to draw up a contract. But contract is arbitrary in another sense in as much as the contractors decide or do not decide in particular cases to enter into a contract with each other. 'The identical will which is brought into existence by the contract is only one *posited* by the parties, and so is only a will shared in common and not an absolutely universal will', as Hegel writes in his *Philosophy of Right* (par. 75).

If one takes the perspective of contract as fundamental, then first society as a whole and, subsequently social relations within society tend to be seen as taking place for the sake of the reasons present in the contracts, i.e. need in general, benevolence, advantage and so on. One fails to discern a more foundational reason within which these immediate reasons eventually have their justification. The perspective of contract is the perspective of those who enter into it; their advantage – even mutual advantage – is the foundational reason; they are not involved in anything greater than themselves.

In contract a shared common will is brought into existence which is properly embodied not in words alone but in the adjustment of rights. Contract adjusts the world and makes it responsive to, indeed the embodiment of, the mutual posited will of the contractual partners. Its perspective is the limited perspective – which in the end cannot be sustained – of the partners, conceived not fully as persons and so escaping from the limited perspective of this contract but precisely as contractors. The perspective of contract can be sustained only by deciding in advance what is to count as reason so that even in the case where to make a contract seems the only reasonable course the reason in question is still a contractual one.

Within a wholly contractual perspective there can be natural rights but they tend to be considered entirely as rights of the individual against society.[5]

Aristotle, in the *Rhetoric* (I, xiii, 1373b and I, xv, 1375a), takes as his example of a conflict between conventional and natural justice (I, xiii) or between written and unwritten law (I, xv) the story of Antigone in Sophocles' tragedy who buried her brother Polynices against the law of the ruler, Creon. But the way of speaking about the conflict is not that *she had a right* that was not acknowledged in the law, as if the right belonged to her, but rather that *it was right* that she should do this even against the written law for 'she declares that it is just, though forbidden, to bury Polynices, as being naturally just'.

What is at issue here is a difference in perspective. It is not a crude opposition where, on the one hand, there is the possibility of natural over against conventional justice, while, on the other hand, this possibility does not exist. In both perspectives there exists this opposition but it appears differently in each case.[6]

We may ask how Aristotle considers 'the law itself a kind of contract'. It is not that justice is a contract, nor that one enters into a contract to ground laws[7] but that particular laws, and even a particular legal system have some of the character of contract for there are different laws and different systems in various countries (1360a) and even though 'there is a general idea of just and unjust in accord with nature, as all men in a manner divine' still often 'there is neither communication nor agreement between them' (I, xiii, 1373b). The particular laws participate in the just, more or less well, but the particular laws are invented, posited and agreed by men.

Furthermore, if one accepts with Michel Villey,[8] that there is in Aristotle a distinction between 'justice' meaning 'virtue' and 'justice' meaning a particular defined virtue having to do with assigning to each his own, then once again it is easy to see how Aristotle would see particular laws as attempting to legislate in the general case for this just distribution, and particular judgement as not merely applying the written law but attempting, with its aid, to discern what is just. What is just then is not contracted but there is something like contract involved in a society's effort to establish schemes for the regular discerning of the just. Natural rights, therefore, are neither before nor distinct from justice although they are before and may be distinct from particular laws. Freedom, too, is not thought of as before justice but as being freely just: 'the written laws involve compulsion; the unwritten do not' (*Rhetoric* I, xiv, 1375a) – the contrast is this: within one context you are compelled by the law to do what otherwise you would not do, within another context you are compelled by the written law and its enforcers to do what otherwise (if the law is just) you would freely do. To act unjustly is not freedom.

The two contexts are more different emphases than outright contradictions and writers working dominantly within one context are rarely wholly oblivious of the way in which similar questions arise within the other, e.g. although what I have called here the Hobbesian context stresses the individual over against the whole (which was not altogether Hobbes' own intention) nonetheless theories of law and politics that have been constructed within this context have had as a central question the good of the whole. However, one does find the suggestion that sometimes rights are so fundamental that the good of the whole must be sacrificed so that these rights might be preserved. Indeed, Ronald Dworkin seems to think that this is what taking rights seriously means.[9]

In that seemingly innocuous sentence is the kernel of the difference between the two approaches. For one, the good of the individual can be opposed to the good of society; for the other, this opposition is impossible. The contrast is both rhetorical and conceptual and is complicated by the fact that one context can be interpreted from the perspective of the others.

If society is conceived as a contract, then, however much the idea of contract is an idea of reason as Kant thought, however vehemently it may be said that the contract did not take place in history, however impossible it may be to escape the contract, in some sense the contractors are conceived as separate from the contract and so as separate from society. They may be thought to have rights prior to the contract and it may be thought that some at least of these rights cannot be taken away in the contract. Furthermore, within the contract theory, society is the contract, i.e. is constituted by the contract, prior (whether that 'prior' be interpreted historically or logically) to the contract society simply is not. If there are rights before the contract, then the contract may recognise them but cannot constitute or confer them: these rights are imprescriptable. If there are rights that in some sense cannot be taken away in the contract these rights are inalienable.[10] Society, then, is in some respects at least less comprehensive than the individual who retains rights against the contracted society. And these rights must be honoured against the good of the society.

If, on the other hand, society is not contracted but is the whole of which the individual is a part, then the good of the part is subordinate to the good of the whole and apparently the individual loses all rights over against society.

But what is the whole of which the individual is a part? Is it a contracted society or something else? Here is where difference of perspective enters in, for it is misleading to understand the term 'society' within the non-contractual perspective as it is understood within the contractual perspective. The whole of which the individual is a part is not contracted society but the society of which contracted society is an imperfect specification. This means that although society is not a contract, particular societies are in a sense contracts.

Particular historical societies are in a sense contracts. The sense is metaphorical. Rather than the fairly specific term 'contract' with its implication of free agreement, the term 'construct' can be used. For 'construct' covers political action from free agreement to violence. Society, then, is not a construct although particular historical societies are.[11]

This has important consequences for the meaning of assertions like the 'good of society is more important than the good of the individual'. For different forms of society have different ends, e.g. 'the end of democracy is freedom, of oligarchy wealth, of aristocracy things relating to education and what the law prescribes . . .' (Aristotle, *Rhetoric* I, viii, 1366a). Each construct defines the part as well as the whole so that 'individual' has a different meaning in a democracy, an aristocracy, an oligarchy, a tyranny. In other words, as the particular historical society is constructed so too is its citizen. But as society is not a construct neither is its citizen. The tension then is no longer between society and citizen but between concrete historical constructs and the idea. The crucial discovery made by Heracleitus, Plato and Aristotle is that the present society is not the idea and this discovery transforms the meaning of the conflict.

The idea is wrongly conceived as a known ideal against which the actual must be measured. There can be a conflict between actuality and ideal and, indeed, this is the manner in which the conflict between idea and construct appears historically. But the ideal is itself only another historical construct and is itself subject to critique by the idea. The idea, then, is specifically effective only by being reduced to a construct which is itself open to criticism.

The idea is present in the dialectic between actuality and ideal but is contained by neither arm of the opposition. This dialectic occurs not only, nor even mainly in political discourse, but in each human relation, and in all its aspects, which is to say that the human is always present as incomplete in relation to an idea which can never be specified. From the liberal tradition I have taken the opposition between citizen and society and replaced it in another context in which it is shown to be the more fundamental opposition between construct and idea.

Specified rights belong to the construct and so are not absolute. They are attempts, necessarily incomplete, to embody the idea. Although rights are sometimes expressed in the imperative mood as commands, they are more properly expressed in the indicative mood as descriptions of the just relations between persons. Now the just relations between persons is specified in the law but this specification is always subject to the fundamental criticism exemplified in Sophocles' *Antigone.* And the justice against which the specification is measured is not another written law or precept but precisely the unwritten, the unspoken, the unspecified.

> There is then, as all divine, a general (or common) just and unjust by nature, although there may be neither communication nor agreement. The idea that men share is not a general idea of natural justice and injustice as the idea that there is a natural justice and injustice. *Rhet.* I, xiii, 1373b.

The liberal tradition which has, I think importantly, stressed the liberty of the individual against society, thinks of rights as rights of the individual against society. But rights, in the context being worked out here, are conceived as the right relations between members of society. The question of wrong must be faced. It is not the only question and not even always the most pressing political question but it is a perennial question: what right has a person to do wrong? The liberal tradition has been able to tackle this question and the common answer is a version of Mill: a person should be prevented from doing wrong only when what he is doing interferes significantly with the welfare of others or the rights of others. This has been a useful answer; it has gone some way to prevent undue interference with the private lives of citizens – it has upheld and developed valuable distinctions between, for example, state, society and government. It has, however, rested on a distinction between private and public morality which in the end fails. The natural law tradition has, I think, been embarrassed by the question and the traditional answer has been that the person has no right to do wrong. This answer is not, in my view, incorrect; it becomes incorrect when the assumption is made that if someone has no right to do wrong then someone else has a right to stop him. It is against this assumption that the liberal tradition developed its enormously valuable theory of toleration.[12]

When rights are conceived as right relations the question can be differently posed. The question now becomes: in human society to what extent should evil be permitted? To begin to answer the question we must return to two versions of freedom. According to one version, freedom is permission to do anything whatsoever and any rule is constraint. In the second version, freedom is freely to do what is just. These versions are only apparently contradictory for freedom is both a field and an act. The field of freedom is structured as p and –p; if p is what is just, then –p is what is unjust; but one cannot freely do p unless – p is possible. The free act, in the second version, is freely to do what is just which does not mean that –p (the unjust) can be chosen freely. Unless –p is possible, freedom is impossible because freedom is not p, but the possibility of freely doing p. The total elimination of the possibility of wrong would be also the total elimination of the possibility of freedom and, hence, virtue. So, in human society the possibility of evil remains within a right ordered society. Compulsion is the elimination of –p and so an increasingly compelled society is an increasingly less free society. So although a person has no right to do wrong, the right ordering of society includes the possibility of wrong and the consequent possibility of freedom.

The liberal theory of the limitation of freedom can be replaced into this context for it seems that some maxim like it is required. For it is no longer sufficient to say that if p is just, then p must be commanded (on the other hand, 'if p is not just, then p must not be commanded' still holds) nor can we say 'if p is not just, then p must be forbidden'. The practial question as to whether and how to forbid the unjust or command the just is by no means solved by saying that is unjust or just. Something of the same range as the liberal maxim is required but the liberal maxim won't do on its own because, if taken as a principle, it fails.

The liberal maxim involves the liberal theory of society and, in practice at any given time, it will be used as part of a rich and not theoretically clarified context so that, for example, what counts as undue interference with an individual's privacy will change from time to time while the expressed maxim remains the same. In other words, the maxim is not the kind of thing one can – unhistorically, unculturally, or with certainty – deduce a course of action from. Deductive non-historical certitude is not available, as everyone experiences in their lives and as many tend to forget when it comes to formal politico-moral argument.[13]

The maxim in practice is a reminder, i.e. it puts an aspect in mind. But most maxims are partial and have to be complemented by maxims which seem opposed – maxims do not properly contradict one another because they are not properly propositions. The liberal maxim may be opposed by a maxim which says that a society in which it is not made unduly difficult to discern the good must be preserved and constructed. There are other maxims and more can be invented. My intention is not to develop one and put it forward as the long awaited single maxim. Rather my effort has been to show briefly and to a limited extent what a maxim is.

I have tried to distinguish idea and construct and in this context:

(a) to show that rights are right relations;
(b) to suggest that right relations are not to be wholly compelled;
(c) to indicate why right relations can not be determined once and for all;
(d) to suggest that their discovery is the political enterprise;
(e) to show that maxims are reminders rather than promises in deductive arguments.

Finally, the political enterprise is the attempt through the conversation among citizens to discover the right relations between them. What is fundamentally between them, what guides their historical dialectic, is "the common just or unjust by nature" which all our power can never establish, but which leads us forward.

Notes

1. See on this question Liberato Santoro "An interpretation of Aristotle's concept of the 'Agathon Eudaimonia", *Seminar II,* Cork 1978 pp. 27-29.

2. The doctor in the Middle High German romance *Der Arme Heinrich* is said to 'break his right' if he will not treat a patient. I am indebted to Professor Peter Schaublin of Cork for this reference.
3. Cf. Ronald Dworking, *Taking Rights Seriously,* London, Duckworth, 1977, p. 267: 'Bentham said that any law whatsoever is an "infraction" of liberty, and though some such infractions might be necessary, it is obscurantist to pretend that they are not infractions after all.' Isaiah Berlin likewise thinks of liberty thus and this concept has become the "obviously correct" way to think about freedom.
4. All quotations from the *Rhetoric* are from the Loeb edition: Aristotle, *The "Art" of Rhetoric* translated by J. H. Freese, London 1967, Heinemann, (1926).
5. 'Contract' is used here in a loose sense; the positive law or custom of a community is what effects right within that community. This law need not, of course, be written; there need be no "code"; how right is effected in a community cannot be determined in the abstract.
6. Within the pure theory of law as enunciated by Kelsen in *The Pure Theory of Law,* trans. Max Knight. Berkeley, Los Angeles, University of California Press, 1970, there is no opposition possible between natural and conventional justice because the former – natural justice – does not have anything to do with law even if it exists. This position can be found throughout the book but see especially pages 48-9, 106, 217-21. Kelsen achieves this purity by making a legal system an entirely self-contained set of rules; his basic norm is a presupposition – 'Such a presupposed highest norm is referred to in this book as basic norm.' p. 195; 'Such a presupposition, establishing the objective validity of the norms of a moral or legal order, will here be called a *basic norm (Grundnorm).'* p. 8 – and so the system becomes axiomatic. Kelsen, however, admits that 'It is self-evident that the legal order makes a certain human behaviour the condition of a sanction, because the legal authority regards this behaviour as harmful to society.' p. 112. This self-evident fact is irrelevant for the purely formal concept of a delict as Kelsen goes on to say but it is this fissure in the formal system that gives rise to the question of 'right' law. See also Kelsen: "Justice et droit naturel" in various authors: *Le Droit Naturel,* Paris, P.U.F., 1959, pp. 1-123.
7. Kelsen's basic norm is not presented in the image of an historical contract but its formal position in his system corresponds to the formal position of contract in contract theory. Both, indeed, have to do with effectiveness and so are more than formally related.
8. Michel Villey; *Philosophie du Droit,* Paris, Dalloz, 1975; *Critique de la Pensée Juridique Moderne,* Paris, Dalloz, 1976. The theme is pervasive in Villey's work but see esp. *Torah-Dikaion* in the Critique pp. 19-50.
9. Ronald Dworkin, op.cit. esp. the essay "Taking Rights Seriously".

Although I do not think that there is this split between the good of the individual and the good of the whole, I think it is all too easy to specify the good of the whole wrongly and between this apparent good of the whole and the real good of both whole and individual there can be, and often is, a split. The basic dichotomy, however, is between real and apparent, not between whole and part.

10. Contracted rights are inalienable only if, within the contract, there is no way of alienating them. A constitution which purports to guarantee something only subject to statute gives only a pseudo-guarantee as Kelsen points out (op.cit. p. 143). In an as yet unpublished paper read to the Irish Philosophical Society in November 1977, "Inalienable rights and the Irish Constitution", D. M. Clarke showed that the Irish Constitution gives only such pseudo-guarantees. Kelsen is quite right to think that there is no formal need to think of an inalienable right as a natural or precontractual right, although the reason why the framers of the Constitution may have made a particular right inalienable is because they considered it to be precontractual. But legal inalienability is a part of the contractual arrangement. When it is not it is bombast.

11. cf. A. von Hayek, *Law, Legislation and Liberty,* London, R. K. P., 1976. Hayek understands Adam Smith's "invisible hand" guiding the market as the order that emerges from the interplay of different ideas, even opposed aims, as there is in a game two kinds of order: one is the order of the rules and the other is the order emergent in the game in play. Society, then, may be the result of several decisions, not a centralised decision and yet be an order and in the present sense, a construct.

12. The *locus classicus* for the liberal principle is the fourth chapter of Mill's essay *On Liberty.* But Mill himself in the fifth chapter, entitled "Applications", knows that in practice the principles are maxims and that the correct mode of their application in the concrete is not a deduction. Society, however, is conceived as an organisation with members who have also their own private goals which they must be allowed to pursue. In the end this conception will not suffice but it must be kept in mind in any attempt at a more comprehensive account. The important truth within it must be taken up (*aufgehoben*) otherwise one risks ending up with a totalitarian alternative that has been the perennial temptation of the natural law tradition. The warning given by P. Braud should be kept constantly in mind: "La fragilité des libertés publiques dans les États liberaux resulte du fait que leur universalité est essentiellement théorique, frappée dans des formules juridiques, comme celle de l'article ler de la Déclaration de 1789:" les hommes, naissent libres et égaux en droit, en distorsion sérieuse avec les faits.' "L'insaisissable liberté publique", *Extrait – supplément des Mélanges en l'honneur du Professeur Michel Strassinopoulos,* Paris 1974. Appropriately enough, Professor Braud's

article was withdrawn by the editors of the *Mélanges* itself, which was printed in Greece, for fear of the military regime then still in power. With the fall of that regime the paper was published separately.

13. In "Human rights and the Foundation of Morality" (Seminar II, Cork, 1978, pp. 10-20) F. Dorr develops the theme of uncertainty and tentativeness in political action: 'The rejection of (abstract, unhistorical) proof is not the rejection of the possibility of truth, though it makes it a more tentative and risky affair.' (p; 79).

CHAPTER 6

HUMAN LIFE AND HUMAN RIGHTS

RICHARD A. McCORMICK

There are many aspects of health-care that touch directly on human rights: the right to adequate health care, the right of self-determination (privacy) in acceptance or rejection of treatment, the right to be properly informed etc. I propose to treat one very troublesome problem as an example of the complexity of the question of rights as it touches health: the decision to treat or not to treat defective newborn babies.

This is a problem touching the most basic of human rights, the right to life. Put simply: if we *ought* to do certain things for newborns, then not doing them is a violation of their rights. Conversely, if we really *ought not* bring all the sophisticated available technology to certain defective newborns, then doing so can – at some point – represent a denial of their rights, a kind of "imposed survival" when this is no longer in the best interests of the baby involved. That rights are involved here no one doubts.[1] But before one can conduct the conversation in terms of rights, one must first analyse what is right and wrong and why. After we have done that, we will be able, by a convenient locution, to assert what are the child's rights. Hence our task in these extremely difficult cases is to discover what we *ought to do,* what we *need not do,* and why.

Drs. Raymond S. Duff and A. G. M. Campbell reported on 299 deaths in the special-care nursery of the Yale-New Haven Hospital between 1970-1972.[2] Of these, 43 (14%) were associated with discontinuance of treatment for children with multiple anomalies, trisomy, cardiopulmonary crippling, meningomyelocele, necrotic gastrointestinal tract and so on.

A considerable body of ethical literature has developed around these problems.[3] It differs both in conclusion and in criteria. Thus, for example, David Smith (in what Paul Ramsey calls "the best article to date on the morality of neglecting defective newborns,"[4] – a judgement I do not share), after rejecting euthanasia turns to withholding treatment. He concludes that it is wrong "unless (1) it can be argued that the action is necessary to protect the personal life of at least one specifiable other person or (2) the infant cannot receive care in any other form."[5] Practically this amounts to a prohibition of "letting infants die" in the case of the vast majority of newborns.

At the other end of the spectrum is an interdisciplinary group that met in 1974 at Sonoma, California. In answer to the question "Would it ever be right not to resuscitate an infant at birth?" they provided broad, accordion-like categories to illustrate their affirmative answer.[6] For instance: if the quality of life is and will be intolerable as judged by most reasonable people; if the infant has no chance of a normal life; if "the infant is clearly below human standards for meaningful life"; if the death of the infant would minimise the suffering of the parents; if the death of the infant would avoid unbearable costs to the family; if the death of the infant would avoid emotional burdens to its siblings, etc.

Two things should be noted about such approaches. First, they are conclusions. What is of greater methodological importance is how they were arrived at. Second, they represent attempts to formulate a more basic value judgment: the claims that newborn life makes upon us, particularly in conditions of overwhelming handicap and future burden or suffering.

Traditionally the moral claims (and statements of justice) were formulated in terms of the means available to preserve life. Some were said to be ordinary, others extraordinary. Ordinary means are morally obligatory; extraordinary means are not *per se* morally obligatory. A means (medicine, surgery, etc.) was said to be ordinary if it could be had and used without grave inconvenience and offered a reasonable hope of benefit to the patient. If it lacked either of these characteristics (therefore, if it was excessively burdensome *or* offered no reasonable hope of benefit) it was said to be extraordinary and, as a general rule, was morally dispensable.

Increasingly it has become clear that these terms are code terms that disguise the type of judgment being made in at least very many cases where incompetents are concerned. The terms were always highly relativised to the condition of the patient, so much so at times that "extraordinariness" was more a description of the patient's condition than of the means used. In our time, with enormous strides in pain management, resuscitative devices, third party carriers (e.g., Medicaid), many life and death decisions centre heavily around the benefit to the patient of a proposed intervention. For example, will the proposed surgery keep the patient alive, but in a (for lack of a better term) merely vegetative state? Will resuscitation save the patient but in a highly dysfunctional, perhaps comatose, condition due to anoxia? These are the types of questions that are so often associated with decisions in intensive care units, especially neonatal intensive care units. They are, straightforwardly, concerned with the *kind of life* we are going to give some patients to whom we bring the powerful technologies now available to us. There are many ways of disguising this decisional ingredient; but it is always there and is a *quality of life* criterion.

Let me attempt to clarify this by citing a pastoral letter of the bishops of the Federal Republic of Germany.[7] The bishops are alarmed that euthanasia is being presented as a form of care for the dying (*Sterbehilfe*). Therefore they outline what should be regarded as true care for the dying. It includes the following: alleviation of suffering; creation of an atmosphere of solidarity and trust so that the sick person realises that his humanity is esteemed; provision of spiritual solace and support.

Finally a death worthy of man means that:

> Not all medical means are used if death is artificially postponed by doing so. This is the case, for example, when life can, in fact, be lengthened by means of medical measures, an operation perhaps, but when, unfortunately, despite the operation, or as a consequence of it, the sick person will suffer from severe physical or mental disturbances in the period thus wrung from death. In this situation the decision of the sick person not to undergo another operation is to be considered morally justifiable.[8]

The bishops then pose the question about the moral duty to use artificial supports indefinitely such as the respirator. Their answer is extremely interesting and deserves to be cited in full.

> As long as there is any possibility of the sick man recovering in this way, we will have to use all such means. Also, it is the duty of the state to ensure that even costly apparatus and expensive medicines are available for those who need them. It is quite

another matter when all hope of recovery is excluded and the use of particular medical techniques would only lengthen artificially a perhaps painful death. If the patient, relatives, and doctors decide after considering all the circumstances not to have recourse to exceptional measures and means, they cannot be accused of usurping illicitly the right to dispose of human life. The doctor must, of course, obtain first the consent of the patient or, if this is no longer possible, of his relatives.[9]

A very interesting and easily overlooked aspect of this statement is the term "recovery." The possibility of recovery determines, in the bishops' statement, whether certain life-supports and interventions need be used or not. If recovery is possible, they should be used. However, it must be noted that the notion of "recovery" is not without problems. "Recovery" can mean at least three things: (1) return to the state of health enjoyed prior to illness, a full state of health; (2) return to a lesser state, perhaps one characterised by "severe physical or mental disturbance"; (3) return to spontaneous vital functions without consciousness. All of these represent forms of recovery in the sense that death has been stayed. Now it seems clear that if the bishops would not deem obligatory (for the patient) the medical interventions that produce the latter two categories – a point they explicitly make – then they would not include them under the term "recovery." This suggests that "recovery" implies a certain level of recovery or quality of life; for if the means need not be used by the patient and the reason is that they do not produce "recovery," then the term clearly means not just staving off death, but also a certain quality of life. What the term "recovery" really means, then, in the pastoral is "*sufficient* recovery" and that is subject to quality-of-life assessment.

I believe that Rabbi Daniel Goldfarb is correct when he writes:

If doctors were prohibited from stopping any respirator which they once start, there is the possibility that they would be reluctant to use such machines at all . . . We know that ultimately, whether we like it or not, we are forming opinions and making evaluations, not on the basis of prizing life itself, but rather on the basis of judging the *quality* of a person's life. The ghastly euthanasia program carried out by the Nazis under Hitler (killing, among others, thousands of 'racially valueless' children) makes us Jews very wary of judgments in quality-of-life situations. Nevertheless, the questions cannot be avoided.[10]

May we use the notion of "sufficient recovery" when dealing with the newborn? Or is it a violation of their right to life to make such qualitative judgments? The problem can be posed in still another way. In a study of the living will Sissela Bok proposed the following as a good example of such a will:

> I wish to live a full and long life, but not at all costs. If my death is near and cannot be avoided, and if I have lost the ability to interact with others and have no reasonable chance of regaining this ability, or if my suffering is intense and irreversible, I do not want to have my life prolonged. I would then ask not to be subjected to surgery or resuscitation. Nor would I then wish to have life support from mechanical ventilators, intensive care services, or other life prolonging procedures, including the administration of antibiotics and blood products. I would wish, rather, to have care which gives comfort and support, which facilitates my interaction with others to the extent that this is possible, and brings peace.[11]

That is, I believe, a statement which is thoroughly Christian in its ultimate attitudes toward life and death. The question is: may it be applied to the newborn, to one who has no ability to share in the decision and who has had no chance at life? Or is such a "substituted judgment" discriminatory?

It should be noted that the key phrase in the Bok will is "if my death is near and cannot be avoided . . ." Once the newborn are in such a condition, no one would want to prolong their dying. On this basis, the prestigious Paul Ramsey has developed an analysis of "medically indicated treatment," "treatment not medically indicated" for the incompetent.[12] Briefly, he argues that if death is impending and unavoidable then further curative attempts are not called for. If, contrarily, the patient is not dying, then life-preserving efforts are mandatory. To omit them on the basis of a projected quality of life would be unjust, indeed, would constitute involuntary euthanasia. For this reason Ramsey states that he would rather be charged with morally justifying first-degree murder than to add a feather's weight on the balance in favour of quality of life judgments.

There are several problems with this analysis. First, Ramsey makes things a bit too easy by dividing the world of patients into the dying (death impending) and the non-dying. But there is a vast grey area in between. When should a patient be said to be "dying" so that continuance of a respirator is said to be "aimlessly prolonging dying"? Increasingly, the notion of "dying" is dependent on the technology available. Some years ago a child born with certain anomalies was dying; but not now because the condition can be corrected or neutralised. Thus fifteen years ago 80% of the children born with spina bifida died. Today 80% survive. Similarly, is a patient on dialysis dying or not?

Second, this policy would force us to treat any non-dying incompetent patient with life-saving measures regardless of the patient's condition. Let Karen Ann Quinlan be an example. As I write, she is a fifty-five pound girl with neurological damage so extensive that she is in what the New Jersey Supreme Court called a "persistent vegetative state." There is absolutely no hope for her return to a cognitive, sapient condition. Would Ramsey really want to put Karen back on a respirator to tide her over a pneumonia crisis? Or give her major surgery? Would he really give a hydranencephalic baby (complete or almost complete lack of the cerebral hemispheres) a kidney transplant or major surgery because he would give this to a normal baby? Some such babies survive 3-5 years and are not, in Ramsey's terms, dying. I believe his policy would force such decisions. I am further convinced that nothing in the Judaeo-Christian tradition suggests such conclusions. As between the dying and the non-dying, I believe there is a third category of incompetents: patients who will die without our intervention but who can be saved.

How this problem ought to be formulated or conceptualised roots firmly in our perspectives on the meaning of life and death. Some years ago, writing explicitly as a theologian, I attempted to approach the question in terms of love of God and neighbour.[13] Such love sums up briefly the meaning, substance and consummation of life from a Judaeo-Christian perspective. What is or can easily be missed is that these two loves are not separable. St. John wrote: "If any man says I love God and hates his brother, whom he sees, how can be love God whom he does not see?" (*1 John* 4:20-21) This means that our love of neighbour is in some very real sense our love of God. The good our love wants to do Him and to which He enables us, can be done only for the neighbour, as Karl Rahner has so forcefully argued. It is in others that God demands to be recognised and loved. If this is true, it means that in Judaeo-Christian perspective, the meaning, substance and consummation of life is found in human *relationships,* and the qualities of justice, respect, concern, compassion and support that surround them.

On this basis I developed a guideline to help in decisions about sustaining the lives of grossly deprived and deformed infants. That guideline is the potential for human relationships associated with the infant's condition. If that potential is simply non-existent or would be utterly submerged and undeveloped in the mere struggle to survive, that life has achieved its potential and no longer makes life-sustaining claims upon our care – which is not to say that it makes no claims upon our care.

This quality-of-life ingredient was always present in the understanding of the distinction between ordinary and extraordinary means; but it did not receive the prominence it is now receiving.

The criterion of minimal capacity for human relatedness or experience has received a good deal of commentary by theologians and philosophers. Some has been favourable, some quite critical. It has been objected that it is practically impossible to say in the early days of life what potential an individual baby has. It has been further objected that using such a criterion denies the equal value of every life. Also it has been argued that physical life as the condition of other values and achievements is to make of it a *bonum utile,* an instrumental good, in a way that is inherently dualistic.[14] There is no need to respond to these serious concerns here since I have attempted to do so elsewhere.[15] They are serious objections but I believe appropriate responses are available.

The one who has understood this proposal best is Paul Ramsey. He clearly grasps that where the position "ever so slightly admits quality-of-life criteria,"[16] the emphasis should be on "ever so slightly." Yet Ramsey then turns to the Sonoma conference and writes:

> In commentary upon this allegedly independent operative moral policy, the authors, I regret to have to point out cited Richard McCormick's article "To Save or Let Die." This was in support of the ethical proposition that an infant in order to be

saved must "have some inherent capability to respond affectively and cognitively to human attention and to develop toward initiation of communication with others." Clearly McCormick's position was misused and abused in this summary of this conference's determinations; yet his language was invoked, and his standard of minimal personal inter-relatedness was *used* – and then abused by vast extension. Clearly, in decisions to resuscitate at the first of life or decisions to discontinue treatment once begun, McCormick would allow no reference to whether others who should bear that burden of care are up to it or not. Clearly he would not allow considerations to be brought in about the patient's predictable future based on correctable social circumstances that deprive a patient of familial or institutional medical care. Clearly McCormick would not endorse the practice of directly killing infants in neonatal intensive care units. Clearly McCormick does not weigh in the balance "impact on siblings," or "wanted by parents," or "needed by society." His standard is limited exclusively to conditions inherent in the defective child. I am confident also that he would not endorse replacing infant A by infant B because the latter has a better prognosis for developing its human potentiality and relating with God and with fellowman. What we should do for an individual patient depends only on that particular patient. Abuse of an ethicist's position, I well know, is no argument against it. Still I think it is fair to ask McCormick to recognise the enormity of the task of containing his standard, which already is racing through medical ethical deliberations today. I ask this, first of all, because quality of life *to the patient* was the first concern at this conference. I ask this also because his original position allowed neglect based on a particular patient's overwhelming difficulty in achieving human relatedness; and because the next quite logical step is, for the same reason, to bring on death and not only to let die. This next step is in some sense an entailment of his position, at least in the case of infants without minimum capacity for interrelatedness who refuse to die soon enough from simply the withdrawal of treatment. The latter inferences were not an abuse – like the wide ranging quality-of-life judgments and benefits to others, which the Sonoma conference proceeded to draw out from McCorkmick's position in the course of its deliberations.[17]

Here Ramsey refers to the "enormity of the task of containing his standard, which already is racing through medical ethical deliberations today." Ramsey is right to raise this question. It is easy to take a general guideline (potentiality for human relationships) and stretch it beyond recognition. Therefore I want to reduce the enormity of this task by attempting to specify it with some subordinate, exception-stopping rules. But first, it is necessary to say it is in no sense an "entailment" of this position, as a next step, "to bring on death and not only to let die." If the position "entails" this, then the traditional prerogative of competent patients to forego certain life-sustaining measures "entails" the prerogative of killing themselves.

The capacity for relationships can be specified as follows.

(1) Life-saving interventions may not be omitted for institutional or managerial reasons. Included in this specification is the ability of *this particular family* to cope with a badly disabled baby. This is likely to be a controversial guideline because there are doubtless many who believe that the child is the ultimate victim when parents unsuited to the challenge of a disadvantaged baby must undertake the task. Still, it remains an unacceptable erosion of our respect for life to make the gift of life once given depend on the personalities and emotional or financial capacities of the parents alone. No one may be allowed to die simply because *these parents* do not feel up to an arduous task. At this point society has some responsibilities.

(2) Life-saving interventions may not be ommitted simply because the baby is retarded.[18] There may be further complications associated with retardation that justify withholding life-sustaining treatment. But retardation alone is not an indication.

(3) Life-sustaining interventions may be omitted or withdrawn at some point when it becomes clear that expected life can be had only for a relatively brief time and only with the continued use of artificial feeding forever.

(4) Life-sustaining interventions may be omitted or withdrawn when there is excessive hardship, especially when this combines with poor prognosis (e.g., repeated cardiac surgery, low prognosis transplants).

The criterion originally proposed read: "if that potential [for relationships] is simply non-existent or would be utterly submerged and undeveloped in the mere struggle to survive, that life has achieved its potential." The second two guidelines are *examples* (only) of instances where the potential for relationship is "submerged and undeveloped in the mere struggle to survive." The first two are instances where there is minimal potential and hence where life-sustenance in crisis is called for unless *other circumstances* come into play. There may be other specifications useful in "containing the standard." I would not argue that these are the only specifications possible. However, they do provide *some* guidance for at least *many* cases.

Finally two things should be noted here. First, these rules do not make decisions; they do not replace prudence. They are simply attempts to provide some outline of the areas in which prudence should operate. They do not replace parental-physician responsibility but attempt to enlighten it. Dr. Raymond Duff is of the opinion that if the parents are loving, agonising persons, their decision will be correct and we should settle for it. I cannot accept that. It is "procedural morality." If parents can make mistakes – and they can and have – then there ought to be some criteria (even if general) by which we can judge the decision to be right or wrong.

Secondly, to the extent that these guidelines are accurate, they aid prudence in the pursuit of justice. That is, they spell out as accurately as one can and ought what are the claims of nascent life on our care. Therefore, they specify the right to life in newborns. If they are accurate they should also serve the purpose of sharpening our focus on the right to life and health in other areas as well.

Notes

1. Cf. André E. Hellegers, M.D., "The Johns Hopkins Case," *Ob. Gyn. News* 8 (n. 12, June 15, 1973) 40.
2. Raymond Duff and A. G. M. Campbell, "Moral and Ethical Dilemmas in the Special-care Nursery," *New England Journal of Medicine* 289 (1973) 890-894.
3. For example, James M. Gustafson, "Mongolism, Parental Desires, and the Right to Life" *Perspectives in Biology and Medicine* 16 (1973) 529-559; David H. Smith, "On Letting Some Babies Die," *Studies* 2 (1974) 37-46; John Fletcher, "Attitudes Toward Defective Newborns" *Studies* 2 (1974) 21-32; Leonard J. Weber, *Who Shall Live?* New York: Paulist Press, 1976; Paul Ramsey, *Ethics at the Edges of Life* New Haven: Yale University

Press, 1978; Albert R. Jonsen and Michael J. Garland, *Ethics of Newborn Intensive Care* Berkeley, Calif.: University of California, 1976. Further references may be found in the above entries.

4. Cf. Ramsey as in note 3, p. 183, n. 41.
5. Smith as in note 3.
6. Jonsen and Garland as in note 3.
7. "Das Lebensrecht des Menschen und die Euthanasie," *Herder Korrespondenz* 29 (1975) 335-337.
8. ibid., p. 335-336.
9. ibid., p. 336.
10. Daniel Goldfarb, "Try to Define 'Death'" *Keeping Posted* 22 (1976) 7, 17-18.
11. Sissela Bok, "Personal Directions for the Care at the End of Life," *New England Journal of Medicine* 295 (n. 7, August 12, 1976) 367-369.
12. Ramsey as in note 4.
13. Richard A. McCormick, S.J., "To Save or Let Die," *Journal of the American Medical Association* 229 (n. 2, July 8, 1974) 172-176.
14. For some of these problems, cf. Weber as in note 3.
15. Richard A. McCormick, S.J., "The Quality of Life, the Sanctity of Life" *Hastings Report* 8 (n. 1, February, 1978) 30-36.
16. Ramsey, *loc. cit.*, 227.
17. ibid., 238-239.
18. Thus, with most commentators, I am convinced that the decision in the John Hopkins case was wrong and in violation of the rights of the baby.

CHAPTER 7

HUMAN LIFE WITHIN LIMITS

MARTTI LINDQVIST

Life and Moral Values

> Human culture taken as a whole may be described as the process of man's progressive self-liberation. Language, art, religion, science, are various phases in this process. In all of them man discovers and proves a new power – the power to build up a world of his own, an "ideal" world. Philosophy cannot give up its search for a fundamental unity in this ideal world. But it does not confound this unity with simplicity. It does not overlook the tensions and frictions, the strong contrasts and deep conflicts between the various powers of man.[1]

The theme "human rights" has certainly to do with human self-liberation. The quotation above, taken from the famous book of Ernst Cassirer, indicates how complicated this process of self-liberation really is. On one hand we must assume that there is a fundamental unity in the world as a whole. On the other hand, however, every-day realities seem to be very controversial and confusing.

Thirty years ago the nations of the world proclaimed the *Universal Declaration of Human Rights* based on the conviction that 'recognition of the inherent dignity and of the equal and inalienable rights of all members of the human family is the foundation of freedom, justice and peace in the world'. What really matters is not so much the wording of the declaration, which reflects a particular historical situation, but the basic idea of declaration itself. Out of the horrors of the second world war grew the conviction that the international community must have a *moral design*. As a matter of fact the preamble of the declaration assumes that there is a 'natural law' of morality which is shared by all members of the 'human family'. Therefore, human rights should never be mixed with civil rights even if we do emphasise the right of each state to sovereignty – including the right 'freely to choose and develop its political, social, economic and cultural systems' as well as "to determine its laws and regulations'.[2]

It is evident that the *Universal Declaration of Human Rights* is based on humanistic assumptions. Human dignity is seen as the focus of universal morality. Historically, the modern concept of 'human rights' seems to have several roots. According to the most common theory, the idea of human rights stems from the Enlightenment. However, as Wolfgang Huber and Heinz Eduard Tödt among others have shown, the basic ideas of the Reformation opened new perspectives which have contributed to the understanding of human rights. Although the 1776 *Bill of Rights of Virginia* cannot be interpreted as an outcome of a "Christian Philosophy', it certainly comes closer to Christian self-understanding than the documents of the Enlightenment.[3] For our purposes it is not necessary to analyse the historical background of human rights. It is enough to note the general humanistic approach to value questions implied by the very concept of 'human rights'.

If 'all human beings are born free and equal in dignity and rights', this means that the value of a person is not based on his or her individual qualities. Human life as such has an intrinsic significance. The mere fact that all human beings participate in the same life is sufficient to constitute the value of each person.

The concept of 'civil rights' presupposes that the actual value of a human person is connected with his or her membership of a political community. Of course, civil rights can be motivated by more general humanistic ideals but the question remains why citizenship in a state can be decisive for the concrete rights of a person. If there is a universal moral community, the value of human beings can never be expressed *only* in terms of civil rights.

1 OPPORTUNITIES AND LIMITS

Life is More than Human Rights

Arnold Toynbee has given an interpretation of human history as a process of continuously expanding possibilities leading to the 'revolution of rising expectations'.[4] This is in accordance with Cassirer's concept of 'man's progressive self-liberation' quoted above. For two reasons this is more true today than in any earlier period of the history of humankind. Firstly, after the second world war industrial nations have gone through an economic and technological expansion without equal in the history of mankind. Many people believed that the time was present to overcome material scarcity definitively. Secondly, the mechanism of 'rising expectations' is based on concrete comparisons between people in different economic, social and political situations. World-wide communication has improved to the extent that almost everyone can compare his or her life-situation with that of other people in different parts of the world.[5]

Against this background it is very understandable that there is a tendency to an overall approach to economic, social and political issues in terms of human rights. The rights of nations and the rights of individual people have become the leading concept in dealing with the 'world moral order'. In my opinion, however, this is a rather limited interpretation of the realities of life. There can be no responsible morality if we are focussing only on the human rights' issue at the same time forgetting other elements which are necessary in order to sustain a meaningful life on the globe. In his famous book *A Theory of Justice* John Rawls discusses thoroughly the concept of right in a much wider sense than that of human rights. In order to show the interplay between different variables I use here the 'upper part' of Rawls' schematic diagram:[6]

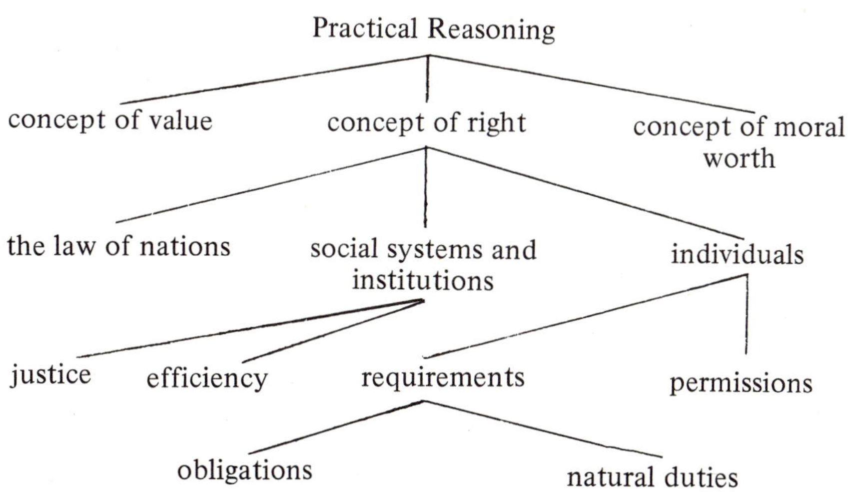

In his theory Rawls also suggests a certain order in which the various sorts of principles are to be acknowledged in the original position. For our purposes, however, it is not so important. The following points seem to be relevant for us:

1. The concept of right has to do with three levels of the human community: (a) individuals, (b) social systems and institutions, (c) the law of the nations.
2. Justice is not a property of individuals and their actions, but a predicate of social systems and institutions.[7]
3. The concept of right cannot be understood correctly if reference is being made only to the things human beings are entitled to. Speaking about rights means speaking about duties and obligations.

The *Universal Declaration of Human Rights* can easily give the impression that the essence of those rights lies in their permissive character. This emphasis is very typical of a liberalistic world view. However, 'this liberalism has spent itself because it has become irrelevant. Its sacred premises of individualism, unbridled competition, and unlimited growth are no longer compatible with our social experience . . .'[8] What we must learn is that basically the concept of human rights refers to our responsibilities and obligations. Self-liberation is meaningless without self-limitation. Our inherent human dignity not only entitles us to the basic requirements of life, it also presupposes that we are ready to behave according to our dignity.

Human Rights – Rights of Nature

The concept of human rights has clear limitations. Its basic intention is to protect individual human beings against the arbitrary use of power on the part of the state and other social institutions. At the same time, however, this concept gives the impression that all other values are of secondary importance. A human person is an end to be achieved. Therefore all institutions and material things are means towards its achievement.

This may sound like an overstatement. However, the emancipation of humankind from direct dependence on nature gives evidence for that point of view. The struggle for justice is seen as one of redistributing material, social and intellectual resources between human beings. Nature is merely the setting where this historical struggle takes place.

The time has come to re-evaluate this approach. The man-machine-nature model is no longer valid as a responsible interpretation of life values. Since the famous debate on the 'limits to growth' there is a new sense of our responsibility for nature. Two models of thinking seem to be emerging.[9]

On the one hand there are people who insist on the importance of making a clear qualitative distinction between the rights of human beings and the value of nature.[10] They point out that the only meaningful way to deal with value questions is to relate them always to the rights of persons. We have to take care of nature because otherwise we would hurt ourselves, our neighbours and the generations not yet alive. Protection of nature is *for the sake of human beings.*

On the other hand some people argue that the traditional anthropocentric view of life has been one of the root causes of the present crisis. Therefore, the concept of human rights is not wide enough to cover our moral responsibilities. I quote David R. Griffin:

> . . . *no* being should be treated as a means to our ends without due consideration of its own rights as an end in itself. This "due consideration" may lead to the conclusion that our objective (but not absolute) rights are such as to justify over-riding the objective (but not absolute) rights of the being(s) in question . . . But the beings used as means are not 'exploited" in the strict sense if their own value and rights are given due consideration. As long as the logic of liberation is not carried through consistently and applied to *all* beings, its defence remains arbitrary and its application capricious, and no group of beings is safe, even in theory, from exploitation.[11]

This discussion is, or course, partly academic. It seems to have certain theological implications (theology of creation, and of history) which do not fall within the scope of this presentation.[12] What matters for us is the new emphasis that human rights cannot be dealt with in a responsible way without taking into account ecological concerns and our moral partnership with the rest of creation.

Human Rights and the Common Good

The exact content of the concept of the "common good" is very difficult to define. It varies from one situation to another according to different social ideologies, cultural traditions, needs and existing resources. Perhaps one can say as Alan Gewirth has put it:

> . . . it is clear that the common good is an egalitarian concept, particularly in that aspect of it which consists in utilising the resources of the society to provide equality of opportunity for achieving the values which living within the society makes possible.[13]

Each of us knows that the concept of the common good has been used many times as a pretext for neglecting basic human rights. This cannot be defended. However, if we do believe in the necessity of social institutions there is also a valid use of that concept.

In my opinion two considerations are important on this point. Firstly, distributive justice is a basic common good both within and between nations. Therefore, individual self-liberation has to be limited in order to promote distributive justice. In many cases this means that maximum use of human rights is not responsible because it would threaten basic rights of other people and of other nations. This is especially true as far as the excessive consumption of limited material resources is concerned.[14]

Secondly, there are "communal goods" which cannot be decided according to individual wishes and preferences. This might be the question which has been most neglected in the present debate on human rights. Cultural heritage, social stability, national security and self-reliant development are good examples of collective values which are not matters of individual preference. The society has a legitimate right to protect and promote these values using appropriate legal means.

The question of the common good becomes still more complicated as soon as we touch international issues. The WCC conference on human rights, held in 1974,[15] included issues of human survival, cultural identity, and self-determination of the nations in its list of basic human rights. In my opinion, it would be conceptually more clear not to use such a wide definition of human rights. Anyway, the issues are interrelated. Therefore, in planning for international strategies to promote social justice the main areas of human rights, new international economic order and disarmament have to be kept together. They form three 'clues' to the establishment of a responsible international community based on fair and sound moral values.

II TOWARDS A THEORY OF HUMAN RIGHTS

Many attempts have been made in order to create a comprehensive theory of human rights.[16] I am not in a position to form my own theory. What follows is an attempt to give a general frame of reference for dealing with these issues. It is based on a classic anthropology where human beings are seen from three main perspectives: (a) material (physical), (b) social (communal) and (c) personal (spiritual).[17]

Material Aspects

In the recent debate on human rights more and more emphasis has been put on the basic material requirements for a meaningful human life. Human beings are part of the physical world and totally dependent on it. Both the opportunities and the limits of human life are provided by physical nature. Therefore, it is reasonable to suppose that basic human rights include the more important material requirements of food, clothing, housing and necessary health care.

However, it has to be taken into account that although the additional use of material resources, (compared with the minimum requirements stated above) widens the possibilities of human self-liberation, the "utility limit" of those resources diminishes as the level of consumption increases. Because of the limited nature of material resources at certain point this "utility limit" becomes negative undermining the possibility of distributive justice.

Also the *quality* of material consumption is important. It must adapt itself to the processes of nature. This is the only way to guarantee the sustainability of human society on the globe.[18]

Social Aspects

To say that we are social beings is true in a double sense. On the one hand, with regard to our human relationships, the persons who are close to us contribute significantly to our sense of security, self-respect and dignity. Our personal development is to a large extent determined by the quality of the human relationships in which we are involved.

On the other hand we meet the social reality when participating in different social institutions. The crucial question is to what extent an active and creative participation is possible. The need for self-determination is commonly understood to be basic for all human beings. Only when this is recognised can individuals experience that they are responsible subjects of their own lives. This is not necessarily a statement in favour of a certain type of political system but rather it proposes a *social design* which can be applied to different political systems. The recognition of social rights does not exclude the diversity of economic, social and political systems.

The difficulties of including the social needs of human beings in codified catalogues of human rights are evident. The area of informal social relationships seems to be particularly far beyond the possibilities of juridical statements.[19] The state and other social institutions can certainly contribute to conditions which are favourable for the development of this kind of personal care in the human community. The area of economic, social and political self-determination is directly connected with legislative measures.

Personal Aspects

In order to become a whole human being a person has to create a relationship with himself or herself. This area of human development has to do with our self-understanding and self-respect. The questions concerning the meaningfulness of life can be answered only by people themselves. It is very understandable why many of the earliest documents on human rights are so concerned about the freedom of conscience. It is the heart of all personal integrity, and this leads us to one fundamental conclusion. We can criticise with good reasons the first *UN Declaration of Human Rights* because it does not take seriously enough the material and social security of human life. However, the most important idea is there – i.e. that human life loses meaning without personal integrity in thoughts, moral and political convictions and religious beliefs.

People are not only "creatures". They are also creative subjects of history trying to shape their own lives and to reform their physical and social environment. By definition this is something which has to be done by the people themselves. How they succeed in these efforts is partly dependent on the moral and juridical codes accepted and followed by social institutions. It must be clear that the bodily integrity of a person is part of his or her human dignity.

A Model For Evaluation

There has been much discussion concerning the way different societies have "specialised" views on human rights. On onc hand it has been said that this is fully justified due to different political systems and different stages of economic and social development. On the other hand a deep concern has been expressed that this kind of "specialisation" undermines the whole idea of human rights.

I try to give my own interpretation of this question using the following very schematic graphs:[20]

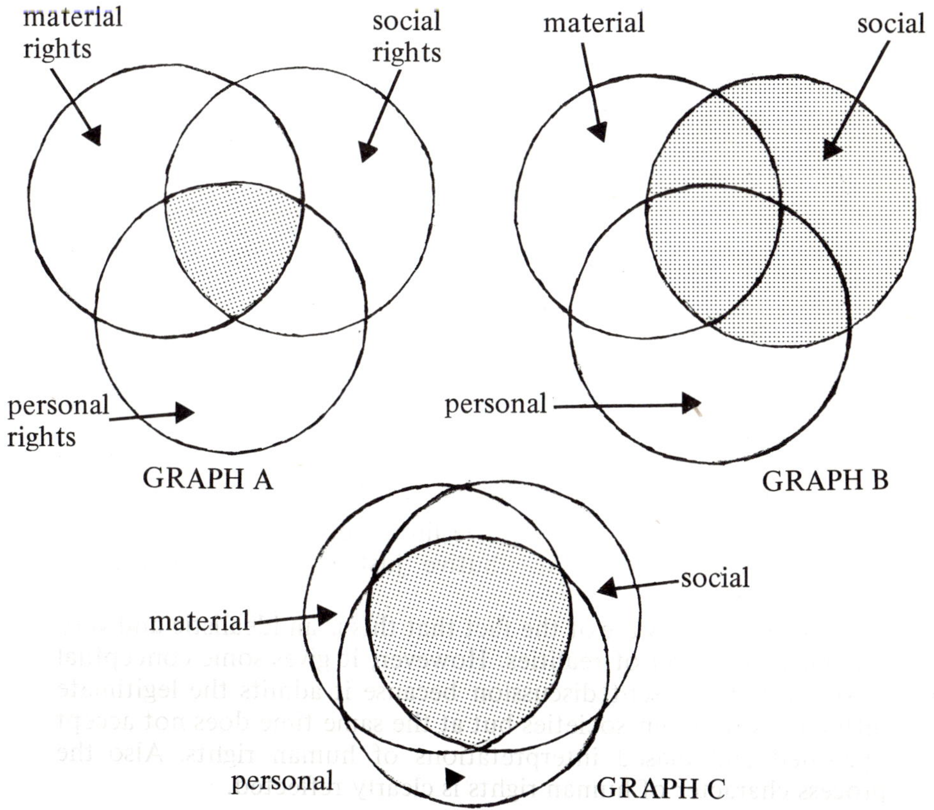

In graph A, three basic areas of human rights are shown by three circles which are partly intersecting. The circle form of each area indicates that there are objective limits for human self-fulfilment in all three areas but at the same time also unused real opportunities. The section surface which is shadowed represents a balanced realisation of human rights in a certain historical situation. The scope of this area varies from one society to another according to objective resources available. Due to the process character of the implementation of human rights the goal in each situation is to widen the range of real opportunities for each single individual.

Graph B shows a situation where the emphasis is put on one of the three sectors of human rights (material, social or personal). What happens is that there are increasing opportunities for human self-liberation in certain questions (in this case within the social/communal sector of human rights). The development, however, is not balanced, but takes place at the expense of other human rights. In this particular case the social sector is developing in a direction which threatens the material and personal well-being of individuals. We can, of course, imagine situations where this kind of development is taking place in the material or personal sector. The actual point is this: It is possible that work for human rights in a certain area is not in accordance with the very nature of balanced human development.

The ideal situation is reflected in Graph C. The strategy for implementation of human rights takes into consideration the existing opportunities in all three areas. This means that social institutionas are being developed in such a way that when they provide more opportunities for social participation they at the same time support the satisfaction of material needs and people's personal fulfilment. This can be called an *organic* development of human opportunities within the objective limits, determined by material resources, demands for distributive justice and ambiguities of human beings.

I am very well aware of the fact that this is an idealistic and very general description of realities. However, it gives some conceptual clarity to the present discussion because it admits the legitimate differences between societies but at the same time does not accept one-sided and biased interpretations of human rights. Also the process character of human rights is clearly reflected.

The strategies of individual people and groups interested in the promotion of human rights will vary according to differing socio-political situations. I quote a document on human rights from the Lutheran World Federation:

1. Constructive and critical participation in the positive sharing of power. This is possible where legislature, judiciary, and government themselves grant human rights to their citizens as public subjective rights and shape the legal system and political process accordingly.
2. Active and critical resistance to that power which shows itself incapable of learning. This finds expression in public complaint where human rights are violated or denied, if necessary at the bar of international public opinion.
3. Critical passive resistance to that power which shows itself incapable of learning. This is appropriate where the ruling power prevents all public pursuit of human rights. Such resistance sustains awareness of the fact that a life protected by the role of law, i.e. the enjoyment of human rights, is the due of every citizen. A conformist justification of the ruling, but illegitimately acting, power is in this way refused.[21]

III CONCLUDING REMARKS

A Hierarchy of Human Rights?

What has been said above indicates that a balanced view of human rights is very important. The implementation of those rights has to follow the general pattern of whole human development. Many forms of the misuse of power are due to simplistic and one-sided interpretations of human rights.

The question is, however, more complicated. There is a danger that in highlighting certain violations of human rights we underestimate more burning issues.

There are no clear-cut answers to these questions. I tend to think that we need some kind of "minimum model" of human rights which is balanced in itself but gives high priority to very basic material, social and personal rights. Coming back to the graphs presented above, I would say that we have to define that minimum area of balanced intersection which is necessary for preserving human dignity. In my opinion, this will include questions like the protection of a person's physical integrity, freedom of conscience, access to basic material necessities of life, support of family life and opportunity to participate in the political decision-making process.

Christians and Universal Human Rights

My task was to deal with the problem of universal human rights. Therefore I have not taken up specific theological issues which are, of course, very important. Because I am a theologian and I have to integrate these aspects in my own personality I conclude my presentation with a few remarks concerning the relationship between universal human rights and the theological understanding of human rights.

It was said earlier that although there are certain connections between the history of Christianity (especially in the Reformation's concept of freedom of conscience) and the history of human rights the latter cannot be derived from the former. The human rights issue is, by definition, something which belongs to all people regardless of their different backgrounds and convictions. It is the responsibility of all Christian people to share this concern with other human beings without religious reservations. At the same time they will give their specific insights based on their faith. These insights do not separate people from each other but deepen the common search for freedom and justice. This has been stated very clearly in the book *Christ and Humanity* published by the Lutheran World Federation:

> The Christian ethos remains oriented to the universally human and does not seek anything specifically Christian. While it stems from a new, a Christian, understanding, it struggles to maintain this understanding only with a view to enriching what is universally human and in order to achieve authentic humanity. It is sustained by the hope that in the process of history man will, in the light of faith, increasingly find himself and will discover that which makes his existence as man human.[22]

Notes

1. Ernst Cassirer *An Essay of Man* An Introduction to a Philosophy of Human Culture London, Yale University Press, 1966 p. 228.
2. This is one of the 10 basic principles in the Final Act of the Conference on Security and Co-operation in Europe. Prof. Osmo Apunen of Finland

has given an interesting interpretation concerning the value structure in the Final Act (see E. and M. Weingartner (ed.) *Human Rights is more than Human Rights* A Primer for Churches on Security and Co-operation in Europe, Rome, IDOC 1977 pp. 159-163).

3. W. Huber and H. E. Tödt *Menschenrechte* Perspektiven einer menschlichen Welt Stuttgart. Kreuzer Verlag 1977 pp. 124-130.
4. Toynbee's theory and its relevance to the present discussion on human rights has been dealt with by R. J. Niebanck 'Human Rights – Theological Perspective' mimeographed. New York, Lutheran Church in America, 1978 p. 4.
5. As a matter of fact the UN has become a major forum where comparisons of this kind are being made, resulting in new policy statements.
6. J. Rawls *A Theory of Justice,* London, O.U.P. 1972 p. 109.
7. This aspect of social justice is thoroughly discussed by W. K. Frankena 'The Concept of Social Justice' in *Social Justice* (1962) pp. 1-29.
8. G. H. Brand *Human Rights: Rhetoric or Reality,* pp. 5-16.
9. see Lindqvist *Economic Growth and the Quality of Life,* Helsinki, Finnish Society for Missiology and Ecumenics, 1975.
10. This point is typically held by T. S. Derr *Ecology and Human Liberation:* A Theological Critique of the Use and Abuse of our Birthright. Geneva, World Student Christian Federation, 1973.
11. D. R. Griffin 'Human Liberation and the Reverence for Nature' in *Anticipation* Geneva – WCC – no. 16 1974, p. 30.
12. It seems to me that J. Moltmann 'Theologishe Erklärung ze den Menschenrechten' in Moltmann and J. Lochman (ed.) *Gottes Recht und Menschenrechte* Neukirchen – Vluyn, Neukirchener Verlag 1977 has taken a different stand on this question than Huber and Tödt op. cit.
13. A. Gewirth 'Political Justice' in *Social Justice* (1962), p. 168.
14. see S. Parmar 'Ethical Guidelines and Social Options after the Limits to Growth Debate' in *Anticipation* no. 18 (1974), p. 21.
15. W.C.C. *Human Rights and Christian Responsibility:* Report of the Consultation, St. Pölten, October 1974, Geneva, W.C.C. 1974.
16. In my opinion, one of the most interesting theories in this field has been presented by Huber abd. Tödt op. cit. It is based on three basic concepts: freedom, equality and participation. This theory was adopted by a Lutheran World Federation consultation on Human Rights in 1976. see J. Lissner (pref.) *Theological Perspectives on Human Rights,* Geneva. L.W.F. 1977.
17. A Finnish social scientist has made an interesting comparative study on the quality of life in the different Nordic societies. He defined the human needs according to three categories which are very close to those which I am using: 1 needs of 'having'; 2 needs of 'loving'; and 3 needs of 'being'. – E. Allardt *Hyvinvoinnin ulottuvuuksia,* Porvoo – Helsinki, Werner Sodestrom Osakeyhtio 1976.

18. The concept of a "Just, Participatory and Sustainable Society" has become one of the key issues in the work of the World Council of Churches. see P. Abrecht (ed.), *Faith, Science and the Future,* Geneva, W.C.C. 1978.
19. cf. G. Wingren 'Human Rights: a Theological Analysis' in *The Ecumenical Review,* 27 (2) 75, pp. 124-127.
20. This interpretation can be understood as an application of my analysis concerning the meaning of the 'quality of life' concept. In Lindqvist op. cit.
21. Lissner, op. cit., pp. 40-41.
22. Ivar Asheim (ed.) *Christ and Humanity,* Philadelphia, Fortress Press, 1970, p. 23.

CHAPTER 8

HUMAN RIGHTS AND INDUSTRY

DAVID E. JENKINS

"It nowhere recognises the right of the working-man to a life worthy of a human being, to independent activity, and opinions of his own".[1]

"The most obvious facts are the most easily forgotten. Both the existing economic order and too many of the projects advanced for reconstructing it break down through their neglect of the truism that, since even quite common men have souls, no increase in material wealth will compensate them for arrangements which insult their self-respect and impair their freedom".[2]

"The worker is controlled by forces over which he has little or no influence – by the limits of his education and qualification; his environment; the siting of factories and of schools; 'town-planning'; problems of housing accommodation; economic and social pressures . . . And who cares? . . . He has never seen his boss. The managing director is as far away and mythical a figure as the Mona Lisa or Whistler's Mother; the shareholder a mere cipher which everyone ignores. He has lost the relationship of shared labour, the interest and incentive of even minor achievement . . . He can no longer see himself as a human part, however lonely, of the total enterprise that is British Leyland or Courtaulds or Joseph Lucas or whoever it might be. His days are recorded on a time band, his efforts on a mechanical counter, his rewards on a punched card untouched by hand. His thoughts are not recorded at all, since it assumed that he doesn't have any".[3]

Industry as we know it is generally assumed to have developed out of the "industrial revolution" which was launched in Britain in the 1760's by the invention of the spinning jenny, and James Watt's steam engine. There is, of course, a considerable history behind these inventions as well as behind all the other strands (developments in transport, metallurgy, engineering, sources of power etc.), which combined to produce this "revolution"; but between say 1760 and about 1830 developments were so rapid and so extensive that the revolution can properly be dated in this way. For example, in the years concerned the consumption of raw cotton went up by about twelve times and the population of Great Britain doubled from eight million to sixteen million, while coal production quadrupled and, between 1800 and 1835 iron output likewise was multiplied fourfold. The explosion of production and of population led to the wide spread of the factory system and the great growth of industrial towns. The face of the land was changed and the conditions of life of the majority of the quickly growing population drastically altered.

It is necessary to refer to these truisms in order to remind ourselves that the subject of human rights in industry is not one perhaps rather specialised and technical issue within the broad field of human rights as a whole, since industry is not just one of many institutions or classes of institutions within our society. It is the major shaping force of our society. Consequently problems of human rights that arise within industry or because of the impact of industry on our society are critical both for the very concept of "human rights" and for the realistic development of human rights, or of whatever human good or value that phrase is supposed to point towards in our society.

It is clear that the cost of industrial development from say 1778 to the present has, in terms of human suffering, been immense. It is also clear that the workers in industry, i.e. those who have provided the labour force for payment of a wage, have had to "fight for their rights" in a very basic and elementary sense. It has taken militant organisation and at least sporadic actual fighting with owners, police and soldiers to obtain any recognition by society and its legislative bodies that wage-earners as a class have any standing or claims as human beings at all.

For industry as such and as hitherto organised makes certain demands. Any sort of production line imposes an intense and inflexible discipline. You do not have to be a romantic or a revolutionary to recognise that in a factory-type organisation men are subordinated to the needs of machines and their interconnections. In 1884 Engels wrote,

> Let us turn to another side of the factory system which cannot be remedied by legislative provisions so easily as the diseases now engendered by it . . . The supervision of machinery, the joining of broken threads, is no activity which claims the operative's thinking powers, yet it is of a sort which prevents him from occupying his mind with other things. We have seen, too, that this work affords the muscles no opportunity for physical activity. Thus it is, properly speaking, not work, but tedium, the most deadening, wearing process conceivable. The operative is condemned to let his physical and mental powers decay in this utter monotony, it is his mission to be bored every day and all day long from his eighth year. Moreover, he must not take a moment's rest; the engine moves unceasingly; the weals, the straps, the spindles hum and rattle in his ears without a pause, and if he tried to snatch one instant, there is the overlooker at his back with the book of fines. This condemnation to be buried alive in the mill, to give constant attention to the tireless machine is felt as the keenest torture by the operatives, and its action upon the mind and body is in the long run stunting in the highest degree.[4]

Things have improved since then and nobody is now compelled to be bored all day long from his eighth year. A considerable amount of reflection, effort and planning as well as much legislation, has been and is being directed to improving working conditions, finding ways of reorganising production processes into units which can be both experienced more personally and contributed to more personally and so on. But the fact remains that production processes, complex systems and large-scale organisations (or the inter-locking of small organisations in large-scale networks) impose immense constraints on, and make great demands of, all those who work in them and who depend for their "livelihood" on this work.

It was apparent from a very early stage in the development of the factory system that people needed to be protected against some of its effects. It also rapidly became clear that people needed to fight for themselves against it, as I have already indicated. Parliamentary legislation in Britain began as early as 1802, with a very weak Apprentices Act, and by the 1830's, "Factory Acts" were beginning to appear and be passed. But for a long time this type of legislation was concerned with children and with women, i.e. with those human beings who were the weaker members of society and who could be assumed to be in need of protection on grounds which came from the assumptions of the older family-based and traditionalist society. To interfere in the condition of employment of "free and adult" men who must be assumed as capable of looking after themselves was quite another matter. What legislation there was was extremely limited in scope and easily avoidable, until the notion of appointing Inspectors to oversee the application of it became acceptable. Even so the opposition to any interference with the freedom of industry and commerce and the rights of employers and owners was very fierce.

An extract from a speech of William Cobbett's in the House of Commons, quoted by John Fielden in his *The Curse of the Factory System,* published in 1836, may serve as a reminder to us of how easily "human rights in industry" get swallowed up in "issues of public policy" or "the demands of production". (Both matters which, as I shall later argue, cannot be ignored either in any realistic approach to this issue). In ironic mood Cobbett has been reminding the House that at various times "the glory of our country" has been held to be the Navy, our maritime commerce and extensive manufacturers, the Land or the Bank. He goes on:

> but now, a most surprising discovery has been made, namely, that all our greatness and prosperity, that our superiority over other nations, is owing to 300,000 little girls in Lancashire. We have made the notable discovery, that, if these little girls work two hours less a day than they now do, it would occasion the ruin of the country; that it would enable other nations to compete with us; and thus make an end to our boasted wealth, and bring us to beggary.

It is, I think, very necessary to be aware that a long and remarkably consistent history of speeches and arguments such as those which Cobbett is deriding goes a long way to explaining, if not necessarily justifying, a certain reluctance among Trade Unionists to restrain the exercise of their present rights and temper the force of their current demands because of the threat of inflation and other dire economic perils which are called in aid by those who continue to run (or attempt to run) government and industry. The perils may be real and the need for restraints realistic and urgent but this would only serve to heighten the urgency of the issue of who should trust whom about what – an issue which lies at the heart both of the struggle for human rights in industry and of the struggle to produce a humane and constructive collaboration and consensus in an industrial society.

Alongside the development of legislation and to some extent around attempts to promote it there grew up, as is well known, workers' agitation and workers' organisation. Both these manifestations of the reaction by manufacturing workers to the conditions of their work and of their whole lives were viewed by established opinion and established authorities with great suspicion and hostility. Strikes, the organised with-holding of labour in order to bring pressure to bear on employers or owners in the interest of the workers, were held to be illegal and in restraint of trade, and viewed as little better than riots (to which they sometimes led), or even as rebellion. The development of Labour Unions was likewise opposed and harassed by legal and other means. (e.g. Paid officials were said to be exploiting the pockets of the workers who contributed to their support). Commonplace as all this is it is an essential precondition of any realistic discussion of human rights in industry that we should remain constantly aware that the attitude of these in positions of influence and power in the industrialising societies of the nineteenth century (and later!) to workers' attempts to organise and exercise countervailing force seems to have been "Cet animal est méchant, il se défend", (This creature *is* wicked, it defends itself!). Industrialisation has apparently had an extraordinarily direct relationship with dehumanisation.

None the less some at least of the labourers refused to accept this and as the nineteenth century progressed Trade Union development grew and worker MPs began to appear in Parliament. Out of this emerged the twentieth century Labour Party and the situation which we now have with Labour governments; "the power of the Trade Unions" and so on. From the middle of the nineteenth century a combination of growing awareness in some quarters of the humanitarian need to regulate some of the worst miseries of industrial life and pressure from the agitation and the organisation of workers served to promote a growing amount of legislation and, with the help of some influential utilitarians, to initiate or extend State intervention in the ordering of society. This intervention began to deal not only with the direct regulation of industrial and factory conditions but also with the broader conditions of life in an industrial society. Health and sanitation became matters for Parliamentary legislation and central government activity, education also and eventually housing, town-planning and pensions. Industrial society could not be left to itself. The dynamics of industrial organisation and expansion seemed to require countervailing organisation, whether on the part of workers' collectives or on the part of the State to work for the restraint or suppression of dehumanising developments and to begin to face up to the vast human and social problems which industrial development produced.

The continuation of this process through and after the Second World War led in this country to the launching of the Welfare State with its underlying assumption that every man, woman and child had, as human beings, certain rights to a certain standard of social provision for their needs from the cradle to the grave. From the 1960's legislative form began to be given to the idea that an actual right to work or to remain in work needed to be defined and protected, as distinct from rights and regulations about payment for work or conditions in work. Thus we have had legislation like the *Contracts of Employment Act* (1963), the *Redundancy Payments Act* (1965) and the *Employment Protection Act* (1975). All this can be seen as attempts to establish and preserve the objective recognition of the rights of men and women within industry and within industrial society by positive, interventionist legislation. We have, it may be said, increasing legislative attempts to respond to the growing awareness that everyone who is a "subject" of industrial activity and industrial organisation has an equal right to be treated as a human being and this "treatment as a human being" includes much more than being protected from the grossest forms of exploitation and practical misery.

Here we are confronted by a critical question. Does the above sketch refer to the central thrust by which our society is properly and hopefully seeking to respond to the vital issue of human rights in industry and of human rights in an industrial society? Or does it simply indicate a series of largely ineffectual skirmishings around the main political and human issue of our industrial times? This central issue is the necessary fight of the workers against the ruling and owning classes for ownership and control of the means of production. To pose this question is, of course, simply to reflect the diagnosis of Marx and Engels that the source and cause of idustrialisation's undoubted evils and miseries lies, despite its almost unbelievable achievements in the expansion of production and in the multiplication of wealth, in "Capitalism", i.e. in the private and limited ownership and exploitation of the means of production and therefore, in effect, of the lives and livelihoods of the producers (i.e. the workers).

It would seem futile to discuss Human Rights and Industry without facing up to this formulation of the central problem. For if our society is largely shaped by industry and if industry is focussed on the production of goods and services then there would seem to be a strong case for at least investigating the suggestion that the basic right of every man and woman is to equal ownership. and control over the products and conditions of his or her labour. If this right cannot be established then it looks as if men and women must always be at the mercy of those who do control means and processes of production.

That this tradition is "alive and well" (or that this "sickness" continues) is well illustrated in the current UK Ford workers' strike. There has been a fierce reaction to a Company suggestion that part of a wage increase should be related to "Attendance Money", i.e. payments dependent on clocking-in on time, avoidance of absenteeism etc. From the perspective of those who are worried about inflation and bad productivity records this seems a blatant example of irresponsibility and of refusal to accept elementary and obviously required disciplines. But how does it appear from the perspective of a tradition which has been obliged for the last 150 years or more to struggle against the grip of "them" on everything one has to do or can hope for?

Thus the question of the ownership of the means of production seems a very good question for focussing the problems of industrial society and of human rights within it. For it is a way of focussing on the questions of who pays what costs and who obtains what benefits and it relates this to *human* terms rather than just to terms of economics, of capital and of money-values. *Who suffers* poverty, ill-health, boredom, arbitrary orders, lack of opportunity to think or to contribute and *who enjoys* freedom for discretion, the right to issue orders, expansive style of life and a sense of being in control rather than under it?

But while the questions pointed to by raising the issue of the ownership of the means of production seem central to humane living in an industrial society the solutions pointed to or implied by the notion of social ownership of the means of production seem at least insufficient and, quite probably, both simplistic and naive. In any case evidence is steadily accumulating to suggest that whatever the ownership of the means of production *the organisation* of production continues to generate many problems, not least vis-a-vis the rights of both individuals and groups.

An interesting and suggestive discussion of this issue is, for example, provided by the Yugoslav philosopher and sociologist, Svetozar Stojanovic, in this book *Between Ideals and Reality.*[5] His main concern is to rescue Marxism from the Stalinist false route developed in Russia and to relate valid Marxist insights to the Yugoslav experiments in developing true worker ownership of and control in industry. His positive points cannot be made use of here, only his testimony to continuing difficulties in organising an industrial society.

Thus he writes,

> The days are past in Yugoslavia when the establishment transparently rationalised about their inability to concede that to strike is a right of the working class in socialism. This rationalisation consisted of the typically ideological explanation that 'the workers cannot strike against themselves'. But this has been shown to be a mere mystification, since it is not the working class which is in power, but rather its representatives. The history of socialism demonstrates that the latter have frequently pursued their own interests rather than those of the workers. This can reach such proportions that the working class is forced to defend itself not only by means of the strike, but also through political demonstrations, and even with arms (as in Hungary).[6]

The relation of "workers' control" groups to society at large is touched on at many points:

> The danger presented by group ownership and group self-government is not very discernible in an economy composed of small enterprises. But how much autonomy in the distribution of income can a self-governing society allow a working collective composed of a few dozen workers in a highly automated plant in which it is has invested huge resources? Some

> theorists claim that in such cases the problem is one of a conflict between the nature of decision-making and the nature of ownership. But they are slaves of the legal fiction of social ownership. Ownership is not a metaphysical entity which exists independently of decision-making and control. In the instances cited above, individual groups dispose of social property in a largely monopolistic manner.[7]

And on the internal running of industry he has such remarks as:

> One of the consequences of an uncritical attitude toward self-government is the confusion of self-management with day-to-day management. . . . When democratic bodies omnipotently meddle in operative leadership then, of course, there is neither true self-management nor professional and responsible leadership. It is not at all surprising that such groups do not even contemplate making use of modern scientific achievements in leadership and management, and that the degree of working hierarchy and discipline demanded by any modern society, self-governing society included, is absent.[8]

Industry, in fact, has its own demands.[9] Men and women also continue to have their own demands and contribute their own mistakes or distortions. Thus whatever may be held to be appropriate moral and sociological judgements on the developments of industrial society from 1778 to 1978 we have to face the demands and pressures of industry and of production as we now encounter them.

If industry is to be kept operative, then some disciplines imposed by the productive processes will have to be observed. If men's labour is to be made easier by machines and its effects multiplied by machines then up to some point, and in some way or another, men will have to fit in with machines. The ideal, of course, is that machines should serve men and there is a constant demand for experiment and adaptation both within industry and in the understanding and operation of the links between industry and society. But the development and running of industry will still impose its own demands. These extend to the requirements of organisation at a variety of levels and to the problems of the bureaucracies which are both necessary to enable complex organisation and also a source of interference with both the industrial purposes and the human experiences of such organisation because bureaucracies breed their own demands. Problems of size are never going to be settled, only grappled with, and it is practically certain that the ideal of everybody belonging to a basic group which permits face-to-face and free decision-taking and is the basic and effective unit of power is as utopian in industrial management as it is in the political sphere. Industry, moreover, will always be subjected to varying constraints to do with the use and availability of resources, while in the foreseeable future it will be constantly disturbed by technological obsolescence and innovation. It seems likely that creativity and ingenuity will continue somewhere or other in the world and will be applied somewhere or other in the world so that no one's industry is able to remain a closed or settled system for long. Finally, on the more directly human side there is little sign that productive systems can run for long without coming up against problems of motivation, incentives and differentials. There may be differing views and practices about "ownership of the means of production" but problems seem to be common about the actual operations of these means. Industry, like any other major product of human activity and history, is neither encompassable nor controllable by any theory.

The demands of industry fall (and so far always have fallen) very unevenly among those who work in it, the rewards of industry have been very unevenly distributed and a strong case can be made for saying that industry has and does have some effects and requirements which are dehumanising on all associated with it or affected by it. All this has to be faced against the evident fact that it is the industrial multiplication of wealth which has been the necessary basis of, or accompaniment to, the increasing human opportunities of the last two hundred years, whatever threats we may now be facing. It seems, therefore, that the organising of countervailing interventions against the dehumanising effects of that industry which has so many desirable and desired products is an absolute necessity for any positive approach to the problems of human living in the world. It is in this context that the notion of human rights in industry can be most usefully explored. Taking the measures necessary to obtain or develop certain "human rights" could be, and, indeed, already has been, a source of vital tools or weapons for working for and fighting for improvement in society and for justice and humanity within society.

Like the State, industry is both a necessity for and a problem to human living in society. Both the State and industry promote human living and threaten it, they enable humanity and they oppress it. It is necessary, therefore, to seek means of establishing rights *over against* the threats and oppressions of industry and also to develop rights *on behalf* of that which promotes and enables greater humanity within industry.

All the protective and regulative legislation from the early Factory Acts onwards should be seen and judged as part of the attempt to define and develop the rights of workers over against the demands of industry, whether these are understood as the personal demands of such as owners or the impersonal demands of systems. Since systems of production have their own demands, regardless of ownership, it is clear that means are required for protecting the human rights of workers whatever the system by which society is organised. In this connection it is important to notice that workers' rights are positively jeopardised if the powers of running the State and the powers of running industry are too easily identified, for then whose is the necessary countervailing power? Further, if protective regulation is to be effective then it is necessary also to establish and empower means of inspection, recognised dispute procedures and tribunals to which appeals can be made. Otherwise rights which have come to be recognised or conferred as part of the process of establishing workers as independent human beings within, and therefore sometimes over against, industry cannot be made good. Finally, history has shown that the possibility of establishing these rights over against industry has depended on the development of protective structures and collectives by those who originally had no power and no recognised rights. In view of the system's demands already referred to, it would seem that the maintenance and development of human rights in industry and in industrial society depends on the recognition of the right to form such protective collectives. Countervailing power to such collectives may become necessary but this would not invalidate the importance of their existence and the recognition of their right to exist.

Protection of that which is human needs, however, to be extended into promotion of that which is human. Hence also the need to develop rights on behalf of that which enables greater humanity within industry. It is in this context that the so far very imperfectly worked out discussion about workers' participation and the provision of information to workers' representatives should be located and worked on. Other examples of moving towards "rights on behalf of positive humanity" are to be found in various forms of State intervention to protect jobs, enterprises and communities from being at the mercy of purely commercial and strictly industrial factors and in the provisions of recent Health and Safety legislation for worker representation in the definition and monitoring of consequent local regulations. All the examples given represent threats to the running of industry as well as, or instead of, positive contributions, at any rate given the present climate of much industrial relations. And it is clear that neither the means nor the will to operate them successfully yet exist. Yet since industry is so decisive an influence in the life of our society, it seems inevitable that some such attempt must go on being made to work out a more positive balance of power, responsibility and opportunity among all employed in industry. How the "rights" of the various parties concerned should be defined, recognised and handled, has not yet begun to be clear. Most of the necessary work has yet to be done.

As this necessary work of discovering, establishing and enabling more generally extended and enjoyed rights in industry is carried on it will be necessary to be sensitive to at least the following influences from the past which continue to be pressures in the present and to some currently pressing questions which greatly affect the future.

The pressures from the past which are still very much alive include the long history of "class distinction". The active evidence for this includes the humanly degrading demands for discipline often expressed arbitrarily or peremptorily by all grades of management. There is also the continuing evidence of double standards. On the one hand this is to be seen from "the perks" which go with white-collar jobs and with salaried or managerial status. On the other hand there is also the "double standard" concerning the behaviour which is socially demanded of workers' collectives over against other less publicly recognised "pressure groups". This is well set-out by Fred Hirsch in his *"Social Limits to Growth"*,[10] as follows:

restraint over politically organised economic power, which is likely to take the form of disruptive power, has to be considered in the context of what restraint, if any, is exercised on independent acquisitive power in the sense of market opportunities. The relevant entity is the combination of direct (independent) and indirect (disruptive) acquisitive power. It is one-sided to expect those who command relatively great organisational or political power to restrain its exertion, in the collective interest, if no similar restraints are applied to the exercise of relatively great independent acquisitive market power by other individuals in the collectivity. Yet this asymmetry is endemic in almost all liberal discussion of the issue.

This is the heart of the trade unionist's objection: 'In a free-for-all, we are all part of the all'. Workers organised in unions are asked to restrain their use of disruptive economic power, while individuals who are able to exert greater acquisitive power without recourse to disruptive power remain free to do so.

This sort of issue makes it clear that "human rights in industry" falls very near the centre of the critical social problem of the relations between political power and economic power. This is further underlined by the long history and continuing experience by workers of powerlessness. Conditions of work and access to what have hitherto been generally recognised to be the regular means of livelihood (i.e. a wage) are at the mercy of what, to the workers, are wholly external and arbitrary forces. This becomes sharply clear when plants of singular importance to the viability of particular communities are marked out for closure. No amount of organisation and agitation eventually make any difference, save possibly on the size and distribution of redundancy payments. This is why the central social provision of at least some mitigating "rights" (e.g. to lump sums, extended unemployment pay, training schemes, etc.) are essential and also why attempts to develop increased information, consultation and participation are also essential. But the basic powerlessness remains. This, combined with the long and continuing experience of "them and us", makes it clear that "rights" are, for the foreseeable future, bound to be weapons in a conflict as well as tools in building up more balanced collaboration.

Such experiences and pressures increase the difficulties but also the urgency of questions which are now emerging as our industrial society seeks to find ways forward into a future which is both sustainable and increasingly humane. It may be that the development of a common understanding that these questions exist and that they are proper and necessary questions for all sections of our society could be an essential part of providing that necessarily changing but working social consensus which is required if our society is to hold together while it works out new practical expressions of rights and duties and new social structures for the necessary balancing of powers.

One such question might be formulated as "What are the rights which workers should have established, recognised and enforceable so that the community can be mutually recognised to have a right to expect and, through possible sanctions, up to a point, enforce acceptance of the discipline of production and provision of goods and services"? This is a question about the relation between workers' rights, consumers' rights and citizens' rights. Marxist attempts to reduce these three to the rights of workers and Market-theorists attempts to reduce them to the rights of consumers seem practically false and humanly dangerous. It may be that a sensitive, urgent and realistic probing of issues of human rights in industry and in an industrial society could be an important practical way in to that revival of original political thinking and inventiveness which we seem to require.

A sub-ordinate problem in this area is of the form "When do collective rights which were historically necessary as tools *and weapons* become so potentially oppressive or disruptive that there has to be counter-organisation to challenge them?" The issue of the closed shop clearly fits in here. In the light of considerations which I have been trying to point to in this paper I would simply register two observations. The first is that the realities and human pressures of this issue cannot be dealt with by a hotted-up version of a debate (fight) between the proponents of the classical rights of the individual and the proponents of the Marxist rights of the (workers) collective. Secondly, the issue cannot properly be regarded as closed or as a touchstone of loyalty to "the cause". There is, for example, an observable tendency for officials of Trade Unions or professional bodies to justify industrial action by their members on the grounds that the relevant decisions were "taken democratically". Such action is, of course, not democratic. It is the exercise of tribal power made possible by the tribal possession of some element of at least quasi-monopoly. The action may be both necessary and righteous, perhaps precisely because "democracy" is so sadly lacking. But to speak of it as "democratic" is to head back in the direction of the conflicts of Hobb and probably to strengthen a trend which might well push people, frightened by the disruptive tendencies in society, to the point where they would be ready to invest power in some specious "Sovereign" for the sake of some stability and some protection.

Thus the continued working at issues and practices of human rights in industry is a crucial matter for our society. The actual definition and establishment of "rights" would seem to be negotiable, provisional and relative to historical and technological developments. In view of the demands of production and the necessities of an organised society it seems clear that rights must go with duties and all rights are limited by other rights. The critical question for us is probably whether our society can find ways of enabling sufficient participation and achievement in the adjustment of rights while keeping the necessary production of goods and services going and not allowing any set of "rights" to overwhelm all others and so become an unchecked tyranny or such an unbalanced exercise of tribal demands as to disrupt the capacity of society to produce and to survive.

Notes

1. F. Engels, writing of a report of a parliamentary commission on the factory system, in *The Condition of the Working Class in England,* published in German in 1845. See p. 198 of the Panther edn. of the English translation of 1892, ed. E. Hobsbawn.
2. R. H. Tawney, *Religion and the Rise of Capitalism,* The Holland Memorial Lectures, 1922, Harmondsworth, Pelican 1938, p. 278.
3. Cited from material recently prepared for a British Council of Churches study on unemployment by a sometime shop steward in the motor industry.
4. F. Engels, op. cit., p. 206.
5. Svetozar Stojanovic, *Between Ideals and Reality,* New York, O.U.P., 1973, (orig. publ. in Belgrade 1969).
6. ibid., p. 113.
7. ibid., p. 124.
8. ibid., p. 128.
9. see *The Times,* 17.10.78, Report on speech by Mr. Hu Chiao-nu, President of the Chinese Academy of Social Sciences.
10. Fred Hirsch, *Social Limits to Growth,* London, Routledge, Kegan, Paul 1977, p. 155.

CHAPTER 9

HUMAN RIGHTS IN THE CHURCH

The Contemporary State of the Canon Law

FREDERICK R. McMANUS

Introduction

Although the topic which I propose to treat is extremely broad, "Human Rights in the Church," for my purposes, I shall consider only the canonical determination of the human rights in the ecclesial community – and that determination not so much in the more significant and Spirit-guided custom of the church but rather in the written enactments of ecclesiastical authority. I shall consider both the declaration of rights within the church community, as these may or should be found in the canon law, and the protection of rights by means of canonical procedures and formalities. With regard to the latter, I take it there will be little dispute: the written canonical tradition is sound enough, if weak in practice: it needs development and strength. With regard to the former, the inclusion of enumerated rights in the canon law, I speak from a tradition and mentality formed by the experience of a written Constitution and Bill of Rights and thus strongly incline to the inclusion of such statements in the law.

It may be argued, of course, that written affirmations of rights are not always needed, that rights should instead be the unwritten assumptions of a free society, including the society of the church. Perhaps more tellingly, it may be argued that written declarations of rights lead to apathy or false security. It is almost futile to recite the long list of canons and canonical traditions if they are not observed by those with power in the church community – just as it is almost futile to confront certain governments with the *United Nations Declarations of Rights* or the like.

Yet I believe strongly that the experience of my own country demonstrates the formative and educative force of such declarations, that the restraints upon the powerful can in some ultimate fashion be enforced, that there comes a time when the abuse of authority can be corrected without rebellion, or schism, by reliance upon the constitutional affirmation of rights and its acceptance by the society. For more than a decade we have recognised that the church should discern the signs of the times. And one sign, it seems to me, is the utility, if no more, of solemn asseverations of rights and duties.

In what follows I will try to trace, rather selectively, the efforts made in this direction by council and popes on behalf of all the churches and some contributions made by the church in the United States.

The Code of Canon Law

Only the briefest survey of the post-Code of Canon Law and preconciliar state of ecclesiastical law on human rights in the church is feasible. The present situation is the fruit of a long canonical tradition in which the protection of rights, if not their enunciation, is a significant and Christian dimension. But this has been diluted and sometimes nullified by exceptions and by a breakdown in process.

Much could be said about the human rights of the ordained ministers of the church, rights which they share with all the baptised, but the clergy are, after all, voluntarily committed to the exercise of the pastoral office – and the exercise of their rights within the community may properly be circumscribed and limited by this fact. Nevertheless, many of the restrictions upon the ordained may well be questioned, as such restrictions grow more and more remote from the genuine needs of a fruitful ministry within the Christian community.[1]

Perhaps something parallel can be said of 'religious' and all those who by public dedication subject themselves to special limitations upon their human rights within the church. Whether they are, theologically and canonically, lay persons or ordained ministers, the limitations placed upon them arise from a commitment or consecration which is voluntary and which does not affect the members of the church as a whole.

Two points may be made quickly about the ordained ministers and, to the extent that a parallel can be drawn, religious. First, the presumption in the exercise of human rights should be in favour of freedom; obedience to the gospel is not at stake. Second, there is an irony in that the restraints are greater upon those with lesser responsibilities; perhaps the reverse should be true.

Our concern, however, is with the human rights of all the baptised, rights to be declared and rights to be vindicated. Looking only to the successful if imperfect 1917 Code of Canon Law, we do find basic statements or assumptions of rights. It can be urged, for example, that canon 682 has a fundamental breadth so as to include rights of every kind. To render this canon effective in the church community is something else again, and of course it is improperly restricted to lay persons unless the following is clear: First, bishops, presbyters, and deacons are *laici* as well as *clerici* in their dependence on other members of the clergy.[2] Second, the ministry of the whole church in the sharing of spiritual goods must be acknowledged as one not limited to a paternalistic and patronising clergy. Third, the expression, "in accord with the norm of ecclesiastical discipline" should not be employed in canon 682 or elsewhere as an escape hatch or device to limit rights and freedoms. Perhaps a stronger indication, this time in a canon placed among the general norms rather than misplaced in the part *De Laicis,* can be found in canon 19. This is a statement of the presumption of freedom.[3]

The 1917 Code of Canon Law cannot be reasonably criticised for not developing an affirmation of rights at length and as a distinct statement; this was hardly its purpose. At the same time the expression of rights should not be ignored, from the most general "no one may be compelled against his or her will to embrace the Catholic faith"[4] to the most specific, like the right to marry[5] and the right to Christian burial.[6] Sometimes, without affirming a right, a whole complex of canons rests upon a recognition of rights; for example, the law on associations rests upon the right to assemble and associate freely.[7] More to the point, the very obligations imposed upon those who hold the pastoral office, for example, those affecting sacramental ministrations, are certainly both recognition of rights and attempts to assure their exercise.

Finally, the procedural law is designed if ineffective to assure that every right can be enfored by a judicial trial "unless the contrary is expressly indicated."[8] Rights of appeal,[9] rights to petition for the exercise of rights,[10] all are included in the elaborate procedures. Even non-judicial, administrative processes are provided.[11] The law includes highly developed procedures so that the gravest ecclesiastical penalties may not be unjustly imposed, although it then vitiates such guarantees by permitting simple denial to priests, for example, of any ecclesiastical appointment or faculty.

A middle course should be steered. The 1917 Code of Canon Law does look to the protection of rights. But its ineffectiveness cannot be stressed too strongly. Both the declaration and the means to vindicate rights remain weak. That this problem exists is not the assertion of some shrill complainers. In November 1967, the Synod of Bishops accepted without dissent the principles for the revision of the Code of Canon Law.[12]

The Doctrine of Rights

My purpose under this heading is not to deal with the doctrine or philosophy of rights within the church, but to suggest that the assertion of human rights has an inevitable impact upon the canon law. Even when the assertion of human rights is thought to be safely directed to societal issues outside the church, its application to the church community cannot be entirely avoided.

1. Under this heading I would mention, first and very selectively, the encyclical letter of Pope John XXIII, *Pacem in terris.* In the context of peace and order, the pope listed the several rights of individuals.[13] He asserted the responsibility of civil authorities to ensure that these rights are acknowledged, respected, coordinated with other rights, defended and promoted.[14] "The public authority of the world community, too, must have as its fundamental objective the recognition, respect, safeguarding, and promotion of the rights of the human person."[15]

A parallel may be drawn with the principle of political subsidiarity. The assertion of this principle in the sphere of civil society has led to its ready application in the ecclesial society, where it affords a theoretical and even pragmatic pattern of conduct, if only weakly articulating the mystery of the local church vis-a-vis the communion of churches which is the universal Church. Similarly the assertion of human rights in the social and political sphere leads to an inescapable parallel recognition of rights in the church.

2. A good example is the conciliar declaration on human freedom.[16] Admittedly the document is directed toward religious freedom immune from coercion extrinsic to the church not with

freedom within the church: it was difficult enough for the framers to reconcile continuity and change without facing questions of rights and freedoms within the Christian Church itself. Yet the enunciation of the principle is still valid for the society of the church.[17]

John Courtney Murray felt that n. 7 was the most significant statement in the declaration[18] as it expressed in more philosophical and eloquent terms, the principle of canon 19 on the strict interpretation of laws which restrict the free exercise of rights.[19] In spite of its context and purpose, it is applicable to all rights and freedoms in the church community as well as to human society at large.

3. Much the same can be said about the Pastoral Constitution *Gaudium et spes* issued by the Second Vatican Council on the same day in 1965.[20]

While we can understand the hesitations and even reluctance with which those in authority review the application of such assertions to the church itself, there is already a great awareness of the application evidenced as we shall see in the projected revision of the Code of Canon Law. And it is not out of place to mention that rights within the church, over and above the human rights common to all men and women, have a special title and source, namely, the common dignity derived from rebirth in Christ.[21]

But the significant issue is first the recognition of rights in the church and then the implementation of those rights – canonical implementation in the context of this paper.

4. To give a final example, the 1971 session of the Synod of Bishops addressed questions of justice in the world, largely in terms of political and social problems. After proclaiming the message of the Gospel to which the church bears witness, the Synod faced in some degree the practical problem of justice within the church itself.[22] The context of its assertions is the church's role in educating for justice and in collaborating for justice. As within the church community there must first be a renunciation of privilege and an examination of Christian witness to poverty before either education or collaboration will be acceptable, so first the protection of human rights in the church must precede any claims for respect for ecclesial rights, much less power and place.

In the United States

Ten years ago the question of rights in the church came to a head in the United States, perhaps chiefly in respect of the rights of the ordained but also with a concern for the rights of all the Christian people. These had been vindicated in principle by conciliar statements and by papal pronouncements; they had not been vindicated in practice, nor were the remedies of the canon law available or effective.

Two contributions of a corporate character by the Canon Law Society of America, in one case with the collaboration of The Catholic University of America, and formal action by the United States National Conference of Catholic Bishops should be summarised. As will be seen, they constitute an American contribution, and in some sense a contribution of Anglo-American law, to the development of a better defined sense of human rights in the church.

In October 1968 the symposium on rights, already mentioned, was held at The Catholic University of America under the cosponsorship of the Canon Law Society and the University's School of Canon Law.[23]

I will not attempt to recapitulate the 1968 papers and discussions or the appendix to the collection, which offers valuable guidance in the drafting of declarations of rights.[24] The position paper, however, should be summarised:

The document begins with an explicit preamble which situates any consideration of the definition of rights in the ecclesial body.[25]

After theological, historical, and legal considerations the document places its declarations within the framework of the conciliar constitution *Gaudium et spes,* the papal encyclicals, and two civil documents of modern society, the American *Bill of Rights* and the *United Nations Declaration of Rights.* The important influence of the last two documents can best be understood as flowing from the conciliar experience. In that experience, especially as reflected in the pastoral constitution and the *Declaration on Religious Freedom,* the interaction of human society and Christian teaching is acknowledged. The development of Christian recognition of rights admittedly and gladly takes into account the growth in human perspectives.[26]

There is an evident relation between that position paper, in the form of a declaration of human rights, and the subsequent report on *due process* and the action of the Conference of Bishops in the United States. The concluding sections of the 1968 document provided for effective remedies with fair and impartial procedures.[27]

The National Conference of Catholic Bishops of the U.S. took up the question of human rights at three successive meetings in 1968 and 1969. Its concern was directed to the vindication of rights by due process rather than to their abstract definition, and the concern grew from mild interest to a firm resolution.

The final resolution, passed in November 1969 and given the *nihil obstat* of the Apostolic See in October 1971, acknowledged and recommended to the diocesan Bishops a report prepared by the Canon Law Society of America and submitted by the Bishops' Committee on Canonical Affairs. The report *On Due Process*[28] deals with conciliation, arbitration, and judicial process, as well as structures for administrative discretion, but it begins with a preamble which is a declaration of human rights in the church.

The preamble concludes:

> The dignity of the human person, the principles of fundamental fairness, and the universally applicable presumption of freedom require that no member of the Church arbitrarily be deprived of the exercise of any right or office.[29]

Each of the enumerated rights is derived from a conciliar or papal statement and is carefully documented. After a brief but thorough discussion of the meaning and needs of procedures to protect rights, initial emphasis was placed upon a process for conciliation.

In spite of appearances to the contrary, practitioners of law in the United States are not in principle litigious. But the settlement of grievances and disputes out of court in the ecclesial society is suggested not out of the analogy between canon law and the law of human society, but out of evangelical injunctions. Even the maligned Code of Canon Law may be invoked to this effect.[30]

1. Concretely, the report offers at the first level several recommendations for effective conciliation: face-to-face dialogue of parties to controversy, participation of an impartial conciliator, common recognition that concrete applications of rights must be achieved rather than vindication of abstract principles, avoidance of delays and concealment of relevant information, and the obligation of parties to demonstrate Christian love.[31]

2. At the next level a "process for arbitration" is proposed for the cases where conciliation fails. The definition is that accepted in civil proceedings.[32] In making this proposal, which is described in principle and then completed with a model process, the Canon Law Society was extending the norm already found in the 1917 Code of Canon Law.[33]

The process of arbitration demands greater formalities, a record of the proceedings, and competent, impartial persons to make the judgment. It is recommended that in many instances the arbitrators be chosen on a basis wider than diocesan, with the possibility of regional panels of arbitrators, but with each local church free to determine details.

Since the transgression of rights and similar grievances not infrequently involve ecclesiastical authorities, it is in the process of arbitration, as here conceived, that the Bishop of the local church must voluntarily submit himself to the judgment of an arbitrator or arbitrators. When the conference of Bishops of the United States approved and recommended the process of arbitration, it was with the understanding that each bishop accepting the process would indeed forego his canonical rights in some degree, by accepting in advance a decision which might be unfavourable to him. Some Bishops feared that they might be surrendering an inalienable right or that they had, in this regard, no capacity to bind their successors. For some, at least, the *nihil obstat* of the Apostolic See was enough assurance on these scores.

3. Recognising the inadequacy of the present ecclesiastical judicial system[34] – and especially the exemption of the Bishop from subjection to it – the report added the following, to deal with the third level in the resolution of differences and the vindication of rights:

> It is the recommendation of the Society, therefore, that pending the establishment of administrative tribunals as part of the revision of the Code of Canon Law, Ordinaries delegate jurisdiction either to existing diocesan tribunals, or to newly created experimental tribunals, for the resolution of disputes between persons in the church and administrative authorities or bodies within the diocese . . .[35]

The question of administrative tribunals, as part of the revision of the procedural law of the Latin Church, will be taken up in another context. Unlike the progress for arbitration, which had enjoyed some initial success in American dioceses, the delegation of judicial power seems not to have taken place. There are different ways of looking at this. From one viewpoint, it is a weakness that the Bishops may not recognise their pastoral power and capacity to set up judicial processes over and above the common or general canon law but not contrary to it, simply as an exercise of their native pastoral responsibility. This is a matter clearly determined by the conciliar decree *Christus Dominus,*[36] demanded by the nature of the local church and the principle of ecclesial subsidiarity, but too little appreciated in the practical life of the church. On the other hand, it is surely not desirable to invite the development of judicial litigation. If, as the American document suggests, a formal process of arbitration should be a last resort after Christian conciliation fails, a judicial process should be extraordinary and ultimate.

4. The authors of the Canon Law Society proposal were not content to deal with procedures in cases of grievance, whether conciliation, arbitration or judicial trials. Problems of rights in the church society should not arise if there is "an atmosphere of Christian living in which disputes are less likely to appear."[37] This points to an important qualification of the usual and popular concept of due process.

It is the substantive implications of due process that were most easily overlooked, in the legitimate and timely search for just and equitable procedures, especially those already described. Substantive due process goes beyond this and constitutes "a principle of justice according to which no one is to be deprived of the exercise of any right without adequate justification, without sufficient reason."[38] Going beyond procedures to right wrongs, therefore, the 1969 report has a significant section on "structuring administrative discretion." This touches what may be more sensitive and more telling than any *post factum* vindication of rights. When those who administer or execute the law act, they must act, and must be seen to act, fairly. Uncontrolled and unchecked exercise of power leads to arbitrariness and injustice.

In the detailed appendices to the report, the specifics of conciliation and arbitration, are only models, but in this instance – the introduction of substantive due process into administrative decisions – the appended recommendations have very wide implications and deserve to be summarised.

First, discretionary administrative power should be confined and controlled by "a clear delineation of the competence of the particular administrative organ or individual administrator."[39] Second, it is suggested that administrators and administrative bodies should state their policies, publish "the considerations, the criteria, the standards that will guide decisions to be made in individual cases."[40] Such policies should themselves be the fruit of an open policy-making process. Third, "written findings of fact and reasoned opinions in support of administrative decisions should be issued whenever discretionary power is exercised in such a way as adversely to affect the rights of persons in the Church." Fourth, fairness is demanded as much in extra-judicial discretionary determinations of ecclesiastical administrators as in the most solemn ecclesiastical trial. Due process then means a great deal more than the resolution of disputes or the redress of grievances.

I do not wish to exaggerate either the success of these norms in the United States or their influence upon the broader scene of the Latin Church and the revision of its Code of Canon Law. Nonetheless, that revision, for all its halting progress and manifest weaknesses, is an opportunity not to be missed, an occasion to declare rights and to protect them procedurally and otherwise.

Projected Fundamental Law of the Church

In 1959, at the same time as he announced his intention to call a general council, Pope John XXIII recognised the need for a complete revision of the Code of Canon Law. In the debate about every disciplinary decree of the Council, this revision was taken for granted and it proved a ready means of disposing of specific questions as being too particularised for conciliar action. After the first period of the Council, Pope John established a Commission of cardinals for the purpose on March 28, 1963, but the Commission's activity did not get under way in earnest, with the collaboration of large numbers of consultants in more than a dozen *coetus studiorum* until after the completion of the Council.

Among the projects of the Commission, distinct from and in some ways prior to the revision of the Code, is the *Lex Ecclesiae Fundamentalis*. It was conceived as a fundamental code which contains the constitutional rights of the church as a preface to the two different codes of the Latin Church and of the (Catholic) Eastern Churches.

The first two drafts that were circulated for the comments of the Episcopate in 1971[41] had countless deficiencies as a constitutional statement: theological, ecclesiological, ecumenical, canonical. The document confused those elements which are truly necessary if the *Ecclesia* is to be the authentic Church of Christ with very contingent elements; it offered an image of the church as primarily a quasi-political society of governors and governed; its use of conciliar sources was found to be highly selective and neglectful of the biblical and sacramental emphases to be seen in the constitution *Lumen gentium;* it used the very term *ecclesia* equivocally; and it was inadequate in its well intentioned effort to define and declare the rights of the members of the church.

It is with this last element alone that we are directly concerned. Some fifteen canons deal with the "fundamental duties and rights of the Christian faithful."[42]

In some sense it is difficult to speak harshly of these proposed canons of the Fundamental Law. Their purpose is sound enough, and they represent a measure of progress. Yet they seem to be vitiated both by their incompleteness and by their inclusion of so much language of compromise, not to mention the problems found in other parts of this projected constitutional law as these affect rights and their protection.

Fourteen of these canons mention *iura Christifidelium* but almost all contain qualifications ot reservations. The fundamental problem is fear of freedom and rights, almost a pessimistic tone which befogs the good intentions. One balanced judgment of the canons on rights concludes:

> The fundamental prerogatives . . . are so restricted and qualified that it is often difficult to discern which is stressed the more: the right, or the restrictions on the right . . . Canon 19 then places a final, and rather arbitrary, qualification on all of the rights set forth, leaving the whole statement considerably weakened and diluted. In addition certain prerogatives are expressed so vaguely (e.g. the right to participate in the government of the Church – canon 13, § 3) that one is left with the impression that no real right has been guaranteed at all.
>
> It must also be stressed that this part of the schema . . . does

not assure adequate remedies in the event of the violation of rights. Indeed, the interpretation of these rights rests in the hands of the very persons whose interests could often be most effectively served by restricting them . . .[43]

The further revisions of the 1971 schema have not yet been published or circulated among the Bishops or others, but the process of revision has been reported, sometimes in detail, in the pages of the Commission's journal, *Communicationes.* It must be confessed, however, that these indications do not suggest any fresh orientation of the draft on rights (although many basic changes in the structure of the document have been introduced).

This report on the Fundamental Law is necessarily incomplete and tentative. It must be noted, moreover, that one of the weaknesses of the current recodification, namely, lack of coordination, is especially apparent in the relation of the Fundamental Law to the series of schemata now in circulation for comment. Even a cursory study of the other schemata indicates that no clear decision has been reached about the inclusion or exclusion of constitutional canons, presumably belonging in the Fundamental Law, in the books and titles of the Code of Canon Law. Despite this methodological weakness an opportunity to see other Roman versions of the canons on rights as well as the canons on the protection of rights remains.

Projected Code of Canon Law: Rights

When the draft of the *Lex Ecclesiae Fundamentalis* first received wide publicity, one judgment was that, if the schema were promulgated "nothing would happen in the practical order". This is less true of the revision of the Code of Canon Law of the Latin Church, which may be expected to have a more pragmatic significance, if and when the process of recodification comes to term and the code is published. So far as human rights are concerned, because of the vast quantity of canons now in draft form, it is necessary to concentrate upon two areas:

(a) a relatively brief statement of rights within the church, related in some parts to what was projected for the Fundamental Law but in expanded and in some ways improved form;

(b) the guarantees and protections of rights, principally through procedures.

First of all, the projected canons on rights, circulated among the members of the episcopate and others in early 1978,[44] are entitled "obligations and rights of all Christian believers." They are found within the schema *De Populo Dei,*[45] formerly *De Personis,* and are carefully located so as to be equally applicable to lay men and women and to the ordained or "sacred" ministers of the church. It would be easy to comment in the greatest detail, both positively and negatively, upon these canons. Some of them have a familiar ring and may be said to express well the minimal expectations of human rights and freedom within the church.

One general hesitation has to be expressed, not necessarily substantive in all cases. Unquestionably some of the canons are couched in cautionary terms, and occasionally what the canon gives in the main clause it takes away in a subordinate clause or in an adjective or phrase. This is cause for concern, partly because it reveals a grudging spirit in the formulation of the canons. The canonist would find much to quarrel with in the inconsistencies of language in the canons, but in the more profound concern for guarantees of human rights such niceties are secondary.

If one compares these canons, in the form circulated in 1978, with the canons of the *Lex Ecclesiae Fundamentalis* of 1971, the following is evident:

1. Several of the norms are familiar enough and have been restated with lesser changes only. These include some generalities and a few specifics concerning the right to association, the right of inquiry or investigation, the right to a just and equitable trial in the judicial or administrative order, the right to free expression – at least in the still patronising and restricted terms employed in ecclesiastical documents. In at least one instance however, the right not be punished with penalties created *ex post facto,* the 1978 canons are considerably weaker.

2. On the other hand, considerable progress over 1971 is evident in the right to confidentiality or privacy, for example, and in the specifics of the right to redress and recourse. The elements of due canonical process are rather carefully determined: the right to be judged by a competent tribunal, right to be heard, right to legal assistance, right to know the name of one's accuser, right to know the reasons for judgments, but no reference to the right to incriminate onself. The formal inclusion of certain other rights, although still in rather general terms, represents a genuine development:

the right to participate in liturgical celebrations, right of choice among diverse forms of spirituality.

3. There is an awareness of enlarged possibilities of administrative recourse in the case of the violation of rights, a matter to be considered separately in the schema of canons *De Procedura Administrativa.*

4. Perhaps most important of all, the possibility of the abuse of power by ecclesiastical authorities is explicitly acknowledged by canon 34.

On balance, something like a declaration of human rights in the church has been achieved in this 1977 draft *De Populo Dei,* the projected second book of a new Code. It demands refinement and considerable improvement so that some of the hesitations and possible escape clauses may be eliminated. It needs to be seen in the wider framework of all the canons which deal with rights of the ordained, for example, and which are beyond the scope of this survey. Finally, it must be related to the guarantees of the protection of rights and redress in cases of grievances, which is the next matter to be considered.

Projected Code of Canon Law: Procedures

Looking now to other parts of the recodification, we find little radical change affecting our concern except in the schema on administrative procedure. Some of the basic norms from the 1917 Code of Canon Law have been retained in the several drafts.[46] Attention must be paid, however, to the efforts to simplify and improve judicial procedure, to the extent that this may be invoked to redress the violation of rights.

The schema of canons corresponding to the fourth book of the 1917 Code, *De Processibus,* was circulated for comment in 1976 under the title, *De Modo Procedendi pro Tutela Iurium seu De Processibus,*[47] an indication from the beginning of good intentions. The projected seventh book of the new code is indeed for the purpose of protecting rights. Perhaps it is even unfair to deny that the revision is radical, because major steps toward simplification of procedure – and thus more equitable and expeditious resolution of cases – have been taken.

The procedural law, according to the introductory notes which accompanied the consultation, requires "That justice be administered surely and quickly so that each one of the people of God may rely upon the protection of his or her rights by means of a procedural system that is rapid and clear."[48] An immediate defect in principle is evident from the same introduction (and from the *principia* of the revision approved by the Synod of Bishops in 1967): the usages of various nations, embodied in civil tribunals, are given only token recognition on the grounds that recourse to the Apostolic See will be jeopardised if the procedural law is not everywhere substantially the same. An overall view is that the drafters, in their effort to balance decentralisation and the "unitary organisation of justice" preferred the latter.[49]

Many features of the revision are admirable: the greater, if still limited, role given to lay persons even as judges; greater autonomy for judges in the light of their greater stability; removal of inhibitions upon religious as plaintiffs. The same can be said of the direct simplifications; respect for the consciences of non-Catholics who do not wish to appear before a priest, so that proofs will not be lost on this account; recognition of a certain probative value of the statements of parties; participation of advocates at the interrogation of witnesses and some recognition of civil usages in regard to interrogations; the introduction of a so-called summary process considerably broader in use than the previous summary matrimonial case. Finally, the simplifications in matrimonial cases in general, introduced by the apostolic letter of Paul VI, *Causas matrimoniales*[50] of March 28, 1971, have been incorporated – not, however, the broader concessions of the so-called American procedural norms.

The application of all this to the actual vindication of human rights within the church is extremely problematical. The judicial tribunals have been rarely available in actual practice for the redress of grievances among believers, much less those involving allegations of abuse of ecclesiastical power. Conceivably, such a situation could change, and no one would deny that it is desirable to have judicial and judicious avenues of relief in extreme cases. Similarly no one should seek needless litigation, but some of the old inhibitions remain, such as the reservation to the Roman See of cases involving Bishops.

Perhaps a greater recognition of the signs of the times – and of human rights which need to be protected – is found in the development, still tentative, of an administrative procedure. Although belonging properly to the seventh book of the new codification, the schema of canons on this subject was issued separately in 1972.[51]

The schema *De Procedura Administrativa* represents a departure in church law in order to provide that, within limits, recourse to special and new tribunals may be an alternative to petitions addressed to the Pope and the other Bishops. A distinction is made between hierarchical recourse, already available to those aggrieved by ecclesiastical decisions and actions, and the planned style of national and regional administrative tribunals.

This development, promised in the *principia* of recodification, is described by the Pontifical Commission as arising from "the necessity of having more suitable protection of physical and moral persons in relation to decrees issued by those who have the power of governance in the Church."[52] A first step in this direction had been taken, so far as the Apostolic See is concerned, when Pope Paul VI reformed the Roman Curia in 1967.[53] The highest tribunal, the Apostolic Signatura, was given a new section competent to judge administrative decisions taken by executive authorities in the church. The purpose of the projected canons is to permit the Conferences of Bishops to set up similar administrative tribunals, whether national or regional, of first instance and even of second instance or appeal.

In connection with the American beginnings of new processes of conciliation and arbitration, I drew attention to the priority and greater significance of *due process* in the making of administrative decisions, rather than limited to the resolution of controversies and the redress of grievances. Perhaps the few canons on decrees or decisions which are to be issued are the most important, requiring ecclesiastical authority, before acting, to seek the necessary information, to hear those affected by the decisions, to communicate the information and reasons for (and against) decisions.[54] Most of the schema is of course devoted to the processes of recourse against decisions which are alleged to violate the rights of individuals or communities. Only the administrative actions of an ecumenical council or of the Bishop of Rome are exempt.

Conclusion

Apart from our own topic of rights in the church, the recodification of disciplinary law for the Latin Church has some broad pitfalls. Granted the inadequacy of the present schemata and the great methodological problems ahead, there are twin dangers in substance and principle: one is that the momentous reflections and decisions of the Second Vatican Council not be implemented in spirit and promise as well as in letter; the other is that the conciliar plateau be accepted as a static and enduring reality, without embracing the developments in church life since 1965.

The first statement of Pope John Paul II in his address to the Cardinals on October 17 1978, indicates that the new Bishop of Rome recognises these dangers and, we may hope, will act vigorously and incisively to avoid them.

If Pope John Paul II succeeds in his declared intention of implementing the decisions of Vatican Council II, its application to the recodification of the canon law and to the declaration and protection of human rights in the church through the canon law should be obvious. Commitment to the exact and faithful implementation of the conciliar decisions and mentality is the enemy of compromises and dilutions of the conciliar promise. Recognition of the further unfolding of conciliar purpose in the light of subsequent experimentation and today's changing circumstances is the enemy of static rigidity and intransigent literalism.

Our considerations may be summed up as evidence of the great signs of progress in the legal and canonical appreciation of human rights in the church – let us not minimise the progress in any way. But there is equal evidence of weakness and hesitations yet to be overcome if the canon law is to be one among many of the ecclesial instruments to define and assure rights in the church community.

Notes

1. e.g. *Codex Iuris Canonici* [=CIC] 137.
2. Since 1973 only bishops, presbyters, and deacons are considered clerics (ordained or sacred ministers) in the Latin Church. Effective January 1 of that year, the subdiaconate, minor orders, and tonsure were suppressed, and the canonical status of clergy abolished for those who do not pertain to the three sacramental orders. See Paul VI, motu proprio *Ministeria quaedam,* motu proprio *Ad pascendum,* August 15, 1972: *Acta Apostolicae Sedis* [=AAS] 64 (1972): 529-540.
3. CIC 19. cf. A. Flannery (ed.) *Vatican Council II: The Conciliar and Post Conciliar Documents* Dublin, Dominican Publications, 1975, p. 804. n. 7.
4. CIC 1351.

5. CIC 1035.
6. CIC 1239, §3.
7. CIC 684-725.
8. CIC 1667.
9. CIC 1879.
10. CIC 1693.
11. CIC 2147-2167.
12. *Principia quae Codicis Iuris Canonici Recognitionem Dirigant* [=Principia], Vatican City, 1967, n. 6-7. Later published in *Communicationes* 1 (1969), pp. 82-83.
13. April 11, 1963: *AAS* 55 (1963): 257-304.
14. Ibid., 274.
15. Ibid., 294.
16. *Dignitatis humanae,* op.cit. n. 7.
17. N. 7.
18. "Religious Freedom" in Walter M. Abbott and Joseph Gallagher, *The Documents of Vatican II* (New York, 1966), p. 687, note.
19. CIC 19: "Laws that establish a penalty or restrict the free exercise of rights are subjected to a strict interpretation."
20. *Gaudium et spes* (on the Church in the world of today), December 7, 1965, n. 26: in Flannery op.cit.
21. Ibid., n. 29.
22. "Justice in the World," Vatican, 1971.
23. James A. Coriden, ed., *The Case for Freedom,* Washington, Corpus Books 1969.
24. This is the work of Charles M. Whelan, S.J., Ibid., pp. 167-170.
25. Ibid., p. 5.
26. Ibid., pp. 12-14.
27. Ibid., p. 13.
28. *On Due Process,* revised ed., (Washington: National Conference of Catholic Bishops, n.d.). An account of the several resolutions of the conference of bishops, their relation to the report of the Canon Law Society, and the *nihil obstat* is given in an introduction, "The NCCB on the Subject of Due Process," (pp. 1-3), dated March 1, 1972, by Bishop Joseph L. Bernardin, then general secretary of the conference.
29. *On Due Process,* pp. 4-5.
30. CIC 1925.
31. See *On Due Process,* pp. 13-15.
32. Ibid., p. 15.
33. CIC 1929.
34. See CIC 1557, §2, 1°.
35. *On Due Process,* p. 17.
36. See II Vatican Council, decree *Christus Dominus* (on the pastoral office

of bishops in the Church), October 28, 1965, n. 8a: in Flannery op. cit.
37. *On Due Process,* p. 17.
38. Ibid., p. 40 (in the "Commentary" by R. T. Kennedy).
39. Ibid., p. 31.
40. Ibid., p. 32.
41. *Schema Legis Ecclesiae Fundamentalis,* Vatican City, 1971. The volume contains the first two drafts with extensive reports on each by W. Onclin. Only the 1971 revision, called the *textus emendatus,* is considered here.
42. Canons 10, 12-24 incl.
43. Study Committee of the Canon Law Society of America, "A Critique of the Revised Schema on the Lex Fundamentalis," *American Ecclesiastical Review* 165 (1971): 9.
44. The drafts of the codification have been circulated in several parts, for example, the canons on sacraments, on religious, on penalties, etc. The five final drafts or schemata, dated 1977 and made available in early 1978, are on general norms, on the people of God, on the teaching office of the Church, on the sanctifying office of the Church, on property. Although these drafts are, like earlier ones, marked "reserved" and thus not for publication, an English translation was distributed by the U.S. National Conference of Catholic Bishops and made generally available. See Canons 17-38 incl.
45. *Schema Canonum Libri II: De Populo Dei* Vatican City, 1971.
46. These canons are found in *Schema Canonum Libri I: De Normis Generalibus* Vatican City: Typis Polyglottis Vaticanis, 1977.
47. *Schema Canonum de Modo. . . .* Vatican City, 1976.
48. Ibid., p. v.
49. Ibid., see *Principia,* n. 5: *Communicationes* 1 (1969): 80-82.
50. March 28, 1971: *AAS* 63 (1971): 441-446.
51. *Schema Canonum de Procedura Administrativa,* Vatican City, 1972.
52. Ibid., p. 5.
53. Paul VI, ap. const. *Regimini Ecclesiae universae,* August 15, 1967: *AAS* 59 (1967): 885-928.
54. Canons 4-7 of the schema *De Procedura Administrativa.*

CHAPTER 10
STRASBOURG

A System of Supervision for the Protection of Human Rights in Europe.

*MICHAEL O'BOYLE**

Introduction

The Strasbourg system instituted by the *European Convention on Human Rights* has been in operation for twenty five years.[1] It constitutes a remarkable feature of the process of European integration. The purpose of this paper is to examine its rationale, its concrete achievements and its developments, actual and potential, as a regional instrument for the protection of rights.

The structure of the system is well known. It is sufficient here to sketch as briefly as possible its most important elements. These are as follows:

(a) The Convention, based on the *Universal Declaration of Human Rights* contains a wide list of civil and political rights to be observed by the High Contracting Parties, including the rights to life, liberty, speech, assembly, association, family life and correspondence and freedom from torture and inhuman or degrading treatment (Arts. 2-14).

(b) It also establishes the European Commission and Court of Human Rights as organs of supervision to ensure the observance of its provisions.

(c) It provides for inter-state complaints within the framework of a collective guarantee of its provisions by all its signatory states. More important, in practice however, it provides for a right of individual petition to the Commission by individuals who claim to be victims of a violation but only vis-à-vis those states which have specifically accepted the competence of the Commission to hear individual cases by lodging a declaration to this effect with the Secretary-General of the Council of Europe. (Arts. 24 & 25).[2]

(d) It provides for the possibility of a friendly settlement of the case between the parties, or a decision as to the question of breach by the Court. The Committee of Ministers is charged with the responsibility of supervising the execution of the Court's judgment. If the case is not submitted to the Court, the Committee of Ministers shall decide by a majority of two-thirds whether there has been a violation. If satisfactory measures are not taken by the State concerned the Committee shall "consider what effects shall be given to its original decision and shall publish the report" (Art. 32).

Rationale

The Strasbourg system has an inbuilt and inevitable contradiction. The more successful the Commission and Court function in terms of the importance and dimension of the issues examined and the solutions arrived at, the more likely that politicians will question the legitimacy and appropriateness of its role as part of the machinery of Western democracies for the protection of human rights.

Developing public awareness of the significance of the Strasbourg system, in itself an important contributory ingredient to its success, has also generated alarm and criticism in some quarters at the prospect of an international court subjecting national laws and practice to constitutional scrutiny. A suitable context for the expression of opinions such as those was provided after the decision of the Court in the *Tyrer* case.[3]

The case concerned the use of the 'birch' as a form of judicial corporal punishment. The Court, confining itself to the facts of case, concluded that it constituted degrading treatment contrary to Art. 3 of the Convention. In its decision it stated that the belief that judicial corporal punishment deters criminals was irrelevant. A punishment does not lose its degrading character just because it is believed to be, or actually is, an effective deterrent or aid to crime control. The fact that the punishment was carried out in private did not deprive it of its degrading character.[4] Nor did the Court consider it relevant that the applicant was birched for an offence of violence or that as an alternative to a period of detention it might have less adverse effects. In arriving at its conclusion the Court stressed that the birch was a form of institutionalised violence which might have adverse psychological effects and that it constituted an assault on a person's dignity and integrity compounded by the aura of official procedure surrounding it.[5]

The case was ripe for controversy from the start. It was clear that there was general support for the use of the birch in the Isle of Man, based on popular beliefs as to its deterrent effect. More importantly, it looked as though the application would provoke a minor constitutional crisis between the Manx Government and Westminster over the potential difficulties of enforcing a decision requiring abolition of the birch. Under the Convention, the United Kingdom Government would be legally obliged to give effect to the binding judgment of the Court (Art. 53). However, it was not clear that the Manx Government, proud of its regional autonomy and local customs, would be prepared to introduce the requisite legislation. To compound matters, the applicant, during the examination of his case by the Commission, sought to withdraw his application and, on being refused, took no further part in the proceedings.[6]

The decision of the Court attracted substantial criticism. One commentator expressed his personal exasperation in the following way.

> His own physical assault on his victim, causing actual bodily harm, was apparently an unrelated matter, nothing to do with human dignity. Has there ever been a better example of using strict legal interpretation as a foundation for dogmatic political waffle? As far as these Mandarins were concerned, public order could go to pot and public opinion could take a running jump . . . Thus we have the remarkable spectacle of an Italian lecturing the Manx people on the right way to deal with violent crime. It is like the grasshopper reading a homily on industry to the ant . . . I am certainly prepared to reverse my earlier views about birching or about any other system of punishment if I should come to the conclusion that its adoption was the only way of maintaining the safety of streets and homes in Britain. And I shall not be influenced by the cloudy transcendentalism on the subject of distant and somewhat introverted foreign functionaries. Salus populi suprema lex.[7]

Such criticism represents more than mere disagreement with the views of the Court as to its balancing of the various factors involved in its decision. It reflects a view which challenges the legitimacy of international machinery for the protection of rights composed of several elements. Firstly it is urged that it is unacceptable and an infringement of national sovereignty to have fundamental and controversial political issues relating to every sphere of legal, political, social and economic life examined by an international tribunal composed of foreign judges. It constitutes a usurpation of the role of the national legislature, executive and judiciary who are in a better position than the international judge, by virtue of their closer contact with the "vital forces" of society, to weigh the various interests involved and come to a decision. Furthermore, while a system of international supervision may be necessary in respect of countries where human rights are known to be regularly abused, it is not necessary for democratic West European countries, who already enjoy a high level of protection which they are committed, by virtue of their democratic political philosophy, to maintain.[8]

This form of criticism is a variant of the traditional doctrines of national sovereignty and domestic jurisdiction, both of which stress the principle of non-interference in the internal affairs of another State. Together they constitute the most important conceptual obstacles to the development of effective forms of international supervision.[9] Given that the Strasbourg system is ultimately dependent on the consent of States in accepting and renewing the right of individual petition and the compulsory jurisdiction of the Court and in being willing to accept and implement decisions of the Court and the Committee of Ministers, it is both valuable and important to be clear on the answers to such criticism. The following points can be made.

1. It is accurate to observe that national sovereignty has been diminished in principle by a State's full participation in the Strasbourg system. In the context of a particular application the organs of the Convention can examine important national issues and find a State to be in breach of its international obligations. Under the treaty such a determination is binding on the State in international law and its practical effect will be to require the State to change the offending law or practice. The power of the Committee of Ministers and of the Court would seem, however, to stop short at prescribing in detail the actual rectifying measures the State should adopt.[10]

2. It must be accepted that the State, being fully advised of the attendant consequences of accepting the obligations of the Convention, has taken a 'policy' or 'value' decision that adherence to a system of international supervision of human rights is more

important than a rigorous conservation of national sovereignty. The basis of such a policy decision may involve factors ranging from a desire to be seen participating in the institution of a 'collective guarantee' of human rights either for national or international consumption; an earnest and sincere value concern for human rights standards and their enforcement; recognition that ratification of the Convention is an important step towards European integration; belief that ratification of the Convention may make it easier to gain entry into the EEC.

3. The Strasbourg system is by its nature a system of last resort or outer supervision. It is founded on the principle that its machinery of protection is subsidiary to the national systems safeguarding human rights.[11]

4. An anlysis of the work of the Commission and Court leaves no doubt as to the necessity in modern Europe of a system of supervision. While it is clear that some cases are of marginal importance, brought about by oversight or mere inadvertence on the part of administrators or legislators, others concern areas of policy that a State may consider defensible or major questions of fundamental importance such as the use of wide emergency powers to deal with terrorist activities or the behaviour of troops of military occupation.[12]

Achievements

The impact of the system in operation goes beyond a mere statistical tally of the number of cases registered or held admissible by the Commission, or decisions of the Court and the Committee of Ministers.[13] At one level it can be seen in terms of the types of cases examined by the Commission and Court dealing with fundamental issues relating to a wide variety of minimum civil and political rights. While it is accurate to observe that the Convention consists of an enumeration of general rights expressed in broad language, subject to equally general qualifications[14] it must be appreciated that the significance of the system lies in the developing interpretation of these standards by the Commission and Court. Perhaps the most significant achievement of the Convention has been the elaboration of the content of Conventional rights when applied to particular situations, and of equal importance, the development of principles of interpretation.[15] It is in this way that the organs of the Convention have been developing a public law of Europe which, having the status of law, has to be taken into consideration by legislatures, administrators and judges in their routine approach to questions of national law and practice. This process represents the principal value of a system of 'outer' supervision. Those States that have accepted the right of individual petition are aware that if their laws and practice are not ordered in conformity with the standards of the Convention as interpreted by the Commission and Court, or if national law does not provide an adequate and effective remedy where it is alleged that a right has been infringed, the possibility exists for an individual to bring the matter complained of before the Commission. It can be seen that where such an application is held admissible the resulting reasoned decision of either the Commission or Court becomes part of the developing European law of human rights to be studied and absorbed by those States that have ratified the Convention. In this way it becomes immediately apparent why an important factor contributing towards the maximum influence of the Convention is the acceptance by State parties of the right of individual petition.

The Convention can influence national law in two other respects. First, experience has shown that the development of human rights law is closely followed by pressure groups and non-governmental organisations such as the National Council of Civil Liberties, Amnesty International, International Commission of Jurists, MIND, who often rely on the Convention and its case-law in support of suggestions for reform. Perhaps the most important example of this can be seen in the developing campaign in the United Kingdom for a Bill or Rights, enforceable in national courts. The number of admissible applications against the United Kingdom concerning issues that could not be adjudicated on by national courts has played an important role in stimulating the Bill of Rights debate as well as raising the level of judicial sensitivity to the Convention aspects of cases in national courts.[16] Second, in several European countries, notably Austria, Belgium, Federal Republic of Germany, Netherlands, Switzerland, the provisions of the Convention have direct effect in internal law and may be invoked before the Courts to challenge the validity of national laws, administrative acts and judicial decisions.[17] In this way the Convention can be said to increase the level of protection of human rights in these countries by providing the possibility of an effective remedy at the domestic level.

In this context, reference should be made to developments by the Court of Justice of the Communities, who in a series of decisions have stated that in interpreting the Community treaties they will have regard to the Convention as part of the general principles of law to be applied to cases before them. The effect of this development creates the possibility that acts of the Community institution or member States of the Community could be challenged on the basis of the Convention in proceedings before the Court of Justice.[18] It remains to be seen in the developing case law of the Court of Justice how significant this extension of the scope of the Convention will be in practice.

On a more practical level the influence of the Convention can be examined in the light of the positive results achieved through the Convention's system of adjudication. These results fall into four recognisable categories:

First, there are cases where the offending law or administrative practice has been changed as a result of a decision of the Court or Committee of Ministers. The *Golder* case affords a good example.[19]

Second, there are applications which have been declared inadmissible by the Commission but where a friendly settlement has been achieved between the parties.[20] The *Simon-Herald* Case is one such case.[21]

The third category consists of applications which have either been withdrawn by the applicant or declared manifestly ill-founded by the Commission but where the institution of proceedings has resulted in some form of beneficial arrangement with the Government. An example of this is the case of *Karnell & Hardt v. Sweden.*[22]

Finally, there are cases where the complaint has been met with compensation awarded by the Court exercising its powers under Art. 50 to award "just satisfaction" to an injured party. *Ringeisen v. Austria* is an example of this.[23]

Developments

An important feature of the Convention is its developing or evolutionary character in the light of changing social, economic, political circumstances, the pace of European integration and the responsiveness of European States to the protection of human rights. Two important trends are of particular note. It is apparent that the number of 'quality' cases raising important admissible issues of general interest before the Commission and Court is increasing. This can be explained in the light of factors such as greater and better informed media coverage, awareness of the significance and potential of the system in legal education, a better informed legal profession who see Strasbourg as proving a possible avenue of redress. This trend can be illustrated by the following issues which have been raised in recent years:

- the case of compulsory sex education in Danish schools and its compatibility with Art. 2 of the First Protocol (*Kjeldsen, Busk Madsen and Pedersen Case*);[24]
- the compatibility of the use of corporal punishment in Scottish schools with Art. 3 and Art. 2 (First Protocol);[25]
- the interception of telephonic telegraphic and postal communications under special legislation in West Germany and its compatibility with rights to privacy and correspondence under Art. 8 (*Klass Case*);[26]
- interference by the prison authorities with prisoners' correspondence in the United Kingdom (*Prisoners' Correspondence Cases*);[27]
- cases concerning the absolute prohibition, under criminal law, of homosexuality in Northern Ireland and the "age of consent" for private consensual homosexual relationships under United Kingdom legislation;[28]
- an application concerning the prohibitive cost of the remedy of judicial separation in Ireland (the *Airey Case*);[29]

A second trend, of importance for the authoritative interpretation of the Convention, concerns the increase in the number of cases being referred to the Court by the Commission. This reflects the important nature of the issues coming before the Commission and a recognition of the value of a final judicial decision through public proceedings resulting in an authoritative interpretation of great weight.[30] It also reflects an awareness of the problem of 'non-decisions' in the Committee of Ministers where the two thirds majority required by Art. 32 to find a violation of the Convention has sometimes proved difficult to obtain. By referring important cases to the Court this difficulty, which undoubtedly affects the credibility of the system, can be avoided by a technique which is legal, diplomatic and ultimately beneficial.[31]

It is appropriate in this context to mention a potential development which has recently been the subject of a report by the Legal Affairs Committee to the Parliamentary Assembly of the Council of Europe,[32] namely the possibility of widening the scope of the Convention to include certain economic, social and cultural rights such as the right to social security or right to just and favourable conditions of work. Such rights have traditionally been considered as inappropriate for the regime of enforcement of the Convention since their enjoyment depends directly on economic progress. It is beyond doubt however, that in the wider human rights debate these rights are assuming a greater importance. This is attributable in part to the growth of enforceable claims in national law arising out of social legislation and giving rise to legitimate expectations and to the emphasis placed on them by socialist theorists. The question recalls statements like that of Maurice Cranston who expressed the view that economic social and cultural rights "muddles, obscures and debilitates a respectable concept" and that the effect of overloading the Universal Declaration with "affirmations of so-called human rights which are not human rights at all . . . is to push all talk of human rights out of the clear realm of the morally compelling into the twilight of utopian aspiration".[33]

It is now clear that with the passage of time the categories of "respectable concepts" have been open ended. As it stands some rights of an economic social and cultural character are already guaranteed under the Convention, for example, Art. 11 (which includes the right to form and join trade unions), Art. 1 of the First Protocol (the right to the peaceful enjoyment of one's possessions) and Art. 2 of the First Protocol (the right to education). It is also clear that amongst the catalogue of economic, social and cultural rights in the European Social Charter there are rights which are regarded as "fundamental" and which would be capable of sufficiently precise formulation to give rise to legal obligation on the State as opposed to merely setting a standard. The abovementioned report provided the following examples:

- the right to choose or accept paid work freely in the light of the individual's qualifications for the work concerned and of reasonable geographical and economic considerations;
- the right of access to free employment services, occupational guidance and occupational training;

– the right to an adequate standard of living in the event of involuntary employment;
– the right to form a social security system.[34]

Conclusion

The Convention system was regarded as a progressive experiment when it was drawn up thirty years ago. However, both its adversaries and its detractors have noted its limitations. The following features have given rise to criticism as to its effectiveness as an organ of human rights supervision.

– the length of time it takes for a case to be examined from the time of registration to either a decision by the Commission on admissibility or a decision by the Court or Committee of Ministers on the merits;[35]
– acceptance of the right of individual petition is optional and so far only fourteen States have accepted it;
– the Commission is only a part-time body which meets for two-weekly sessions five times a year;
– proceedings before the Commission and Committee of Ministers are clothed with too much secrecy; for example oral hearings before the Commission on admissibility and the merits are in camera, the Commission report to the Committee of Ministers under Art. 31 is secret, and the case-file is confidential;
– the Commission has no power to grant interim remedies such as injunctions, or to intervene in a dispute between an individual and the State;[36]
– the individual cannot refer a case to the Court nor has the individual any *locus standi* before it;[37]
– the requirement under Art. 32 that a political organ, i.e. the Committee of Ministers or their deputies, take the final decision where an application has not been referred to the Court, as to whether there has been a violation creates the possibility of a 'non-decision' which undermines the credibility of the system.[38]
– it is not clear that the Court can make consequential orders directing a State to a particular course of action pursuant to a finding of breach and apart from its powers under Art. 50 to award just satisfaction;[39]
– in the exercise of its enforcement powers where there has been a violation, the Committee of Ministers cannot themselves pre-

scribe the measures to be taken by the State to remedy the complaint;[40]

– Art. 57, which empowers the Secretary-General of the Council of Europe to request a State to report on how its internal law ensures the effective implementation of any of the provisions of the Convention has been under-utilised.[41]

However, the purpose of this paper was to show that the Convention in its present form has achieved concrete results in particular cases over the last twenty-five years which, because of the nature of the system and the general interest involved in the issues, go beyond the boundaries of the specific dispute and have to be taken account of as part of the public law of Europe by other signatory States. The system should not, however, be permitted to rest on its laurels. It is the responsibility of lawyers, politicans, consumers and the public to ensure that over the next twenty five years consistent progress is made to utilise the system for what is can offer, to consolidate the effects that it can have and to make it a more effective instrument of European supervision.

Notes

*All views expressed by the author are done so in his private capacity.

1. For text of the Convention and its five Protocols and specific information concerning ratifications, membership of Commission and Court, see: Council of Europe, *Collected Texts, passim* (1978 edition). For general works see: F. G. Jacobs, *The European Convention on Human Rights* (1975); A. H. Robertson, *Human Rights in Europe* (2nd ed., 1977); J. E. S. Fawcett, *The application of the European Convention on Human Rights* (1969). See also: Council of Europe publications "What is the Council of Europe doing to protect human rights" (1977); and Bibliography relating to the Convention (1978).
2. The Convention has been ratified by 19 of 20 member States of the Council of Europe. Fourteen States have recognised the right of individual petition with the exception of France, Cyprus, Malta, Turkey, Greece. Some States have accepted this right for an unlimited period; others accept it for a specified period, such as five years. Jurisdiction of the Court also has to be recognised by special declaration. (See Collected Texts, op.cit., pp. 601-605). Portugal has just ratified the Convention and accepted the right of individual petition for a tacitly renewable period of two years (Nov. 1978). It also appears likely that both Spain and Lichtenstein will ratify in the near future.
3. Eur. Ct. H. R., *The Tyrer Case,* Judgment of 25 April 1978.

4. Ibid., at p. 11.
5. Ibid., at p. 12.
6. See: Report of Commission, 14 December 1976.
7. See: letter to the Times, 29 April 1978, from Mr. Ronald M. Bell, Q.C., M.P. for Beaconsfield (Conservative).
8. See: e.g., article by Mr. Enoch Powell in the Spectator "Giving away the rod", 21 January 1978.
9. See: Louis Henkin, "Human Rights and Domestic Jurisdiction: in Thomas Buergenthal, *Human Rights, International Law and the Helsinki Accord,* (1977) at p. 25 (published under the auspices of the American Society of International Law); See: comments of the Court in *Handyside* Case on its self-restraint approach to judicial review and the concept of margin of appreciation; Judgment of 7 December 1976, at p. 22, and critique by Cora Feingold, The Little Red Schoolbook, 3 *Human Rights Review* No. 1, pp. 31-42 (1978).
10. The Committee of Ministers takes the view that it can give advice or make recommendations or suggestions under this provision but that such "advice" would not be binding. (Rules of Committee of Ministers for application of Arts. 32, 54, Rule 5).
11. Supra note 9 at para. 48, p. 22.
12. See: remarks on this point by Mr. Teitgen, "The European Guarantee of Human Rights, a Political Assessment", in *Fourth International Colloquy about the European Convention on Human Rights,* Council of Europe publication, pp. 5-6; also, Case of Ireland against the United Kingdom, Judgment of 18 January 1978; Admissibility decisions in Cyrpus v. Turkey, Application Nos. 6780/74 and 6950/75, 2 Decisions and Reports, and in relation to the most recent Cyprus application, No. 8007/77.
13. 8,370 applications have been registered up to 30 September 1978, 198 of them admissible; there have been 14 inter-State cases made up of five complexes; 27 cases brought before the Court which has heard 22; 31 cases referred to the Committee of Ministers; 11 cases have been terminated by a friendly settlement and 13 others by unofficial arrangement between the parties.
14. See, for example, *Handyside Case* for principle of margin of appreciation and principle of proportionality supra note at p. 22; Case of *Ireland v. United Kingdom* interpreting Art. 15 which allows a State to derogate in time of public emergency supra note 12, at p. 48; also the Case of *Klass v. Federal Republic of Germany* concerning the Art. 13 requirement that national law provide an effective remedy where it is alleged that a Convention provision has been violated.
15. "It follows that the obligations undertaken by the High Contracting Parties in the Convention are essentially of an objective character being designed rather to protect the fundamental rights of individual human

beings from infringement by any of the High Contracting Parties than to create subjective and reciprocal rights . . .

. . . A High Contracting Party, when it refers an alleged breach of the Convention to the Commission under Art. 24 is not to be regarded as exercising a right of action for the purpose of enforcing its own rights, but rather in bringing before the Commission an alleged violation of the public order of Europe . . .".

Austria v. Italy, Application No. 789/60, 4 Yearbook 116 (1961), at p. 138.

16. See the favourable proposals for a Bill of Rights modelled on the Convention in "Report of the Select Committee on a Bill of Rights" (House of Lords), 24 May 1978; *"The Protection of Human Rights by Law in Northern Ireland"* (Standing Advisory Commission on Human Rights) Cmnd. 7009 (1977).
17. For detailed studies of the status of the Convention in the domestic law of member States see: Andrew Drzemczewski, *The Domestic Status of the European Convention on Human Rights:* New Dimensions, in Vol. 1, Legal Issues of European Integration (1977); Reports presented by Sir Vincent Evans, Athens Colloquy on Human Rights, Sept. 1978: "The Practice of European Countries where direct effect is given to the European Convention on Human Rights in internal law".
18. See: G. Cohen-Jonathan – La cour des Communautés européennes et les droits de l'homme, *Common Market Law Review,* February 1978; also Report presented by Mr. Robert Lecourt to the Athens Colloquy on Human Rights September 1978: *"Convention Interferences between the European Convention on Human Rights and the Community Law concerning the Community and national judicial control* (Council of Europe Doc. H/Coll. (78)4).
19. Eur. Court H. R.: Judgment of 21 February 1975, Series A, Vol. 18; For other examples of legislative or administrative change consult: *Stocktaking,* a periodic note of the concrete results achieved under the Convention, Council of Europe publication 1977 (DH (77)3); This does not take into consideration amendments introduced in national law to facilitate a State's ratification of the Convention. For example Norway amended its constitution to secure greater religious freedom, as did Switzerland to give votes to women and greater freedom to the Jesuits.
20. See: application No. 4340/69, Yearbook 14, p. 352; For other examples, See: *Alam & Khan v. UK; Poershke v. F.R.G., Knechtl v. UK, Sepp v. F.R.G., Mellin v. F.R.G.* referred to in *Stocktaking* op.cit.; p. 24-34. Friendly settlement has to be "on the basis of respect for human rights" (Art. 28). This has generally been interpreted by the Commission as requiring the settlement to cover the "general interest" aspects of the case.

21. See also the Collection of Decisions 44, p. 101. In this regard mention should be made of the frequency of expulsion cases brought before the Commission. Although the Commission has held that the Convention does not guarantee the right of an alien to remain in a country, it has often stressed in its case-law that explusion to a country where a person fears he will be subject to inhuman or degrading treatment may in certain cases give rise to an issue under Art. 3. In such a situation the President of the Commission may, under Rule 36 of the *Rules of Procedure* request the State not to deport the applicant pending examination of his application by the Commission.
22. Application 4733/71; Yearbook 14, pp. 664, 676.
23. See: Yearbook 15, 1972, p. 678 at p. 692.
24. Eur. Court. H.R., Judgment of 7 December 1976, Series A No. 23.
25. Presently under examination by the Commission; *Campbell & Cosans* v. United Kingdom, Application Nos. 7511/76, 7763/76. An oral Hearing on the merits of these applications was held in October 1978. A further application concerning the use of corporal punishment in an English school was declared admissible in July 1978, Application No. 7907/77.
26. Eur. Ct. H.R., Judgement of 6 September 1978.
27. Presently under examination by the Commission having been declared admissible; *Colen v. United Kingdom,* Application No. 7052/75, 10 Decisions & Reports, p. 154; *McMahon v. United Kingdom,* Application No. 7113/75; ibid; p. 163.
28. Both of these cases have been declared admissible. See: Application No. 7215/75 ("age of consent" case). An oral hearing on the merits of this case was held in May 1978 and the Commission's Report was adopted in October 1978; Application No. 7525/76 declared admissible in March 1978.
29. This case was referred to the Court; Application No. 6289/73: See: Report of the Commission adopted 9 March 1978. The hearing before the Court is scheduled for February 1979.
30. e.g. Airey op.cit.
31. See: A. Drzemczewski: A Non-Decision of the Committee of Ministers under Art. 32(1) of the European Convention on Human Rights: The East African Asian Cases, 41 Mod. L. Rev, pp. 337-342.

    This has only occurred so far in two cases, the *Huber* Case and the *East African Asian Cases.* In relation to the position of the Commission's Report in the Cyprus v. Turkey case it is not yet clear what decision has been taken by the Committee of Ministers.
32. See: Provisional Report on widening the scope of the European Convention on Human Rights, presented by Mr. Craig to the Parliamentary Assembly, largely based on a memorandum submitted by Prof. Francis Jacobs, 13 September 1978 (Doc. 4213).

33. See: Cranston, op. cit., p. 68.
34. See: Provisional Report, op. cit., p. 21. The Report provides three criteria for selecting economic social and cultural rights. The right must be fundamental, universal and capable of sufficiently precise formulation to give rise to legal obligations on the part of the States rather than merely setting a standard, ibid., p. 9.
35. See: A. H. Robertson, *Privacy and Human Rights,* pp. 372-331 on the problem of length of proceedings.
36. See: e.g. *Donelly et al. v. UK,* Application Nos. 5577-5583/72, Collection of Decisions, Vol. 43, p. 149.
37. In practice the applicant's lawyer is invited by the Commission's delegates to address the court, mitigating substantially the force of this criticism. See: A. H. Robertson, Supra Note 1, p. 212.
38. Supra note 31.
39. See: *Ireland v. United Kingdom;* supra note 12, p. 62.
40. Supra note 10.
41. See: A. H. Robertson, supra note 1, p. 268.

CHAPTER 11

ASPECTS OF A JUDICIALLY DEVELOPED JURISPRUDENCE OF HUMAN RIGHTS IN IRELAND

DECLAN COSTELLO

Introduction

In a parliamentary democracy such as exists in this country the effective protection of human rights depends not only on the laws themselves but also on how the Courts interpret them; not only on the limitations which the laws impose on the exercise of fundamental rights, but also on how such limitations are juridically construed. Laws, particularly when contained in a Constitution, relating to fundamental rights are usually framed in very general terms; as a result considerable scope for judicial law-making can exist and the process of the application of the law may lead to a judicially developed jurisprudence of human rights. This, in fact, has been the Irish experience. Enacted law on human rights is to be found in the main, but not exclusively, in the 1937 Constitution, but the law therein established is skeletal in form – the flesh and muscle and sinews of the law are to be found in the judgments contained in the Law Reports. When these are examined the activist role which the Courts have played in carrying out their constitutional functions will immediately become apparent. A complete review of the resulting jurisprudence would obviously not be possible within the confines of this paper. What, instead, is here proposed is an examination of certain features of the law relating to human rights as judicially established in this country and a consideration of the role of the Courts, as well as the role of the law, in protecting human rights.

The Concept of the Law relating to Human Rights in the Irish Constitution

The 1922 Constitution effected a fundamental change in the law relating to the protection of human rights in this country. By enacting a fundamental law with entrenched human rights clauses and by providing for a system of judicial review to protect them a "radical break with the pivotal conception of the modern British Constitution, the doctrine of the Sovereignty of Parliament"[1], occurred. But the break with pre-existing English law was a more profound one than a mere departure from the mechanism by which human rights were protected by the law. Article 2 of the 1922 Constitution declared that all the powers of Government and all authority legislative, executive and judicial were derived from the People of Ireland and that the same should be exercised through organisations established by or under and in accord with the Constitution. This was a rejection of a fundamental concept of English constitutional law that the judicial power of government was derived from the Crown. This change was, of course, of great interest to constitutional lawyers and legal theorists. But it was also a change which, when it came to be considered by the Courts, was found to have had far-reaching practical consequences. The Supreme Court was required to consider[2] whether or not a right to sue the State in tort existed in this Country. In concluding that it did the Court relied on Article 2 of the 1922 Constitution as showing the Royal prerogative of immunity from suit had not been carried over into the law of the Saorstát Éireann as it was inconsistent with Article 2. It followed from this that the prerogative was not part of the law of the State established by the 1937 Constitution and that, accordingly, "Ireland" can be made liable for the tortious act of a servant of the State when acting in the course of his employment.

The break with English legal concepts was taken a step further in the 1937 Constitution. Like its predecessor, the new Constitution contained entrenched human rights clauses and a system of judicial review. The rights which were protected were not the same as those contained in the 1922 Constitution and their exercise was, in important instances, differently limited. Apart from these differences however, the new Constitution contained an explicit statement of the source from which it claimed certain fundamental rights are derived and also a clearly defined theory of positive law. It proclaimed certain basic dogmas of the Christian religion, which were not contained in the 1922 Constitution, and moral and legal principles associated with Christian philosophers were also set out in its Preamble and in those articles most relevant to the protection of human rights.

The Preamble starts with an invocation of the Most Holy Trinity.

The concept of authority as emanating ultimately from God appears again in Article 6 which provides that all powers of Government, legislative, executive and judicial derive, under God, from the people; the moral virtue of Justice which was envoked in the Preamble appears again in Article 34 which provides that "justice" is to be administered in the Courts which are to be established by law. The concept of a moral order which is superior to the legal order appears in the Article dealing with the Family (Article 41) which declares the family to be a "moral institution" possessing inalienable and imprescriptable rights antecedent and superior to all positive law. The right to the private ownership of external goods is explicitly described as a "natural right" and it is described as one which exists antecedently to positive law (Article 43). In the light of the construction placed by the Courts on these provisions a number of principles relevant to the law relating to human rights can be ascertained from them. By proclaiming the Christian beliefs of the people who enacted the Constitution, an assertion is being made that the legal order established by it should be informed by the values which Christians hold. By requiring the observance of the virtues of Prudence, Justice and Charity the pre-eminence of precepts of the moral law is also proclaimed. A relationship between moral law and positive law is established which requires in important respects that positive law should accord with moral law or otherwise be invalid. The fact that certain rights are declared to be antecedent to positive law and to be inalienable presupposes a concept of natural law from which these inalienable rights are derived and which is superior to positive law. The particular concept of the natural law is, by virtue of the proclamation of Christian beliefs, associated with that elaborated by Christian philosophers rather than with the rationalist and secular notions developed in the 17th and 18th centuries.

The break with the ideas of legal positivism, the school of thought which has dominated legal theory since the 19th century and is associated in English legal thought with the names of Bentham and Austin, will be readily appreciated. Legal positivists may well believe in basic Christian dogmas and the value of a moral law, but they would regard both as irrelevant to the proper theory of positive law. For them, laws are commands of the Sovereign; a fundamental distinction they say must be made between the notion of law as it is, and law as it should be; the question of the validity of a law is a purely juristic one and not to be decided by reference to a higher moral law; the ideas of a natural law and natural rights are "nonsense on stilts" (Bentham); positive law is the measure or test of legal justice or injustice (Austin).

Any discussion, however, on the specifically Christian and moral aspects of the Constitution should take into consideration the contribution which they have made, as a result of judicial interpretation, to the protection of human rights. Secondly, it is hoped to show that these aspects of the Constitution are of interest not only to legal theorists or moral philosophers but have had, again as a result of judicial interpretation, considerable practical significance for the protection of human rights in this country.

A review of the relevant case law may, perhaps, appropriately commence with a reference to the most recent decision in which the conclusions of the Court were assisted by reference to the concepts contained in the Preamble – a case in which the Supreme Court was required to consider the validity of a conviction of a young man who was not professionally represented at his trial. In the course of his judgment the Chief Justice (Mr. Justice O'Higgins) stated:

> In the first place the concept of justice which is specifically referred to in the Preamble in relation to the freedom and dignity of the individual appears again in the provisions of Article 34 which deal with the Courts. It is justice which is to be administered in the Courts and this concept of justice must import not only fair procedures but also regard to the dignity of the individual.

The Chief Justice expressed the view that every criminal trial must be conducted in accordance with the concept of justice, and he pointed out that if this was not so the dignity of the individual would be ignored and the State would have failed to vindicate the personal rights which it was required to do under the Constitution. The legislation under which legal aid could be obtained permitted a presiding Judge to make legal aid available on the application of an accused person; but did not require him to inform the accused of his rights. The Chief Justice found that the statutory provisions did not result in justice being administered and in effect rejected the notion that positive law is the measure by which the Courts can determine whether a given law is just or not. A conviction which was entered strictly in accordance with law was quashed.[3]

The importance of the Preamble and the concept of natural law contained in the Constitution were strikingly illustrated in a case in which the Supreme Court decided that the right to privacy in marital relations was a constitutionally guaranteed one and that a law which prohibited the importation of contraceptives was invalid because it infringed this right. Of the four judgments which constituted the majority judgments of the Court three made specific reference to the Preamble in support of the conclusions which were reached. In his judgment Mr. Justice Walsh placed particular emphasis upon the particular manner and form in which fundamental rights were guaranteed and protected. In referring to the judicial function of interpreting the Constitution he pointed out that "the very structure and content of the Articles dealing with fundamental rights clearly indicate that justice is not subordinate to the law" and he added:

> According to the Preamble the people gave themselves the Constitution to promote the common good with due observance of Prudence, Justice and Charity so that the dignity and freedom of the individual might be assured. The Judges must, therefore, as best they can from their training and experience interpret these rights in accordance with their ideas of Prudence, Justice and Charity.[4]

In an earlier case assistance from the Preamble in determining an important principle in the law of human rights was obtained by Mr. Justice Gavan Duffy who decided that the power of internment without trial contained in Part vi of the *Offences Against the State Act* 1939 infringed the right to liberty contained in the Constitution.[5] An amending Bill was referred by the President to the Supreme Court for its opinion as to its constitutionality. The power to intern was drafted in a slightly different form from that contained in the 1939 Act and was found not to infringe the Constitution. There is little doubt that if the Supreme Court had taken the same view of the right to liberty as had Mr. Justice Gavan Duffy, a different conclusion would have been reached.

Mr. Justice O'Byrne placed reliance on the provisions of the Preamble in declaring unconstitutional the *Sinn Fein Funds Act* 1947 (which had provided that all proceedings pending in the High

Court relating to the ownership of certain funds in Court should be stayed and an application made on behalf of the Attorney General that an Order should be made disposing of the funds as provided for in the Act). He pointed to the necessity of giving "life and reality" to the concepts in the Preamble.

He found that the Act infringed the right of private property. Having quoted the relevant Article (which provides that "the State acknowledges that man, in virtue of his rational being, has the natural right antecedent to positive law, to the private ownership of external goods") he went on:

> We do not feel called upon to enter upon an enquiry as to the foundation of natural rights or as to their nature or extent. They have been the subject matter of philosophical discussion for many centuries. It is sufficient for us to say that this State by its Constitution acknowledges the right to property is such a right and that the right is antecedent to all positive law. This in our opinion means that man by virtue and as an attribute of his human personality is so entitled to such a right that no positive law is competent to deprive him of it and we are of the opinion that the entire Article is informed by and should be construed in the light of, this fundamental conception.[6]

The fact that the Constitution emphasised the Christian nature of the State also has had important legal consequences. Article 40, it has been decided, contains a guarantee of personal rights in addition to those rights specifically set out in the Article and it has also been decided that it is one of the duties of the Courts to ascertain what those rights are. Mr. Justice Kenny expressed the view that the unspecified rights which obtain the benefit of the guarantee include "all those rights which result from the Christian and democratic nature of the State". Applying this test he concluded that the right to bodily integrity was a personal right which was constitutionally protected, and he pointed out that he obtained support for this conclusion from the fact that the Papal Encyclical *Pacem in Terris* had declared that every man had the right to life and to "bodily integrity".[7] Mr. Justice Finlay has also relied on the "Christian and democratic nature of the State" when concluding that the right to freedom from torture and inhuman treatment was a constitutionally guaranteed personal right.[8]

Society's concept of human rights changes over the years. As a result Courts may be faced with the question whether a Constitution is to be interpreted according to ideas prevailing when it was enacted or prevailing at the time of the case they are considering. The Supreme Court has reached a conclusion which favours a flexible approach to constitutional interpretation and as a result has helped to ensure the protection of certain rights which 40 years ago would hardly have been considered as appropriate for inclusion in the fundamental law of the State. In reaching these conclusions assistance has been found in the Preamble.[9]

The nature of law, the source of human rights, the relationship of the moral law to the positive law are philosophical and jurisprudential problems which have exercised human thought since the Greek and Hebraic thinkers of pre-Christian times. Certain of the conclusions on these matters which have been associated with traditional Christian thought are contained in the Constitution and the human rights which it guarantees are not expressed in merely juristic concepts. It is, however, clear that, far from being rhetoric or surplusage, the Preamble and the particular manner in which rights have been formulated in the Constitution have, as a result of the process of judicial interpretation, significantly assisted in the protection of human rights which the Courts have been able to afford.[10]

The fundamental rights which Irish Constitutional law protects

What are the rights which the Constitution protects? The 1937 Constitution contains a section of five Articles headed "Fundamental Rights", the first of which (Article 40) is headed "Personal Rights". Having proclaimed the equality of all citizens, this Article contains guarantees relating to the right to liberty, inviolability of the dwelling, the right of free expression of opinion, free assembly and the right to form unions and associations. The next Article deals with the rights of "the Family", which is proclaimed as a "moral institution possessing inalienable and imprescriptible rights". The next (Article 42), with "Educational Rights" and a separate Article (Article 43) is set aside to provide guarantees for the private ownership of external goods. Article 44 is headed "Religion", and contains guarantees relating to freedom of conscience and the free profession and practices of religion. It would, however, be a mistake to conclude that the fundamental rights which are constitutionally protected are only those expressly set out in these Articles; the process of judicial interpretation has shown that there are a good many more. As American experience has shown, Courts in construing a written Constitution may ascertain that, by implication, rights other than those explicitly declared obtain the benefit of Consitutional guarantees. This has happened in this country and the Courts here have been prepared to declare, from an analysis of the text of the Constitution, the existence of certain other implied rights which they will seek to protect. For example, when interpreting the constitutional provision relating to the exercise of the right of the citizen to form associations and Unions the Court has held that there is implied in this Article a right not be compelled to join a Union, a right which the Courts will protect if necessary by injunction or by an award of damages.[11] It has been held that the right to maintain a cause of action in common law for damages for personal injuries is a property right and obtains the benefit of the Constitutional guarantee relating to property rights.[12] And the concept of justice which is contained in the Constitution has been interpreted so as to support a conclusion that the Constitution implies a right to free legal aid in certain circumstances:

> If the right to be represented is now an acknowledged right of an accused person, justice requires something more when because of lack of means, a person facing a serious criminal charge cannot provide a lawyer for his own defence. In my view the concept of justice under the Constitution . . . requires in such circumstances the person charged must be afforded an opportunity of being represented. This opportunity must be provided by the State. Only in this way can justice be done . . .[13].

The Constitution, however, contains a unique feature by virtue of which the Courts will protect fundamental rights which are not specified in it and which are not to be found solely by an interpretation of its text. This feature arises from the wording of Article 40 (3) (1) which provides, in very general words, that "the State guarantees in its laws to respect, and as far as practicable, by its laws to defend and vindicate the personal rights of the citizen". It is now well established that this is a general guarantee of the citizens personal rights, that there are personal rights which obtain the benefit of this section of the Article which are not enumerated in the Constitution, that it is the duty of the Courts, in suitable cases, to ascertain what those rights are.[14] The exercise of this judicial function has resulted in the Courts declaring that the following rights are personal rights and as such entitled to the protection of the Constitution.

(1) Right to bodily integrity[15]
(2) The right to have recourse to the High Court to defend and vindicate the legal right[16]
(3) Right to recover damages against a wrongdoer[17]
(4) Right to earn a livelihood[18]
(5) A Right to work[19]
(6) Right to basic fairness of procedures[20]
(7) The right to free movement within the State
(8) The right to marry[21]
(9) Right to freedom from torture and inhuman and degrading treatment[22]
(10) Right to privacy in marital relations[23]
(11) Right to prepare for and follow a chosen career[24]
(12) The right to a passport

Mr. Justice Finlay has held in a judgment not yet reported (*The State (at the prosecution of K. M. & R. D.) v. Minister for Foreign Affairs:* Delivered 29.5.78) that subject to certain conditions one of the unenumerated personal rights is the right to a passport to avail of facilities which international agreement may confer on passport holders.

It should be added that quite recently the Supreme Court has emphasised the existence of the right of an arrested person to communication, to medical and legal assistance and the right of access to the Courts whilst not finding it necessary to specify whether these rights arose by virtue of the Constitution or under the common law.[25]

The duty of the Courts to ascertain the personal rights which come within, but are not specified in, the provisions of Article 40 (3) (1) arises, in the first instance, from the construction they have placed on this Article. It has been made clear that in exercising this duty they may have regard to other clauses in the Constitution (including the Directive Principles of social policy which are contained in Article 45). However, they are not confined to a mere textual analysis of the Constitution.[26] Accordingly, in adopting this approach the Courts must formulate and define those rights which they consider appropriate for constitutional protection in a Christian and democratic State. Mr. Justice Henchy, formulating the Court's task somewhat differently, considers the "social order" envisaged in the Constitution and the personal right claimed by the Plaintiff in relation to that social order.[27] It is unlikely, however, this approach would lead in practice to conclusions different from those resulting from the test in *Ryan v. The Attorney General.*

Limitations on the Exercise of Guaranteed Rights

Constitutions which contain guarantees of human rights usually place some restrictions on their exercise. How these limitations are expressed and how they are subsequently construed by the Courts can be of critical significance for the protection of fundamental rights and freedoms. The limitations contained in the 1937 Constitution have been differently expressed in different Articles with the result that differing constructions on the limitations have occurred. For example, a considerable difference appears between the limitation imposed on the exercise of the right of private property and that imposed on the right to personal liberty – the right to the private ownership of external goods is declared to be a natural right antecedent to positive law, but the Constitution recognises that its exercise ought in civil society to be recognised by the principles of social justice and it expressly provides that the State may delimit the exercise with the exigencies of the common good. If the Oireachtas enacts a law which delimits the exercise of the right of private property in the interests of the common good, what should the Courts do if the validity of the law is challenged? Is the matter one entirely for the Legislature to determine or have the Courts a supervisory function? These questions were answered very clearly by the Supreme Court as follows:

> It is claimed that the question of the exigencies of the common good is peculiarly a matter for the Legislature and that the decision of the Legislature in such questions is absolute and not subject to, or capable of, being reviewed by the Courts. We are unable to give our assent to this far-reaching proposition. If it were intended to remove this matter entirely from the cognisance of the Courts we are of the opinion that it would have been done in expressed terms as it was done in Article 45 with

reference to the directive principles of social policy, which are expressly removed from the cognisance of the Courts.[28]

Compare the limitations on the exercise of the right to private property with that placed on the right to liberty. In Article 40 (4) (1) the right to personal liberty is stated thus:

> No citizen shall be deprived of his liberties save in accordance with law.

The Supreme Court was required to consider the significance of the phrase "in accordance with law" when a Bill which permitted internment without trial was referred to it by the President for an opinion as to its constitutionality. The Court concluded that the Bill did not infringe the Constitution holding that the phrase "in accordance with law" means "the law as it exists at the time when the legality of the detention arises for determination" The Court added:

> A person in custody is detained in accordance with law if he is detained in accordance with the provisions of a Statute duly passed by the Oireachtas; subject always to the qualification that such provisions are not repugnant to the Constitution or to any provision thereof.[29]

The consequences of this decision were not as far-reaching as might, at first sight, be thought. The decision left open a right to challenge a law which restricted personal liberty on the ground that it was repugnant to the Constitution on grounds other than those contained in Article 40 (4) (1) and did not have the effect that the Courts found themselves unable to assist a person who claimed his constitutional rights were infringed merely because the law permitted it. And, in a later case, the Court exercised jurisidiction to examine a law which restricted the right to liberty of mentally ill persons with a view to considering whether it infringed constitutionally guaranteed rights.[30] It is also worthy of note that the Supreme Court acted on the assumption, which had been expressly made, that a legal restriction on the right to liberty which allowed the detention without charge of a suspect for up to seven days would be unconstitutional unless saved by the Constitution's emergency procedures.[31] It has been suggested that the right of the Courts to review the acts of the Legislature in delimiting the right to private property can be extended to permit a review of acts of the Legislature when it attempts to reconcile the exercise of other rights with the exigencies of the common good.[32]

The right to limit the "personal rights" referred to in Article 40 is, again, somewhat differently framed. This Article, having referred generally to the fact that the State is required to vindicate and defend the citizens personal rights, contains specific guarantees in relation to the right to free expression of opinion, peaceful assembly, and the right to form unions and associations. The liberty accorded to the exercise of these rights is said to be "subject to public order and morality" (a similarly expressed limitation is placed on the right to freedom of conscience and the free profession and practice of religion). Whilst the extent of the power of the Courts to supervise the Legislature when it purports to limit these constitutional rights in the interest of public order and morality has not been extensively considered, the existence of such a power quite clearly exists.[33]

The specific obligations placed on the State by the Constitution in the field of human rights are also somewhat qualified. The State is required to defend and vindicate the personal rights of the citizen, but the obligation is not an absolute one – it is an obligation "as far as practicable" to defend and vindicate them. But here, again, the Courts will supervise the Executive and the Legislature in the exercise of their constitutional duties and will themselves consider whether rights have been properly defended and vindicated. Thus a law which fails in the opinion of the Court adequately to defend and vindicate personal rights will be declared unconstitutional (notwithstanding what is, presumably, an opposing view of the Legislature), and likewise the courts will review the acts of State Officials with a view to considering how they are discharging their constitutional duties.[34]

The power of the State to limit constitutional rights and liberties in times of emergency is also a feature common to all constitutions. What the law permits and how the Courts construe laws which allow derogations from constitutional obligations are naturally matters bearing directly on the protection of human rights.

The Irish Constitution specifically envisages three emergency situations; a time of war, a time of armed rebellion, and a time of armed conflict in which the State is not a participant. (Article 28 (3) (3)). The Constitution cannot be evoked to invalidate a law enacted by the Oireachtas which is expressed to be for the purpose of securing the public safety and the preservation of the State in time of war and armed rebellion. Similar provisions apply in the case of an armed conflict in which the State is not a participant but a condition precedent to the enactment of such a law are resolutions of both Houses of the Oireachtas that arising out of such armed conflict a national emergency exists affecting the vital interests of the State. The powers of the Oireachtas to circumscribe fundamental rights by constitutionally permitted emergency procedures has been analysed and explained by the Supreme Court, when the President referred a Bill (*The Emergency Powers Bill,* 1976) to it for its opinion on its constitutionality. The two Houses of the Oireachtas had previously passed resolutions in accordance with the constitutional procedures; the Bill (which permitted in certain circumstances detention without charge of a suspect for up to seven days) was declared to be an Act "for the purpose of securing the public safety and the preservation of the State in time of an armed conflict in respect of which each of the Houses of the Oireachtas" . . . had passed the relevant resolutions. The Supreme Court held that the Bill was not unconstitutional, but pointed out that whilst this meant that the Constitution could not be invoked to invalidate it, it could be invoked for other purposes. This meant that the validity of a detention cannot be challenged on the ground that the law which permits it is unconstitutional, but the Constitution can be invoked to impugn the validity of the detention if, otherwise, it infringes the constitutional rights:

> A statutory provision of this nature which makes such inroads upon the liberty of the person must be strictly construed. . . . The section is not to be read as an abnegation of the arrested persons rights (constitutional or otherwise) in respect of matters such as the right of communication, the right to have legal and medical assistance and the right of access to the Court. If the section were used in breach of such rights the High Court might grant an order for release under the provisions for habeas corpus contained in the Constitution.[35]

In considering, then, the limitations on the exercise of constitutionally guaranteed rights it must be born in mind that constitutional law, as judicially, developed, provides that (a) laws which limit fundamental rights will be strictly construed and (b) the reconcilation of fundamental rights with the common good is not a matter exclusively for determination by the Legislature.

Judicial Review – the guardians of the Constitution

The legal principles relating to fundamental rights which have been here referred to were developed because the Courts have over the years claimed and exercised a wide jurisdiction in the field of human rights.

The Constitution prohibits the Oireachtas from passing any law which is repugnant to it and it gives jurisidiction to the High Court (and, on appeal, to the Supreme Court) to consider the validity of any law having regard to the provisions of the Constitution.[36] Thus, the superior Courts have jurisdiction to consider whether legislation enacted by the Oireachtas is or is not "repugnant" to the Constitution. In addition, however, the Constitution provides that the laws in force in Saorstát Éireann immediately prior to the date of the coming into operation of the Constitution are to continue in full force and effect "subject to this Constituion and to the extent to which they are not inconsistent therewith".[37] The Courts, accordingly, have jurisdiction to consider whether the "laws" in force in Saorstát Éireann are "consistent" with the Constitution; and "laws" in this context consist of statutes enacted by the Oireachtas established by the 1922 Constitution and pre-1922 Statutory laws which were carried into the law of Saorstát Éireann by virtue of the 1922 Constitution. But the article in question also refers to the non Statutory rules of the common law which were part of the law of Saorstát Éireann and the Courts have jurisdiction to hold invalid common law rules which are inconsistent with the 1937 Constitution. In pursuance of this jurisdiction the Supreme Court, for example, has held that a rule of the common law by which a Court in exercising its discretion in bail applications can take into account the likelihood that further offences may be committed by the applicant is inconsistent with the Constitution and invalid.[38] The Courts, have, moreover, made a distinction between laws enacted by the Constitution and other laws whose validity is impugned. Laws enacted by the Oireachtas enjoy a presumption of constitutionality – other laws do not.[39]

The Court's jurisdiction to protect human rights is not confined to considering the validity of legislation or other non-statutory laws. They will review administrative acts and will grant appropriate relief if such acts infringe constitutional guarantees. In addition, as guardians of the Constitution, the Courts consider that they have jurisdiction to adjudicate on the Constitutional propriety of actions taken by other organs of Government established by the Constitution. If therefore a legislative arm of government wrongly interferes with the judicial organ of government established by the Constitution this interference will render invalid legislation which permits it.[40] And not only legislative acts, but the actions of the Government itself can be reviewed by the Courts with a view to considering their constitutional propriety. It has been authoritatively stated that the Courts have jurisdiction to declare invalid the exercise of the executive power of the State if it is being carried out in a manner contrary to the Constitution.[41]

The Courts have extended their jurisdiction in relation to the protection of human rights, beyond a review of laws, administrative acts or the actions of the Legislature or the Government. They regard themselves as having a duty to assist a citizen who wishes to assert a constitutional right against another citizen and they will, in appropriate cases, grant injunctions to restrain a threatened infringement of a constitutional right, or damages when an infringement has been established which causes a loss.[42] By developing this extensive jurisdiction the Courts have ensured the continued growth of a jurisprudence of human rights in this country.

Conclusion

This paper has dealt with the role of law and the role of the judiciary in the protection of human rights in, it should be stressed, a political society which is based on liberal democratic principles which imply the existence of free elections, a free press, an independent judiciary and a general acceptance of the rule of law. In such a society the gross and flagrant violations of human rights which a despotic form of government may permit are usually absent. But not necessarily so. And certainly the existence of what are loosely referred to as "free institutions" do not in themselves guarantee a constant respect for the rights of all members of the society those institutions serve. Rights can be violated in many ways; through inadvertence, through excess of zeal; on behalf of the State; by individuals or by individuals collectively organised. Every violation of human rights, however, results from an abuse of power. It is the proper business of the law to control the exercise of power when its manifestation may injure others.

From what has been written here it will have become clear that the growth of the law in this country in the field of human rights has been an accelerating one. It is safe to predict that it will accelerate even faster in the years ahead. This is because the application of newly enunciated principles leads to their further refinement and the elaboration of still further ones; because of society's expanding awareness that the number of basic human rights which the law should protect is not static; because of the continuing need to regulate by law the claims of conflicting, but legitimate, fundamental rights, and to reconcile newly defined rights with the common good; because the nature of the common good in a parliamentary democracy is, itself, a changing, as well as an elusive, concept. How the law will develop will be of great importance for the well-being of society.

Notes

1. Kohn *The Constitution of the Irish Free State,* 105.
2. *Byrne .v. Ireland* (1972) I.R. 241.
3. *The State (Healy) .v. Donoghue* (1976) I.R. 225, 348.
4. *McGee .v. Attorney General* (1974) I.R. 284, 310 et seq.
5. *The State (Burke) .v. Lennon* (1940) I.R. 136, 142, 155.
6. *Buckley .v. Attorney General* (1950) I.R. 67, 80, 82.
7. *Ryan .v. Attorney General* (1965) I.R. 294.
8. *The State (C) .v. Frawley* (1976) I.R.
9. *The State (Healy) .v. Donoghue* (1976) I.R. 325, 347.
10. The review of the cases in which reliance was placed on the Preamble was not intended to be an exhaustive one.
11. *Educational Co. of Ireland Ltd. .v. Fitzpatrick* (no. 2) (1961) I.R. 345: *Meskell .v. C.I.E.* (1973) I.R. 121.
12. *O'Brien .v. Kehoe* (1972) I.R. 144.
13. *The State (Healy) .v. Donoghue* (1976) I.R. 325, 350.
14. *Ryan .v. Attorney General* (1965) I.R. 294.
15. *Ryan .v. Attorney General* ibid., 313-314.
16. *McCauley .v. Minister for Post and Telegraphs* (1966) I.R. 345.
17. *Byrne .v. Ireland* (1972) I.R. 241, 325.
18. *Mortagh Properties Limited .v. Cleary* (1972) I.R.
19. *Murphy .v. Stewart* (1973) I.R. 97, 117.
20. *In re Haughey* (1971) I.R. 217, 264.
21. *Ryan .v. Attorney General* (1965) I.R. 294, 313.

22. *The State (C) .v. Frawley* (1976) I.R. 365, 374.
23. *McGee .v. Attorney General* (1974) I.R.
24. *Landers .v. Attorney General* (1975) I.L.T.R. 1.
25. *In re Emergency Powers Bill,* 1976 (1977) I.R. 159, 173. The list of judicially declared rights was not intended to be an extensive one.
26. *Ryan .v. Attorney General* (1965) I.R. 312.
27. *Magee .v. Attorney General* (1974) I.R. 325.
28. *Buckley .v. Attorney General* (1950) I.R. 67, 83.
29. *In re Offences Against The State (Am) Bill, 1940* (1940) I.R. 470, 482. The concept of a deprivation of liberty "in accordance with law" was recently considered in *The State (McDonagh) .v. The Governor of Mountjoy Prison* (Supreme Court: 24 July 1978).
30. *In Re Clarke* (1950) I.R. 235.
31. *In re Emergency Powers Bill,* 1976 (1977) I.R. 159.
32. *McGee .v. Attorney General* (1974) I.R. 310.
33. *National Union of Railwaymen .v. O'Sullivan* (1947) I.R. 77.
34. *The State (C) .v. Frawley* (1976) I.R. 365.
35. *In re Emergency Powers Bill,* 1976 (1977) I.R. 159.
36. Article 15 (4) (1).
37. Article 50.
38. *Attorney General .v. O'Callaghan* (1966) I.R. 501.
39. *The State (Sheerin) .v. Kennedy* (1966) I.R. 379.
40. *Buckley .v. Attorney General* (1950) I.R. 67.
41. *Boland .v. An Taoiseach* (1974) I.R. 338, 370-371.
42. *Educational Co. of Ireland Ltd. .v. Fitzpatrick* (no. 2) (1961) I.R. 345; *Meskell .v. C.I.E.* (1973) I.R. 121.

CHAPTER 12
CHURCH, STATE, AND THE IDEAL OF FREEDOM
GABRIEL DALY

After much thought about the possibility of an interfaith, or at least an interchurch, approach to my topic I reached the unwilling conclusion that such an approach, however appropriate to the occasion, would result in the sort of generalised comment which verges on the bland. 'Human rights' and 'the dignity of the human person' are very abstract terms employed to describe very concrete realities. I have therefore chosen to examine some aspects of the question of Church and State in the context of past and present Roman Catholic theory and practice.

It has become commonplace to point to Constantine's reign as the period in which the Christian Church sacrificed its own freedom and trespassed on the freedom of others by accepting political patronage. While there is clearly much truth in this observation, one should avoid the anachronism of supposing that the alternatives were as obvious to Christians in the early fourth century as they are to us today. Even under persecution Christian thinkers were ready to applaud the Roman imperial ideal, contrasting it with the bellicose tendencies of a host of smaller nations. Origen actually interprets the *Pax Romana* as a preparatory setting for the gospel.[1] The Empire might persecute Christians, but Christians did not therefore consider it to have forfeited its divinely-willed authority. Christians, Origen tells Celsus, are forbidden to fight but they are prepared to assist the emperor by praying for the success of his troops.[2] This willingness to find in imperial politics a setting for the gospel, even while the Empire was actively denying Christians their rights, is an index to what was liable to happen when the emperor found it politically desirable to take the church into partnership.

Instead of denying imperial authority because of the pagan repression of Christianity, some Christian apologists set out to convince their persecutors that coercion was against the natural law. Thus Tertullian's words to the proconsul Scapula have a curiously modern ring to them:

> It is a fundamental right, a privilege of nature, that every man should worship according to his own convictions; one man's religion neither harms nor helps another man. It is not proper to force religion.[3]

We should note that Tertullian is here arguing from the basis of a natural law common to both Pagan and Christian. He even goes on to add a theological argument upon which both Pagans and Chistians might find it possible to agree: the value of sacrifice flows from the freedom of its offering.[4]

The era which followed the Edict of Milan witnessed a progressive disestablishment of the pagan religion and the progressive establishment of Christianity. By the end of the first quarter of the fifth century Theodosius had not merely made the Empire a Christian state, he had proscribed the practice of pagan worship. Religious orthodoxy now becomes a political factor. Baptism did not change Caesar's political convictions, it merely ensured that these would in future have a Christian dimension. The church's first problem was to prevent Caesar from exercising hegemony over the spiritual as well as the temporal. Caesar wanted to make religious uniformity an important factor in imperial unity. It now remained to be seen what stand Christian bishops would take on this seductive offer of State-enforced orthodoxy and whether Tertullian's argument from the *jus naturae* would carry any weight in a church no longer subject to imperial persecution but instead invited to utilise the coercive machinery of imperial government.

St. Augustine of Hippo, who exercised pervasive influence upon the centuries which were to follow, around the year 405 declared himself in favour of the civil coercion of heretics and schematics, specifically the Donatists of North Africa. The circumstances of his decision need not concern us here. His argument, however, is of abiding importance, because it is basically the only one which can be invoked with some semblance of credibility by those who, in any age, favour State support for Christian religious and moral ideals.

Augustine always held that no one could believe against his will. When the Donatist bishop Vincentius complained that Augustine's support for civil coercion in religious matters conflicted with his remarks about the essential freedom of faith, Augustine was driven to find arguments which would reconcile the two convictions. The results are not impressive and in fact lack consistency. Augustine[5] continued, even after 405, to proclaim the essential freedom of faith, but he was now prepared to argue that in certain cases coercion and restraint might have to precede the final achievement of true freedom. If you see a feverish man about to throw himself over a cliff, Augustine writes to Vincentius, you restrain him, and later, when he comes to his senses, he will thank you. The 'thing to be considered when anyone is coerced, is not the mere fact of the coercion, but the nature of that to which he is coerced, whether it be good or bad'.[6] There are, he claims, many Catholics who owe their conversion from Donatism to the coercive measures taken against them. What began in fear and resentment is concluded in love and freedom.[7]

Augustine in effect treats coercion as a sort of *praeparatio evangelica.* He points in justification to the indisputable fact that coercion has in some cases issued in eventually free conviction; but he is also uneasily aware of the *ficti,* those who feign Catholic orthodoxy in order to avoid persecution. He consoles himself that these are merely particular instances of the unconquered evil which is mysteriously present in the heart of man. If coercion increases the number of the elect, God's purposes are mysteriously achieved in spite of the bad faith of those who conform only externally.

Augustine based his argument on what he conceived to be objective and irrefragable truth. Several years before his final acceptance of the spiritual utility of civil coercion he had written '. . . if anyone thinks that to be good which is in fact evil and acts accordingly he undoubtedly sins by thinking in this way'.[8] His notorious gloss on Luke, 14:23 ('Go out to the highways and hedges, and compel people to come in, that my house may be filled') is consistent with his conviction that objective truth justifies the coercion. Let those who are being coerced 'not complain *that* they are subject to compulsion; instead, let them advert to *why* they are being coerced'.[9]

This argument is a fairly clear-cut case of the end justifying the means. It is something more. It assumes that consciousness of being in possession of objective truth in the context of ecclesiastical orthodoxy confers the right to restrain the freedom of dissenters if the opportunity for doing so occurs. If 'objective truth' and the free conscience come into conflict, there can be no doubt which takes precedence for Augustine. His response is paralleled today by those who counter any appeal to freedom of conscience by reiterating the demands of 'the objective moral order'.

Throughout the middle ages the Gelasian doctrine of 'the two swords' was frequently invoked to justify not merely the separation of jurisdictions but also the obligation of the State to assist the church in the extirpation of heresy. Since heresy often involved political disturbance, secular rulers were more than willing to handle the physical details of the church's condemnations, thereby earning ecclesiastical approval for acts of political expediency.

It is unnecessary to discuss further the many appalling instances of coercion and institutional violence perpetrated with the church's blessing throughout the middle ages and beyond. No credible attempt would be made today to defend them. The most important single lesson to be learnt from the church's denial of religious freedom in the past is to note the facility with which theological arguments were propounded and accepted in favour of the cruder forms of coercion. It should prompt us to wonder whether we may today be propounding and accepting similarly flawed arguments in favour of subtler kinds of coercion. One thinks, for instance, of appeals to 'law and order' and 'national security' as justification for repressive measures taken by so many States today.

In the second half of the nineteenth century the Roman Catholic Church defined its attitude to the world of its time. The attitude it struck was one of defensive distrust. This distrust expressed itself in a rejection of the possibility of finding any positive values in religious pluralism.[10] Leo's encyclical *Immortale Dei* (1885) laid down a set of principles which remained normative in the Catholic Church until the reforms of the Second Vatican Council. *Immortale Dei* gave it as a principle that the State is bound to the public profession of the true religion. 'Now it cannot be difficult to find out which is the true religion . . .'[11] From this it followed that the State is bound to the public profession of Roman Catholicism and is thus 'acting against the laws and dictates of nature whenever it permits the licence of opinion and of action to lead minds astray from the truth'.[12] This was a strong, if modified, restatement of

Augustine's argument. Although Leo undoubtedly tempered the teaching of his predecessors and sanctioned limited forms of toleration, his arguments were solidly rooted in Augustine's conviction that freedom of conscience was specified by its object not by subject. Freedom to be wrong was no true freedom and the Christian State might concede it only grudgingly and merely to avoid greater evils.

When the Fathers of the Second Vatican Council addressed themselves to the documents which were to change the Catholic Church's attitude to freedom, they had before them the example of Pope John XXIII's encyclical *Pacem in Terris* which contained these words:

> A man who has fallen into error does not cease to be a man. He never forfeits his personal dignity; and that is something that must always be taken into account.[13]

From the standpoint of traditional Catholic teaching these words opened up a new direction in the theology of freedom. Pope John did not develop the implications of his epoch-making encyclical. But the council he had convened did.[14]

The freedom of man is to be 'respected as far as possible, and curtailed only when and in so far as necessary'. The latter principle had been given its classical statement by John Stuart Mill; here we find a great secular dictum being incorporated into the formal conciliar teaching of the Roman Catholic Church. The former principle, that religious freedom is rooted in the dignity of the human person, makes possible a whole new departure in theolgical thought.

Commenting on the Second Vatican Council's *Declaration on Religious Liberty,* Pietro Pavan, who with John Courtney Murray was one of the principal draughtsmen of the Declaration, has emphasised the ontological roots of the right to religious freedom.[15] By 'ontological' Pavan means 'that the document is concerned not with the *moral* dignity that belongs to a person because of the uprightness of his or her conscience, but with the very *nature* of person . . . It is a dignity that every human person possesses always and everywhere simply by being a person, and not by behaving rightly in the moral field.'[16] We have here an interesting philosophical phenomenon. On the whole, essentialist metaphysics of the sort which had a virtually exclusive hold over the theological field in the Roman Catholic Church down to the 1960's was used to underwrite the claims of objective truth over against those of freedom of conscience and of subjective response in general. Here, however, essentialist metaphysics is pressed into service to vindicate the claims of freedom. This fascinating *volte-face* is described, not very convincingly, by Pavan and Murray as an instance of doctrinal *development.* Most external observers would call it a change of course, and a radical one at that; but Catholic theology, with its traditional emphasis on continuity of doctrine, has not yet been able to forge a hermeneutic which satisfactorily encompasses the tension between continuity and change in Church doctrine. Whether we describe it as development or simple change, this teaching on the dignity of the human person is in remarkably strong contrast to the teaching it replaced. Essentialist analysis has been traditionally used in the service of 'objective truth'. Catholic theologians today may savour the irony of employing it in the service of freedom of conscience. As George Lindbeck has remarked, it cuts across the Protestant tendency 'to make not human dignity but human sinfulness the foundation of religious liberty.'[17] Professor Lindbeck goes on to concede that it has a wider appeal in a world for which the concept of sin is an irrelevance. I shall return to this point later, for I believe that the Catholic and Protestant viewpoints can complement each other in a way which involves no compromise of principles for either.

In the light of the teaching of Vatican II it is now possible for Roman Catholics to argue that in religious matters the State is a radically secular institution and has only one function in respect of religion; to ensure the freedom of all persons and bodies within its jurisdiction. The State is society organised for the purposes of government and public order. The Church is the association of those members of society who profess belief in the person and work of Christ and who share in the public worship carried out in his name. Overlap in membership of the two is purely adventitious.[18]

One of the signal benefits which have resulted from recognising the value of separation between Church and State is that the church is freed from the need to construct complicated and apparently self-interested arrangements with individual states. It can now use this freedom to explore further the implications of its role in the world. It can concern itself more with society than with the State. Where in the past it often sought freedom and status for itself as institution (sometimes sacrificing the freedom and rights of others in the process), it can now attend more to the rights and well being of every man, woman and child in society. Conciliar emphasis on the dignity of the subject should result in Catholic leaders and thinkers showing at least as much zeal in vindicating human rights, including the right to be wrong, as in safeguarding orthodoxy. Indeed reflection on human rights may help to broaden the concept and scope of orthodoxy. It will also help to promote the spirit of enquiry. The church at every level, whether teaching or learning, will have to share in the ambiguities inseparable from the attempts to identify, and then campaign for, human rights. In some case the issues will be clear; in others it will become apparent that one man's rights are another man's deprivation.

There is a hierarchy of human rights. The development and utilisation of computer information and retrieval systems, for example, already threaten the right to privacy in the affluent world. But that sort of problem pales into insignificance beside the right to enough food denied to so many in the poorer countries of the world. The role of the church in publicising this hierarchy of rights is sufficiently clear to need no comment. The church has always recognised its role as the guardian of the poor and the helpless. What was formerly seen as a localised situation – small communities caring for their own poor – has now to be seen on a world-wide scale, and the difficulties in responding to this new challenge are enormous. National sovereignty, itself in some ways a defence against imperial oppression, is frequently a barrier to any kind of effective action in the securing of the most basic of rights such as the right to food, shelter and work. The hungry and the homeless are an open sore in humanity's conscience. Unfortunately, however, power lies not with humanity but with states obsessed by considerations of national sovereignty, security and advantage.

It has been suggested that until the most basic rights have been secured for *all* humankind, we have no business pursuing lesser rights for those who live in comparative affluence.[19] This thesis is, I believe, fundamentally misguided. Any society which is careless of human rights, however sophisticated or ostensibly peripheral, in its own bailiwick is unlikely to care for the rights of the wider community of mankind. Care for human rights is the product of a fundamental attitude of mind and heart. The church's role is thus first and foremost an educational one, namely, continuing self-education mediated to others in ordinary pastoral instruction and in the construction of educational programmes. Christians who are alert to the 'signs of the times' can today appreciate more clearly than ever before that the preaching of Christ is inseparable from the preaching of human rights. Denominationalism in this matter is now increasingly seen as a scandalous irrelevance. The church has now to care, and be seen to care, for the rights of all, irrespectively of confessional allegiance; and this care has to be expressed in ways which exclude, and are seen to exclude, all suggestion of proselytism. This new conviction in no way detracts from the Christian missionary ideal. On the contrary, it should prompt Christians to examine with ever greater sensitivity the problems and challenges of presenting their faith and moral convictions with scrupulous regard for the dignity and freedom of those to whom they bring the good news.

These newly gained perspectives carry serious implications for Church-State relationship. In the past the church approached the State as one institution to another. In the days of the confessional State the church offered guidance, warning and correction on the political implications of being a 'Catholic State'. Where the State was not Catholic, the church made the best of an unsatisfactory situation and sought whatever it could get for itself. The State, whether Catholic or not, was in its turn often glad of church tolerance if not support. With the passing of that age, and of the theology which underwrote the church's political attitudes to it, a new situation is opening up. This new situation involves renunciation by the church of political bargaining-power. The pyramidal structure of the pre-conciliar church facilitated the sort of institutional bargaining which expressed itself explicitly in concordats and implicitly in unwritten working agreements. This procedure occasionally secured for the State, if not actual complicity, at least non-obstructive silence from the church, which was expected to keep its prophets muzzled. There was a feeling among statesmen and politicians that the church could be bought, if the right institutional price was offered. The church felt able to enter into these negotiations with a good conscience precisely because its theology of transcendence extended itself to the institution, the divinely established perfect society whose senior officers were divinely empowered to act in the name of all its members. Its ecclesiology and its theology of revelation supported the view that God spoke to the apex and the base eventually got the message. The theological reforms of Vatican II have made possible a whole new concept of the church's relationship with secular society and the State.

Because of the church's traditional concern for the poor and neglected, its voice will from time to time have to be heard indicating circumstances and conditions in which human dignity is being undermined and its rights denied. This duty of social criticism entails readiness to take risks. The first of these risks is unpopularity. It is virtually impossible to indicate a case of human deprivation without irritating those politicians and civil servants in whose jurisdiction the affected area lies. This sensitivity may be regrettable but it is a fact of life, and it may easily dissuade church members, especially leaders, from making their criticisms. A not uncommon response to social criticism is 'Why don't you do something about it yourself?' Obviously if the critic has it in his power to do something, his credibility and *bona fide* will rest on his willingness to act. In most cases, however, there will be little he can do except campaign for his cause and stand up to the hostility which may greet his efforts.

A further risk is that of exposure to the charge of 'political naïvety'. Since most of the Sermon of the Mount might be so described, this charge should not unduly worry the Christian. The Christian may sometimes have to risk the charge of political naïvety by claiming that the ideal may not be as impracticable as is sometimes suggested. In democracies politicians are subject to the constant action of powerful pressure-groups and lobbies. It may be the task of the church to expose and counter the aims of these groups.

Again, politicians are answerable to the ballot-box, which, for all its evident superiority to other ways of achieving power, can be a tyranny in its own way. The voice of the people is not necessarily the voice of God. Lord Devlin's 'man on the Clapham omnibus' may be clamouring for the death penalty, flogging, and other coercive measures designed to promote 'law and order', but it is no function of the church to bow to these misguided, if admittedly democratic, pressures. Furthermore, large business corporations having interests located in countries with oppressive regimes do not instinctively place human rights on the agenda of their board meetings. Christian bodies directly concerned with human rights have sometimes experienced the financial penalties of their chosen apostolate. Nor is this a matter merely of the church's relationship with the State and with commercial power. It can arise within the churches themselves, and when it does, it is particularly scandalous, since it may destroy the credibility of Christian witness in other spheres as well. People with deep-seated racial or religious prejudices may be dedicated church-goers, and the temptation of the clergy to refrain from offending their susceptibilities can be strong. There are churches whose leaders and members react sharply against the very mention of civil or human rights.

Closely allied with willingness to take risks is concern for freedom of communication. It is often through the communications media that injustices and indignities come to light. The church has a duty to promote and defend the freedom of the communications media, if for no other reason than that such freedom is indispensable to the making known of conditions where power is being abused and where human rights are being damaged, threatened, or neglected. From a theological standpoint this is simply an instance or readiness to listen to the prophetic voice wherever it may be raised. In the Judaeo-Christian tradition there are ample precedents for recognising that prophets can arise from any quarter. The church therefore has a duty to ensure that the prophetic freedom of the media is not merely defended but actively promoted.

The church, like any other person or group in the nation, has a right to influence opinion, to comment on proposed executive or legislative action, and to campaign for or against certain policies. Whereas in the past the Roman Catholic Church often commented and campaigned as a monolithic and authoritarian body concerned with the preservation of orthodoxy and received moral values, the changes of emphasis brought about by the Second Vatican Council entail a careful reappraisal, not of the right to influence opinion, but of the *means,* the mode of action, appropriate to the church in its attempts to influence others.

Any church which has peremptory views on certain moral questions and which is relucant to admit any shading or ambiguities therein needs to take special care over the manner in which it seeks to influence public opinion on these questions. Some moral campaigns are marked by a ruthlessness and intolerance which masquerade as single-minded devotion to virtue and are far from Christlike – almost as if the campaigners believed that the worth and desirability of the object to be achieved palliated any lack of delicacy and sensitivity in the means employed to achieve it. Fidelity to Christ may well be betrayed by the attitudes and modes of action adopted by those of his followers most fervent in their wish to bring about a society which lives by his ideals.

Preachers and teachers have a serious responsibility in this respect, since they operate from a privileged base and have opportunities for moulding opinion not available to most other citizens. Scrupulous regard for the truth, including the truth in opinions he cannot share, is written into the charter of every teacher. Lack of this regard has been mainly responsible for the devaluation of, and the common disesteem accorded to, such words as 'dogma' and 'doctrine'. The normal secular understanding of these words today is an impressive warning of what happens when means are sacrificed to ends in religious matters. We easily forget that moral debate, of the sort which is as open to the reception of ideas as to their transmission, is one of the best means for producing 'informed' consciences and for deepening moral experience and convictions. There is, of course, always an element of risk in true openness to the view of others; but, as Bishop Lesslie Newbigin has remarked, Christ is confessed in the actual risk-taking of genuine dialogue with others.[20] Catholic theology and spirituality, rescued by concilar action from an obsession with caution and security, can now welcome the opportunities for deepening faith offered by open debate within a free and pluralistic society.

A sound theology of the secular is needed especially where a nation comprises a large number of religious believers. It is now as open to Catholics as to Protestants to regard the State as a radically secular body. The First Amendment of the American Constitution was a political expedient with significant theological potentialities. Protestant thought found total separation of Church and State easier to accommodate than did Catholic thought. One reason for this is that Protestantism has traditionally accepted a wider gap between sacred and secular, grace and nature, revelation and reason. Catholic theology shares with orthodox Jewish and Islamic theology an unwillingness to make too radical a separation between these areas. Furthermore, Catholic theology has traditionally been ill at ease with Protestant views on the effect of sin upon human nature. 'Wounded', says traditional Catholic theology; 'radically corrupted', says classical Protestant theology. This topic, so far from being *passé,* is in need of more ecumenical attention than it seems to be receiving today.

The problem facing all theologies with a firm historical perspective is how to respect the autonomy of the secular and at the same time to relate the secular to faith and grace. Medieval theology and church practice met the problem by sacralising the secular, thus paving the way for the Reformation. The Reformers met it by radical separation of the two spheres. Neither expedient is an adequate response to a difficult but inescapable challenge. The dilemma is present in the attempt to delineate the role of the Christian in public life. It faces, for example, the legislator who has to weigh his own personal moral convictions against the possible right of others not to be coerced by the sort of legislation which he might like to bring in. Where ethical consensus is not possible, Christians may find themselves in opposite camps. It cannot therefore be claimed that there is only one possible Christian response to many concrete political, social, and industrial problems and disputes. It is precisely these controversial questions which prove that Christian morality is not specified by content alone but also, and perhaps predominantly, by personal conviction and by the manner in which such conviction is expressed and implemented.

For this and other reasons the church must not allow itself to become the official conscience of the State. Such an arrangement induces an extrinsicist and inauthentic attitude to moral values. Statesmen, politicans, and civil servants need to work out their own moral standards in the actual prosecution of their duties. Respect for diversity cannot be produced by decree or by conformity to an extrinsically imposed set of moral criteria. An 'informed conscience' is not a conscience brought into unconvinced alignment with official teaching; it is a conscience which has carefully pondered the conclusions *and arguments* put forward by official teaching before it forms its own authentic convictions.

If any one church is seen to act as the conscience of the State, citizens who do not belong to that church will inevitably, and probably with justice, view such a relationship as an infringement of their freedom and rights as citizens. A further reason why the church should take care to see that it is not regarded as the conscience of the political establishment is its prophetic role in society. The church has to retain its freedom to make a nuisance of itself even to governments which are generally well-disposed towards Christian moral ideals.

The church's role as 'a sign and a safeguard of the transcendence of the human person' entails two major functions which are rooted in its theological inheritance. It must warn against all kinds of Utopianism and it must base this warning on its conviction of the reality of social and personal sin, together with its even stronger conviction of the reality of God's offer of forgiveness. If properly presented, some of this warning will have relevance for non-believers as well as believers.

Movements for political and social reform are motivated by the conviction that society can and should be changed. The specifically Christian contribution to such thought and aspirations should be marked by wholehearted but unillusioned participation. I have already commented on the Christian duty of involvement in movements which seek to promote and defend human rights and the dignity of the human person. Here I want to draw attention to the unillusioned attitude which should ideally characterise that participation. No political reform or revolution ever brings about the Kingdom of God on earth. Though it may remove some obstacles to the coming of the kingdom, in doing so it inevitably provides obstacles of its own. There will never be an historical embodiment of the totally just and caring society. Even the most ideally conceived State will always manifest sinfulness in its structures and in the manner in which its officers exercise power. A totally just and caring society is always in the making and only partially in the achieving. This sombre truth is hard to live with, because all reforming ideals and programmes are motivated by the possibility of bringing about a better world. The authentically Christian attitude to programmes of reform might be aptly described as redeemed pessimism. It is an attitude fully supported both by Christian eschatology and by the verdict of history. Sound eschatology points to an absolute future when Christ will hand over to the Father a totally redeemed creation. History witnesses to the fact that the removal of one set of injustices is normally accompanied by the causing of a whole new set of other, and perhaps subtler, injustices. Human beings have yet to learn how to bring about complete social equality without destroying freedom in the process. Approximations to the ideal are all that will ever be historically possible.

George Tyrrell, shortly before his early death in 1909, reflected in depth on what he described as 'preliminary pessimism'. 'Idealism', he wrote, 'has its roots in the Eternal, and not in the temporal'.[21] Tyrrell was in no sense advocating a policy of inactivity in the face of temporal evil. On the contrary, it was his argument that 'preliminary pessimism' was necessary if the would-be reformer was to avoid discouragement and disillusionment in the pursuit of his vision. We are not destined, Tyrrell claimed, for a political or social millenium in any non-eschatological sense.

'The posterity we work for is not some final generation that is to enter into the fruits of all the tears and sorrows of the past. Every future generation, even the most distant we can imagine, will have tears and sorrows of its own.'[22] Men and women in the past did not live and suffer for our sakes. 'The good of posterity is the result, not the end, of our living as well and as fully as we can.'[23] 'Man must never be treated as a means, as a stepping-stone for his fellows'.[24] 'To believe that every moral and social problem admits of ultimate solution may be merely a necessary illusion to protect [man] from the apathy of despair, until such time as religion has taught him the duty of fighting for victory in the face of certain eventual defeat . . .'[25] A moment's reflection on the sombre realism of Tyrrell's words will suffice to clear them of the charge of pessimism in any ultimate sense.

They suggest a frame of mind eminently suited to the defence of human rights and the promotion of human dignity. The scientific revolution ushered in an age of Promethean ambitions and expectations. The achievement of some of these ambitions has revealed a dark and fearsome aspect to technological progress. Each technological advance opens up not merely greater material benefits, but also more sophisticated methods of oppression and dehumanisation. There is therefore a sisyphean dimension to human evolution. Human rights, as Jurgen Moltmann has pointed out, 'are to be apprehended as a process, which is unfinished and, historically speaking, unfinishable.'[26] A deliberately-fostered determination to avoid illusion and moral Prometheanism is a necessary element in the political realisation of Christian hope.

This thought leads logically to what I suggest ought to be the second function of the church's role in witnessing to the transcendence of the human person, namely, to speak with political as well as spiritual conviction of the reality of sin and redemption. Sin and redemption are terms which belong to the vocabulary of revelation, and the church is committed to preaching them. The problem lies in demonstrating their relevance to secular society and the State.

The phenomenon of man divided within himself has, with Pauline warrant, been traditionally described by the Christian Church as 'sinful'. Non-believers may reject the term 'sin', but the term 'alienation' has established itself in psycho-social and political parlance. Alienation is the secular equivalent of sin, and the church in no way betrays the integrity of its message by showing a willingness to employ relevant secular terminology to convey that message. The antonym of alienation is reconciliation, which, happily, is a term with both sacred and secular resonance. The phenomenon of alienation, together with the instinct for aggravating it, is built into the human condition. Alienation will always manifest itself where human beings assemble for any purpose, political, social or industrial and do not consciously set out to design means which will foster the attitude of reconciliation. Man does not simply create alienation in his world, he enters that world already alienated, and his unhealed activities merely exacerbate an already present situation. Theologians have traditionally wrestled with this phenomenon under the not very satisfactory rubric of 'original sin'. Whatever terminology we use to describe it, the phenomenon is still there for all, even the most sanguine of social and political engineers, to see. It is a phenomenon with extensive repercussions in all human associations, including the church.

In an age of considerable disillusionment with politics, politicians, and political institutions, the church can play an important role in society by promoting a realistic estimate of the limits of political expectation, and therefore a realistic and tolerant attitude towards professional politicians. Awareness of sin can help to prevent the cherishing of illusions. More than most human crafts, politics needs a realistic sense of sin, and it is the church's duty to point constantly and resolutely to its existence, however unfashionable such an indication may be. The sense of redeemable sinfulness can help to prevent that cynicism and disillusioned passivity in citizens which is a cancer in the body politic. In Christian terms the ideal politician is one who sees himself or herself as a sinful person entering a sinful situation with the determination to expedite the redemptive processes which the grace of God makes possible. The use of power to bring about justice, peace, and reconciliation is redemptive in the religious as well as the political sense. As such it pertains to the good news of salvation and belongs to the Church's proclamation. The challenge facing the church today is how to proclaim this good news in a manner which enables men and women to see that ultimate optimism is raised on the ruins of a superficial and self-sufficient Utopianism.

There need be nothing gloomy or life-denying in the recognition of the pervasive presence of sin in every human enterprise. Conviction about the reality of redemption is, to use the expressive phrase of Julian of Norwich, 'a comfort against sin'. It is life-enhancing, and it enables the Christian believer to live in hope with set-backs of every sort. The reality of redemption is, among other things, a licence to cultivate our sense of humour amid the tears of things.

The doctrine of redemption, or reconciliation, extends to all human relationships and comes into complete and final focus when these relationships are seen to mediate God's plan for bringing creation into oneness with his own Being. It is in becoming reconciled with one another that we become reconciled with God. The entire divine-human process is conceived in freedom, executed in freedom and directed towards the attainment of perfect freedom. We recognise it implicitly, if not consciously, whenever we recognise the dignity and transcendence of the human person. We co-operate in bringing it about whenever we act in a manner which is consonant with that personal dignity and transcendence.

1. Origen, *Contra Celsum,* ii, 30; P.G. XI, col. 850.
2. *Con. Cel.,* viii, 73; P.G. XI, col. 1627.
3. Tertullian, *Liber ad Scapulam,* 2; P.L.I., col. 699.
4. ibid.
5. P. Brown, *Religion and Society in the Age of Saint Augustine* London 1972, p. 263 characterises him as a man of 'mysterious discontinuities'.
6. St. Augustine, *Epist. 93,* v. 16.
7. ibid.
8. *Epist. 47,* 4.
9. *Epist.* 185, 24 (emphasis added): 'non quia coguntur, reprehendant, sed qua cogantur, attendant'.

10. See G. Daly, 'Christian Response to Religious Pluralism', in *Studies,* 67 (1978), pp. 66-76.
11. *Immortale Dei,* English translation in S. Ehler and J. Morrall (eds.), *Church and State through the Centuries: A collection of Historic Documents with Commentaries* London, 1954, p. 304.
12. ibid., p. 313.
13. *Peace on Earth,* English translation, Catholic Truth Society London, 1963, p. 57.
14. Second Vatican Council: *Declaration on Religious Liberty,* art. 2.
15. P. Pavan, 'Ecumenism and Vatican II's Declaration on Religous Freedom', in W. J. Burghardt (ed.), *Religious Freedom: 1965 and 1975: A Symposium on a Historic Document* New York, 1977, p. 13.
16. ibid., p. 15.
17. Burghard, op.cit., p. 53.
18. Second Vatican Council: *Pastoral Constitution on the Church in the Modern World,* art. 76.
19. See for example J. Tweedie, 'My Human Rights are Often Gained at the Expense of Yours', in *The Guardian,* April 20, 1978, p. 11.
20. L. Newbigin, 'The Basis, Purpose and Manner of Inter-Faith Dialogue' in *Scottish Journal of Theology,* 30 (2)77, pp. 253-270.
21. G. Tyrrell, *Essays on Faith and Immortality.* Arranged by M. D. Petre London, 1914, p. 244.
22. Tyrrell, ibid., pp. 248-249.
23. ibid., p. 261.
24. ibid., p. 263.
25. ibid., p. 274.
26. J. Moltmann, *The Church in the Power of the Spirit: A Contribution to Messianic Ecclesiology* London, S.C.M. 1977, p. 181.

CHAPTER 13
CHRISTIAN FAITH AND HUMAN RIGHTS

JÜRGEN MOLTMANN

Human Rights in the Context of Ecumenical Theology

The ecumenical movement originated at a time almost parallel with the formation of the League of Nations, the international peacework and the United Nations. It is, therefore, no surprise that as early as 1948 representatives of the World Council of Churches which was formed in the same year were collaborators on the *Universal Declaration of Human Rights.* Here above all the 'Commission of the Churches for International Affairs' (CCIA) is to be mentioned. The co-workers of the Council and of the Commission participated also in the working out, codification and defence of the later human rights blueprints, especially of the 1966 *International Covenants,* which eventually came into effect in 1976 after protracted ratification through the necessary number of 35 States. Since then all plenary meetings of the World Council of Churches and most conferences of the World Confessional Families have sections, which deal with the clarification and enforcement of human rights.

The above mentioned Commission (CCIA) held a conference in 1974 in St. Pölten concerning 'Human Rights and Christian Responsibility', at which representatives from socialist states and the peoples of the 'third world' took part.[1] This conference represents the high point to date of the ecumenical dialogue concerning human rights. It made a convincing correction to the one-sided western conceptions in that it drew up a catalogue of basic human rights, which begins with the 'right to life'. The basis for the present work of the World Council on the theme 'Human Rights' is the detailed recommendation of Section VI of the 5th plenary meeting of the World Council in Nairobi in 1975.[2]

The World Alliance of Reformed Churches decided at its General Assembly in Nairobi, 1970, upon a programme of study on the theme 'Theological Basis of Human Rights and Liberation'. After intensive work in all member-churches the present writer was commissioned to do a comprehensive study. This was discussed and accepted at the conference of the Theological Department in London in 1976. Together with recommendations concerning 'Theological Guidelines' and 'Some Practical Consequences' it was published as *Theological Basis of Human Rights.*[3] At the centenary meeting of the World Alliance of Reformed Churches at St. Andrews in 1977 this 'Theological Basis of Human Rights' was officially accepted as the "first step toward an ecumenical 'Christian declaration on Human Rights"'. Theological co-operation with the World Council, the Lutheran World Federation, the Orthodox Church and the Roman Catholic commissions as well as an ongoing involvement with the problem, 'Human Rights and Politics', on the other hand was also decided upon.

The Lutheran World Federation decided at its assembly in Evian in 1970 on a study concerning human rights. In summer 1976 it held a summary conference in Geneva and published the results in 1977'[4] under the title *Theologische Perspektiven der Menschenrechte* (Theological Perspectives of Human Rights). The leading writers were Heinz-Eduard Tödt and Wolfgang Huber, who published their works on the theme in Germany in 1977.[5] A series of works by individual Lutheran theologians complete the study referred to.[6]

Already in the Autumn of 1974, the Roman Synod of Bishops had published a *Message concerning Human Rights and Reconciliation.*[7] In 1976, the Papal Commission Justitia et Pax provided a working-paper on *The Church and Human Rights.*[8]

From the sphere of the Orthodox churches no official declarations on human rights are known to me. Therefore, I can only refer to the above stated church documents in the following theological reflections.

If one looks at the content of these theological declarations and church attitudes in the ecumenical sphere since 1948, one can perceive interesting shifts of emphasis in the treatment.

From 1948 until about 1960 the question of religious freedom stood at the centre of the church activity and theological work on human rights. Religious freedom, especially in countries with a socialist state-ideology, but also in countries with state-religions has indeed remained a theme. This is seen in the collaboration of the European Conference of Churches on the Final Declaration on Security and Co-operation of the Summit Conference of

Helsinki in 1975 as well as in the dramatic discussion with representatives of the Russian Orthodox Church at the fifth plenary-meeting in Nairobi in 1975. Nevertheless it is not the principal theme any more. Indeed it was already clear at the plenary-meeting in Amsterdam in 1948 that freedom of religion and freedom of conscience can only be realised in the context of the other individual rights of freedom and protection. Besides, the church cannot wait with its protest until its own religious freedom is threatened. It is there for the sake of man and must raise its voice for the rights of man. The vision from that period of a 'Responsible Society' shows that clearly also.

Since about 1960 another theme has pushed itself into the forefront of the ecumenical meetings, at which the voices from the 'Third World' were becoming louder and louder. It was the condemnation of racism as a serious violation of fundamental human rights. Here also it was very quickly clear that one cannot separate the phenomena of racist inhumanity from political colonialism and economic exploitation in Africa, Asia, Latin America and elsewhere. That means, however, that one has had to learn not to conceive of human rights as 'individual freedom' rights any more. The Fourth Plenary Assembly of the World Council in Uppsala 1968 recognised that 'in the modern worldwide community the rights of the individual are unavoidably tied to the fight for a better living standard for the socially disadvantaged of many nations. Human rights cannot be secured in a world of gross inequality and social conflicts'.[9] Thus came to the fore the knowledge that there are economic, social and cultural human rights, about which the history of freedom in Western Europe has had little to say. The *International Covenants* of 1966 also place the 'economic and social rights' in the primary position and the 'civil and political rights' only in second place. Indeed in what other way shall a human being actualise his 'individual freedom' rights if he does not find the economic and social possibilities for doing so?

While the Marxists since 1948 have repudiated human rights as bourgeois ideology for the veiling of capitalist exploitation, socialist concepts of human rights have for the first time been introduced and discussed through the *International Covenants* of 1966, and since the 1974 St. Pölten Conference. Indeed it says in the Socialist Internationale 'O peoples hear the signals to the last fight: the International is fighting for the human right'. However, there is still a long way to go in the dialogue between east and west on the way to a common understanding of human rights. Hitherto, both still understand them differently and contradictorily to one another.

For all that, other priorities are coming once again into the ecumenical human rights discussion from the peoples of the 'Third World', who are seeking their path to freedom from colonial dependence, cultural alienation and political suppression. In these countries the interest in freedom of the press or in the right to strike is understandably slight. The right to life and to the means which make continued living possible stands in the forefront. The *St. Pölten Report* places, therefore, just like the *Roman Synod of Bishops,* the 'right to life', to nourishment, and to work at the beginning of the catalogue of human rights.

The history of the ecumenical discussion concerning human rights shows a quite striking development from the almost entirely accepted predominance of the western-civil-liberal view of human rights and the social rights of the human community, and, eventually to the perception of the life-interests of the 'Third World'. This development went through many tensions and conflicts, which are still by no means overcome. 'Religious freedom', 'racism', 'economic self-reliance' are still catch-phrases which point in different directions. Becoming all the more important is the knowledge of the inner link that holds the individual, the social and the vital human rights together. Because the concern is with the one human being, with the one human race and with a shared humanity, one must ask about the thread that holds them inwardly together. Many conferences have contented themselves with the drawing up of pragmatic catalogues of necessary and desirable human rights. But such a simple addition does not help because it does not impede the unfortunately inevitable subtraction that in many situations pertains. Certainly there are priorities which correspond to the different situations in which humanity is suffering. But the priorities which are necessary for action turn into ideology if they are deemed absolute. Priorities do not exclude other things but just defer them for the time being.

Christendom, which has trod a common path in the ecumenical movement, has hitherto preserved its solidariy in the 'three worlds' and that in spite of their conflicts. Despite everything, there lives in these tensions the common faith. The ecumenical human rights discussion shows an outstanding openness and flexibility of Christians, who must live in such contradictory situations. On account of that, I believe, the further knowledge, development and furtherance of human rights has become the framework of ecumenical politics and ethics. Liberation, development, passive and active resistance, the overcoming of racism, economic aid to developing countries, nuclear reactors and the building up of a 'sustainable society' are discussed today within the framework of human rights. For Church guidelines on political and social matters gain their universal significance only through reference to human rights. Through its relationship to human rights the Church becomes the 'Church for the World'.

Work on the Theological Basis of Human Rights

Most ecumenical conferences, which among other things deal also with human rights, content themselves with drawing up a list of rights which they consider essential for man's humanity. The arrangement of the rights on these lists then indicates the priorities: 'Human rights, which today are especially threatened'. Thus we find in the St. Pölten Report a 6-point list which begins with the 'right to life', then comes to the 'recognition of cultural identity' and then after that speaks of 'participation in decision-processes', 'freedom of opinion', the right to personal dignity' and 'freedom of religion'. The list of the 1974 Roman Synod of Bishops looks quite similar: after the 'right to life' comes the 'right to nourishment', socio-economic rights, political and cultural rights and the right to religious freedom. However it must evidently already have been felt in St. Pölten that it is not enough simply to draw up such checklists of wishes. Therefore it was said: 'All human rights, be they social, economic, religious or political, are interrelated. They must be taken as a whole. The churches should give them equal importance and seek the application of all of them.' But how can one conceive of human rights as a whole if one knows only the different lists of them? In what consists their unity? From where can one grasp them as an entirety?

Here there are two different approaches. Heinz Eduard Tödt and Wolfgang Huber, whom the *Lutheran World Federation* follows in its 1977 Declaration, propose, instead of drawing up lists and priorities, to replace them by an ideal-typical method of viewing all human rights. One can, that is, see three basic elements

(Sachmomente) in all human rights: they are freedom, equality and participation. In this triad Tödt and Huber see the ideal basic countours of 'human rights'. They use this figure as a hermeneutical key to the understanding of the plurality of human rights. Thus it becomes possible to define what human right in the singular actually is. Of course the uncertainty must be tolerated, that one cannot know how these three dimensions function in the case of each particular right. Indeed 'freedom' and 'equality' lead to contradiction in most cases, since both cannot be simultaneously actualised.

Justitia et Pax and the Reformed *Theological Basis* start out from the distinction between dignity and human rights: there are human rights in the plural, but human dignity only in the singular. Therefore the dignity of man takes precedence over the many rights and duties which are bound up with being human. The dignity of man is the one, indivisible, inalienable and shared quality of the human being. The different human rights portray a wholeness because man in his dignity is a totality. The completeness of the catalogues and lists of human rights is not identical with this totality. The light of totality falls much more from man's dignity on to every fragment of his human rights.

The *Universal Declaration of Human Rights* of 1948, Art. 1, and most political constitutions which establish those human rights as the fundamental rights of the citizens start off from this fundamental anthropological distinction between human dignity and human rights. The dignity of man is not itself a human right but a source and ground for all human rights and all human rights promote respect for the singular worth of man.

First of all we shall follow this distinction. The one, indivisible, inalienable dignity of man can be – as just seen – negatively so phrased that men of different beliefs and ideologies can agree. That is an advantage, for a teaching about human rights must be open for all men and must itself practise religious freedom. However one can proceed a step beyond these negative descriptions of the dignity of man if one goes into the general condition of being human: human dignity lies in the fact, that each particular human being and all human beings are in common 'man'. If this sentence is not to be a tautology, then it presupposes the difference between the existence and the essence of the human being: the human being is a human being and ought to be a human being. His being a human contains his humanity initially only as possibility, but not yet as constant reality. With the hominitas the humanitas is at stake. It can be actualised but it can also be blocked. Only of a man do we say that he acts 'inhumanly' if he violates human rights. With a dog it is not even linguistically possible to say something of this kind.

So, the dignity of man consists therein, that he is a man and should be a man. His existence is gift and task simultaneously. It presents him with the task of actualising himself, his essence, and thus coming into his truth. At this point there is in the Lutheran, the Reformed and also in the Catholic documents a strange polemic against humanism and the modern personal as well as corporate – striving for autonomy. Christian apologetics has again and again in modern European times defamed the will to self-actualisation as irreligious, anti-christian and revolutionary, as if this were the quintessence of egoism. Against that, what is Christian is the championing of the neighbour's right, the defence of the other, thus the renouncing of one's own rights. Against the modern self-actualisation the churches like to place selflessness in love. But the question is, which self is meant. If man's self is his essence as man, then self actualisation has nothing to do with egoism but is one side of the biblical commandment of love: 'love your neighbour as yourself' (it does not say the reverse: love yourself as your neighbour). Love of self is the other side of the love of the neighbour. So without self-actualisation there is also no actualisation of humanity for others! The laying claim to one's own rights does not require justification through love, in the sense more or less, that one really only wants to be there for others, but it is itself a part of the commandment of love.

In the more close characterising of the dignity and the essence of man the distinguishably Christian contribution of theology must emerge. Christians cannot expect that all men agree with their Christian view of man. Therefore there is here no absolutism of the Christian faith. But all other human beings can expect that Christians both say and show what they think of the dignity of man and what they can contribute to the realisation of his human rights. Thus there is here the openness of the Christian faith.

St. Pölten has contented itself with a short confession: 'It is our conviction that the emphasis of the Gospel is on the value of all human beings in the sight of God, on the atoning and redeeming work of Christ that has given to man his true dignity, on love as the motive for action, and on love for one's neighbour, as the practical expression of an active faith in Christ. We are members one of another, and when one suffers all are hurt'.

In the declaration of the *Roman Synod of Bishops* the key sentence reads quite similarly: 'The dignity of man has its roots in the fact that every human being is an image and reflection of God. As a result of this all men are equal with one another in their essence. The entire personal unfolding of man is a manifestation of this picture of God in us . . . The mystery of the Incarnation – the Son of God takes on human nature – throws new light upon the picture of man and his dignity, as it is accessible to our natural understanding. For it is only in the mystery of the Word-made-flesh that the mystery of man is truly brought to light'.

Most comprehensively of all the Reformed *Theologicial Basis* saw the dignity of man in his being in God's image and unfolded this being in God's image in its most important dimensions:

1. The image of God is the man who co-responds to God.
2. Insofar as man co-responds to God, his creator, he comes into his truth.
3. Man co-responding to God is the beginning and the end of the history of God with man in creation, reconciliation and salvation.
4. Man should co-respond to God in his relationship to himself. Man is in this respect a person and for that he has essential rights to freedom.
5. Man should co-respond to God in his relationship to other human beings. Men are in this respect beings and have for that essential community rights.
6. Man should co-respond to God in his relationship to non-human creation. He is destined for jurisdiction over and oneness with the earth and has for that essential economic rights and ecological duties.
7. Finally, man should co-respond to God in the succession of generations. He is in this respect a historical being and has corresponding temporal rights and duties in the succession of generations.

Because it is often emphasised on the Lutheran side, that man's dignity is his being an image of God, one can see here a real convergence of all Christian declarations about human rights.

Where do the differences lie and where are their ambiguities?

Theological Differences and Open Questions

1. The Reformed-Lutheran Difference: The Reformed *Theological Basis* grounds human rights in human dignity and human dignity in man's being an image of God and the being an image of God in God's right to man. It follows therewith the 'theological foundation of right' (J. Ellul) and the direction 'justification and right' (K. Barth). It sees Man's being an image of God in the federal-theological context of the covenant of God. This mode of substantiation has certainly the disadvantage that it is only acceptable for Christians. But it has the advantage that it motivates and activates Christians for human rights and their enforcement, and furthermore as Christians and not just by the way. The Lutheran critique of Tödt and Huber gets underway with the Two-Kingdoms teaching. According to this, human rights are secular phenomena to which Christians can refer not directly as Christians but only indirectly with the help of their 'reason illumined by love'. They recognise, then, in human rights similarities and analogies to the Christian faith. A 'Christian foundation' of human rights is rejected. Nevertheless 'the basis from whence we Christians are to deal with and understand the secular human rights should be examined'. Where does the difference lie between one basis and another? Tödt and Huber analyse in the phenomena of human rights 'elements of transcendence', which point towards the promises of the Gospel. They find 'manifest correspondences between the actual elements of the contours of the human right and the basic contents of Christian faith'. In this way they should like as theologians to deal with human rights in a critically constructive way not to legitimate them. It is not easy for an outsider to grasp the real difference between the Lutheran and the Reformed conceptions. Basically the reflection which 'reason enlightened through faith' takes up amounts to the same thing as the 'theological foundation' of human rights based on God's right to man. The real difference lies presumably in the historical characteristics of the tradition. Since the Puritan revolution the Reformed churches have had a direct part and therefore also a direct interest in human and civil rights. The Lutheran churches have had to make the effort, after

the event, to relate to something in the emergence of which they have scarcely had any part.

However the question remains open as to how the particularity of the Christian faith is to be referred and applied to universalism of human rights.

2. *The Roman Catholic-Reformed Difference:* Here also the prejudgements of the different traditions are operative. In the arrangement of official declarations through *Justitia et Pax* the Thomistic schema of nature and grace is distinctly recognisable: 'all men are distinguished with the same dignity of nature, but it is only in the mystery of the Word of God become flesh that the mystery of man truly becomes clear.' In the Reformed *Theological Basis* the schema of sin and grace is visible: 'For the Christian world God's right to man in this world of sin and inhumanity is manifest through the Gospel of Christ. Because the Godly right of grace is made known to all men through this Gospel, the God given dignity of every man and of all men is simultaneously proclaimed with it'.

Both perspectives, properly understood do not exclude each other. The grace, which nature presupposes, establishes a universal horizon. The grace, which justifies sinners, makes it possible to experience concretely God's justice. In the Reformed Declaration one can see the imago-Dei teaching as a common Christian basis. In the Roman Catholic Declaration the central reference is to the 'light of the Gospel', in which the Church acknowledges human rights, and this finds acceptance by Protestant Christians.

The common concentration on the Gospel of Christ does not limit the universalism of human rights, but rather lights up the broadest sphere from the creation of man to the completion of his history. To understand this, one must distinguish between the order of things and the order of knowledge. The revelation of God in Christ through the Gospel is the way to the knowledge of the dignity of all and of every man as the image of God and to the hope for all men and every man of becoming man in the godly kingdom of freedom. Thus what is known in faith through revelation is presupposed and unfolded through the revelation: creation on the one hand, completion on the other.

However the question remains open here, as to how this knowledge is constituted with a view to human rights.

3. *The Experience of Liberation and the Commitment to Human*

Rights: In the Roman Catholic Declaration the starting-point from the knowledge point of view lies in the explanations of the teaching-body of the church, the task of which it is to bear witness to the Gospel and to preserve the tradition. Thus the starting-point for the individual Christian is the experience of Christ's Church. In the Reformed Declaration the starting point lies in the testimonies of Holy Scripture, which make known to all men the good news of the justice of God manifest in Christ. Thus the starting-point for the individual Christian is the experience of justification in his or her own faith.

However there is in fact yet a third starting-point which is ever present in one way or another in the two mentioned: it is the starting-out from one's own life-experience. Whether as a member of the Church of Christ, or as one who believes in Christ, – our understanding of humanity and of human rights is stamped with our personal and collective life-experience. We experience the inhumanity of a dictatorship, of economic exploitation, of racism or the destruction of nature in so far as we have to live in it. We experience these states of affairs as 'inhuman' if we have been made sensitive through the contrary experience of humanity. Otherwise we would get used to them. We experience the suffering due to unfreedom as a conscious pain if and wherever the freedom has come nearer. We fashion our views of freedom and humanity according to our hopes and our experiences.

He who suffers under racism grasps another part of human rights than he who suffers under ideological dictatorship. And he who suffers from a world growing ever more divided and hostile according as it grows together to one world, for him the totality of human rights is, Christianly-speaking, certainly the experience of the Church of Christ and the experience of Christ in one's own faith, but both experiences stand in the context of the real history of oppression and liberation, of inhumanity and humanity. If one isolated out of this context the special Christian experience, then this Christian experience would become abstract and would not be communicable any more. We have learned from liberation theology to begin there, where we ourselves really exist in our own people. Experience in the praxis of liberation from inhumanity is for Christians and churches the concrete starting-point for the commitment to human rights.

The Task of Christian Theology

The task of Christian theology does not lie in presenting once again what thousands of experts, jurists, parliamentarians and diplomats in the United Nations have already completed. However, Christian theology also cannot dispense itself from the discussion of and the fight for the realisation of human rights. In the name of the creation of man according to the image of God, in the name of the Incarnation of God for the reconciliation of the world and in the name of the coming kingdom of God for the fulfilment of history, the Church is charged with responsibility for the humanity of man as well as for his rights and duties in time. We see the theological contribution of the Christian Church in the grounding of the fundamental human rights upon God's right to man. The Christian faith has over and above the different rights and duties of man to esteem the one indivisible dignity of man in his life with God without, in so doing, excluding other religious or humanistic substantions of human rights.

Christian theology refers to the history of God with man on the basis of the biblical testimonies. This history is about the salvation of man from his sinful Godlessness (Adam) and the liberation from his deathly inhumanity (Cain) and therein about the fulfillment of his original destiny to be the image of God.

In accordance with the Old Testament the theology reflects the liberation of Israel from slavery in Egypt, the covenant of the liberating God with the chosen community and the rights and duties of the people of God which are laid down in this covenant of freedom. The salvation-events: liberation, covenant and the right of God are the concrete content of the biblical testimony of the Old Testament, and furthermore in this sequence. They have power of guidance for Israel and Christendom in particular and through both they have exemplary meaning for all men and nations. Through justice and peace Israel and the Christian world become the light of nations.

In accordance with the New Testament the theology reflects the liberation of man from sin, law and death through the sending, the sacrifice and the resurrection of Jesus Christ. Through the rule of the crucified Son of God the power of the Evil One is broken. In his parousia the freedom of the children of God will appear. The liberation through the mediating death of Christ; the new covenant in his blood and the new rights and duties of the ecclesial community composed of 'masters and slaves, Jews and unbelievers, men and women' (Gal. 3, 28) are the concrete content of the biblical witness of the New Testament. Because Christ in his mission, his sacrifice and his resurrection is the 'visible image of the unseen God', men in his community become his brothers and sisters and tread the path leading to the fulfilment of their human destiny as the image of God in the world. In the grace of God lies the dignity of man.

In as much as Christian theology reflects the liberation, the covenant and the right of God according to the biblical testimonies, it discovers also the freedom, the solidarity and the rights of men today. It therefore awakens pain at the present inner and outer enslavements of man. It calls for commitment to liberation for a life in the dignity, the rights and the duties of the community with God. In a world which is not yet the kingdom of God, Christendom can leave no area of life without the witness to divine liberation, to the covenant of God and to the dignity of man. The biblical witness of liberation, covenant and the right of God leads to a corresponding praxis of the Christian world.

The universal presupposition of the special history of God with Israel and Christendom lies therein, that the God freeing and saving them is the creator of all men and things. In his liberating and saving action therefore the original destiny of all men is experienced and fulfilled. In the designation of man to be the 'image of God' the right of God to all men is expressed. The human rights to life, freedom, community and self-determination mirror God's right to man, because man is destined to be God's image in all life-relations.

The universal goal of Israel's and Christendom's special experiences of God lies therein, that the God freeing and saving them is the fulfiller of the history of the world and will actualise his right to his entire creation in the kingdom of his glory. His liberation and saving action in history thus reveals the true future of man: image of God means the full community of God. Man has therefore a 'right' to future. Human rights mirror the right of the coming God and the future of man. The destiny of man to be the image of God indicates the indivisible right of God to man and therefore the irreducible dignity of man.

Translated by James Corkery S.J.

Notes

1. WCC – CCIA *Human Rights and Christian Responsibility* Vols. 1–3, Geneva, WCC – CCIA, 1975.
   Some of the papers to the Conference published in *Ecumenical Review* 27 (2) 75.
2. David Paton (ed.) *Breaking Barriers:* The Official Report of the Fifth Assembly of the World Council of Churches, Nairobi, 23 November – 10 December 1975, London, SPCK 1976, pp. 119-141.
3. Text and preparatory papers in Allen O. Miller (ed.) *A Christian Declaration on Human Rights,* Grand Rapids, Eerdmans, 1977.
4. Jϕrgen Lissner (pref.) *Theological Perspectives on Human Rights,* Geneva, Lutheran World Federation, 1977.
5. Wolfgang Huber and Heinz Eduard Tödt *Menschenrechte,* Perspektiven einer menschlichen Welt. Stuttgart, Kreuz Verlag, 1977.
   See also Jϕrgen Lissner and Arne Sovik (ed.) *A Lutheran Reader on Human Rights,* Geneva, Lutheran World Federation, 1978.
6. J. Baur (ed.) *Zum Thema Menschenrechte,* Stuttgart, Calwer Verlag, 1977. T. Redtorff "Menschenrechte und Rechtfertigung" in D. Henke (ed.) *Der Wirklichkeitsanspruch von Theologie und Religion,* Tübingen, 1976, p. 161-174. W. Schweitzer 'Bericht' in *Zeitschrift Für Evangelische Ethik,* 1978, 1.
7. In J. Gremillion (ed.) *The Gospel of Peace and Justice:* Catholic Social Teaching since Pope John. Maryknoll (N.Y.), Orbis, 1976, pp. 513-629.
8. Pontifical Commission 'Justitia et Pax' *The Church and Human Rights,* Working Paper no. 1, Vatican City, 1975.
9. N. Goodall (ed.) *The Uppsala Report 1968:* Official Report of the Fourth Assembly of the World Council of Churches, Geneva, World Council of Churches, 1968.

CHAPTER 14
THEOLOGICAL REFLECTION ON HUMAN RIGHTS
ALAN FALCONER

Introduction

In line with thousands of people throughout Europe at the end of the eighteenth century, the Scots poet Robert Burns was greatly encouraged by the publication of the French *Declaration of the Rights of Man.* In his poem, *The Tree of Liberty* he des-describes the significance of the Declaration in the following way:

> Without this tree, alake this life
> Is but a vale o' woe,man;
> A scene o' sorrow mixed wi' strife,
> Nae real joys we know,man.
> We labour soon, we labour late,
> To feed the titled knave,man;
> And a' the comfort we're to get
> Is that ayont the grave,man.
>
> Wi' plenty o' sic trees, I trow,
> The warld would live in peace,man;
> The sword would help to mak a plough,
> The din o' war wad cease, man.
> Like brethren in a common cause,
> We'd on each other smile,man;
> And equal rights and equal laws
> Wad gladden every isle,man.[1]

That such a vision extended beyond Scotland's shores may be seen from the reception given in Belfast to Tom Paine's *The Rights of Man,* a work, which owed so much to the French Declaration and indeed which helped to make it more widely known. Paine's book was soon being called the Koran of Belfescu,[2] or, more popularly, the Bible of Belfast.

Despite the passage of some two hundred years the sentiments of

Burns and his contemporaries are still being uttered by thousands throughout the world who are oppressed, marginalised, and treated as less than human. It is imperative therefore, that as we think of theology and human rights, we keep in the forefront of our minds that in dealing with the problem of human rights, it is not just the question of *rights* that is the subject of our attention, but that of *human* rights.

During the last decade, the phenomena of human rights have appeared constantly as items on the agenda of the Churches throughout the world both in the sphere of practical involvement, and in that of theological reflection.[3] When the decision was taken by the Irish School of Ecumenics to launch its human rights project and consultation, a distinctive theological approach was adopted.[4] The theological enquiry was to involve three stages. First of all an examination of the 'secular' phenomena of human rights, particularly in Ireland, was to be conducted. In the light of this analysis, it was felt that ultimate questions would be raised to theology – questions concerning man and God. Thus the second stage would involve facing up to issues of Christian anthropology and also theology. From this, the third stage would arise. It would involve seeing if a theological framework emerged whereby it would be possible to face up to other human rights issues.

As with any theological enquiry, the adoption of such an approach assumes certain presuppositions. It is important to take cognisance of these briefly at this stage. In general, what is represented here might appropriately be called a *theology of the wayfarers,* to borrow the phrase of Johannes Wollebius.[5] Firstly and emphatically, such a theological enterprise is conducted within the Christian community, and has at its source the Gospel and the experience of that community through the ages which has tried to live the Gospel in its varying situations. This is the central part of the theologian's life-story; as he pursues his contemporary quest.[6] Continually a return to the sources for illumination and clarification is required.[7]

Theology, however, is not merely the re-translation of these sources into contemporary terms. Rather it involves a wrestling with the contemporary situation and with the Gospels in the attempt to articulate the nature of God, and, through the fact of the Incarnation, the nature of humankind. Secondly, then, a 'theology of the wayfarers' emphasises the provisional character of our understanding of God. In the Fathers of the Church this was expressed as the 'incomprehensibility' of God. That is, God cannot be grasped, and therefore cannot be controlled by men and women.[8]

The third presupposition is that history provides the locus of God's Revelation to humankind. We shall return later to the Christian understanding of history, but at this point it is important to stress history as the locus of God's Revelation. 'God is present in human history. He is present in a hidden way. Even the forces which resist Him serve His purpose'.[9] History is therefore an appropriate place to seek God. Since, for the Christian community, God became a human, then the revelation or self-disclosure of God, induces the self-disclosure of the nature of humankind.[10] The 'theology of the wayfarers', then, implies a constant search for the disclosure of God and of humankind in history.

The description, 'theology of the wayfarers', serves to remind us both of the nature of theology and of the mode of investigation appropriate to the discipline.[11] It is also an apposite description of the method adopted for our investigation of the phenomena of human rights. This paper, therefore, will begin with an examination of the phenomena of human rights, after which a theological analysis of the central themes will be conducted.

The phenomena of human rights.

> The causes that estrange men from one another are principally three: i. differences of opinion: we are not able to think of the same things in the same way; ii. hatreds: we cannot admit differing opinions about the same things without friendship suffering as a result. Hence, we cannot differ in our opinions without developing impassioned and prejudiced feelings one against another; iii. open wrongs and persecutions: which are the result of our hates, to our mutual undoing.[12]

Although Jan Comenius, the seventeenth-century Bohemian theologian and 'apostle of peace' precedes the 'age of the Enlightenment', when the rhetoric of human rights came to prominence, his insights are pertinent to the reality of human rights. In the above extract from his work *De Rerum Humanarum Emendatione Consultatio Catholica* he points to the problematic out of which the need for a concept of human rights arises. Having pointed to the reality of conflict, or alienation, in human affairs at the individual level, he then goes on to point to alienation in society, linking the idea of conflict with that of power. He writes:

> 'The first conflict originates in the mind, the second in the feelings, the third in those secretly or openly opposing forces which make for mutual destruction. Oh if it were only possible to gain some insight into the inimical intrigues in philosophy, religion, politics and private affairs we should see nothing but endless attempts at mutual subversion'.[13]

Perhaps to these stresses on the conflicts between individuals and within society, and the power structures at play in these situations, there should now be added, due to the increasing recognition of the nature of our world as a 'global village', the concept of conflict between societies.

This phenomenon of conflict or alienation provides the matrix out of which the struggles for human rights arise. In the purportedly perfect society, there is no place for the concept 'human rights', as the need for it does not arise.[14] Such a perfect society, however, does not exist.[15]

Let us, then, examine in greater depth this situation of conflict out of which the necessity for human rights arises. Before examining the relationship between groups in society or that of the individual to society, let us concentrate on relationships between human beings as individuals.

Human beings continually come to a knowledge of themselves. There is no point at which it is possible for anyone to give a comprehensive and final answer to the question, 'Who am I?' The individual is continually coming to self-knowledge through his or her contact with other persons. To make his or her own self-affirmation in relation to other people, however, requires strength, or what Paul Tillich calls the 'courage to be'.[16] This self-assertion is made in the contact of the self-assertion of other people; it is in human relationships that we come to some sense of our own significance. Rollo May in his work, *Power and Innocence*[17], relates this idea of significance to that of power. These two ideas or realities are intertwined for him. He writes:

> 'A great deal of human life can be seen as the conflict between

power on the one side (i.e. effective ways of influencing others, achieving the sense in interpersonal relations of the significance of one's self) and powerlessness on the other'.[18]

May goes on to affirm that for the individual to mature requires self-esteem, which can only come about through the feeling of having an influence in interpersonal relations. He posits five levels of power present as potentialities in every human being's life[19] : (i) the power to be: the fact that even for the infant, actions elicit responses; (ii) Self-affirmation; (iii) self-assertion: the assertion of our self-affirmation in situations of resistance; (iv) aggression: this arises when self-affirmation is blocked and manifests itself as the taking of someone else's territory for oneself; (v) violence: when agression is ineffective.[20]

Having suggested that the above insights gained from psychotherapy are helpful in understanding the way in which individuals are able to affirm their own significance and thus come to maturity, May points to those uses of power which when exercised by other human beings can either stifle or aid the individual's sense of worth. Firstly those types which *stifle* the sense of significance of other human beings, which, if they are used recurrently can elicit the response of aggression or violence. Here May points to three different modes of power, each of which is self-explanatory viz. exploitative, manipulative, or competitive. By the use of any or all of these, human beings in their desire to assert their own significance, and those of their values, opinion, life-styles and feelings do so in such a way that the significance of the other person in the encounter is diminished or demeaned. Power, however, can be used to *enable* a human being to come to a sense of significance. Here May posits two modes, viz. 'nutrient', that is power for the other person (e.g. a normal parent's care for his children) and 'integrative', that is power with the other person.[21]

Although the above analysis has been described in terms of the relationship of one person with another, Rollo May emphasises that such a sense of self-significance is also affirmed by the individual in his relationship with groups, society or the 'state'. Similarly 'corporate consciousness' is also affirmed according to the contours of his analysis. The individual, then, can either be enabled to affirm his or her self-significance within the encounter with groups operative within society, or he or she can be oppressed in that encounter. Similarly, groups within society can be subject to the same loss of self-significance, as can one society at the hands another society; or such groups and societies can be enabled to affirm themselves.

This experience of the sense of self-significance or the loss of it has been subject to a variety of interpretations and analyses, but the basic experience seems to have been affirmed by the use of terms such as alienation, conflict, estrangement, anomie, repression and marginilisation. It is this experience which provides the background for the necessity of human rights. Human rights emerge as attempts to regulate the conflict between human beings or groups of human beings in such a way as to *protect* the individual or group and also in such a way as to *enable* human beings and groups to grow to maturity. Human rights reflect, then, and engage the two effects of conflict, viz. the destructive and the constructive or creative. Let us examine briefly each in turn.

The negative features of the conflict situation were emphasised by Jan Comenius in a continuation of the passages quoted above. He wrote:

> Conflicts of this kind I call inhuman; for man who has been created in the image of God should be kind, pleasant and generally peaceful. But now when man is divorced from man, when man is incapable of tolerating his neighbour, when one man is raving against another what we witness is a veritable downfall of humanity. Such behaviour cannot be observed in any kind of dumb creatures.[22]

What Comenius is emphasising here is the destructiveness of the conflict situation. To counter this destructiveness, each society throws up its own patterns of religious, social and moral behaviour.[23] In the modern state, such protection is afforded by systems of government and law.[24]

It is evident in the modern state that the concept of *protection* underlies the appeal to a Constitution, Bill of Rights or International Convention. Thus, in the recent report of the Standing Advisory Commission on Human Rights in Northern Ireland, *The Protection of Human Rights in Northern Ireland,* when the arguments are advanced in favour of enacting a Bill of Rights either for the United Kingdom in general or for Northern Ireland in particular, the recurrent words used in the argument are 'guarantees against abuse', 'speedy redress', and 'protecting basic rights and freedoms'.[25] Similarly in its reports, *Contempt of Court and the Law,* the Irish Council of Civil Liberties appeals to the *Constitution of Ireland* in its attempt to protect those who find themselves in breach of the rules of the Courts, since the laws of contempt are not adjudicated through trial by jury.[26] Similarly the recent I.C.C.L. discussion on Children's Rights, and the protection of children so that they can grow to maturity, has been conducted in the context of the *protection* afforded by the Constitution of Ireland.[27] Indeed, whenever human rights are declared to be 'fundamental'[28] or 'inalienable',[29] then what is primarily at stake is the *protection* of the individual, or group, from the exploitative, manipulative or competitive power of other human beings, bureaucracy or the state.[30]

This protection afforded by the legislation for human rights may be deemed 'prospective protection'. In other words, by this means the fact of conflict and its recurrence is catered for. Human rights occur as a phenomenon precisely because there is no resolution to the differences between human beings and groups; the conflict will keep on recurring. Given the fact of conflict, then, rights are declared both as a present protection and as a declaration of intent for the future. This element of prospective protection is apparent in the creation or development of the enunciation of specific rights. Richard Claude, in his analysis of the formulation of human rights, sees the emergence of the middle class and their desire to protect their interests, and those of their children, as the basic element in the enunciation of certain rights.[31] Similarly, Zechariah Chafee Jnr. repeats the view that the initial concern of the settlers in America was primarily to secure their religious liberty from outside interference when they began the process which led eventually to the *American Declaration of Independence,* with its list of rights. That is, they were concerned to secure protection for the present and for the future.[32] The very formulation of 'fundamental rights' emphasises further this element of 'prospective protection'.[33] In this way then the concept of human rights is designed to give protection to those in conflict situations, that is, to everyone.[34]

Conflict however, as well as being destructive, can also induce creativity. Jan Comenius in a continuation of the passages quoted above stressed this aspect of conflict. He wrote:

> If therefore inhumanity is to make way for humanity, we must spare no effort to seek means leading to this end. There are three such means: First, for people to abandon the habit of excessively trusting their feelings, and, by making allowance for common human weakness, to recognise as unworthy of men that they should overwhelm one another with hatred for trifling reasons – in general, to forgive one another . . . All this we shall refer to as effacing the past. Second, for nobody to impose his principles (in philosophy, theology or politics) on anybody else, but, on the contrary, for everyone to allow all other men to express their own views openly and enjoy in peace what is theirs by right. This we shall call mutual tolerance. Third, for all to endeavour, in concerted efforts, to discover what is best, and to that end to bring into agreement their sentiments, their aspirations and their actions. This we shall call conciliation.[35]

Through the fact of specific conflicts, new rights have been enunciated. In a recent discussion paper and questionnaire to those countries signatory to the *European Convention on Human Rights,* a question was posed to each Government: 'Have any views, issues and comments been expressed in your parliament on adding further rights and freedoms to those already protected in the convention? (as for example, right to asylum, right to compensation for miscarriage of justice)?'.[36] In their reply, the Austrian Bundresrat quoted a speech by Mr. Reichl during a debate in 1967. What is said is instructive:

> Undoubtedly, technical means for influencing man's subconscious mind have increased enormously since 1950, when the convention was drawn up. The ways in which human thought, will and feelings can be manipulated are incredible. By using the resources of applied psychology it is possible to persuade the ordinary housewife to purchase two washing machines and temporarily paralyse her willpower. Talk of manipulating the human being brings to mind his intellectual enslavement by those forces which dictate the way in which he thinks. It might well be asked how the convention on Human Rights could and should be supplemented in order to guarantee the protection of individual freedom.[37]

Out of specific conflicts the need for new rights emerges. Thus until the McGee case in Ireland, there was no enunciated right to privacy. Out of this specific case a right was established.[38] Similarly, the conflict in Ireland, which is still not fully resolved between women and employers and the Government over the question of equal pay, and the right of women to be regarded for tax purposes as individuals is another case of the emerging awareness of society of the need to expand the horizons of human rights. In the International sphere, conflict between the interests and aspirations of nations has led to the general acceptance of the right to 'self-determination'.[39]

It is in the situation of conflict that a claim is made for rights and freedoms – and in this claim an expansion is made in society's understanding of what it means to be human. Maurice Cranston stresses the connection between this claim made in the conflict situation and the enunciation of rights thus: 'A right presupposes a claim – if the claim is not made, the question of a right does not arise'.[40] Out of conflict, then, can emerge a greater awareness of the needs of men and women and a greater sensitivity to them.

Most of this discussion on conflict could have been related to the classical civil and political rights enunciated at the Enlightenment and expanded since then. Rights, however, do not solely emerge in the conflict to secure the protection from interference by other individuals or groups. They also emerge as an aspiration. Human rights are values to be protected or encouraged.[41] Thus in the emergence of social and economic rights,[42] conditions are enunciated which are necessary for men and women in their striving for humanity. Thus the International Commission of Jurists stressed:

> The function of the legislature in a free society under the Rule of Law is to create and maintain the conditions which will uphold the dignity of man as an individual. This dignity requires not only the recognition of his civil and political rights but also the establishment of the social, economic, educational and cultural conditions which are essential to the full development of his personality.[43]

Human rights not only relate to a static view of humankind, but also to a view of man – becoming; a striving for a humanity which cannot be defined absolutely at any given stage in history.

Until this point in talking of human rights I have not introduced the notion of 'duties' or 'responsibilities'. In his work *The Concept of Law,* H. L. A. Hart saw the notion of the enunciation of rights in the context of 'promises'. He wrote:

> To promise is to say something which creates an obligation for the promiser . . . When we promise, we make use of specified procedures to change our own moral situation by imposing obligations on ourselves and conferring rights on others.[44]

The whole discussion of the question of human rights is equally a discussion of human responsibilities, a discussion of the application of 'nutrient' or 'integrative' power. To confer a right on a group, or rather to recognise that a person, group or society has a right, entails the responsibility to ensure that that right is conferred. It is the question of responsibility that has made many commentators unhappy about the social, economic, and cultural rights being regarded as human rights.[45] The concept of human rights, however, is about responsibility, that of the state, society, groups and individuals to create the climate in which the specific rights and freedoms may be exercised, and to exercise power for the securing of these. A notable feature of human rights is their universal character,[46] and with this goes a universal responsibility for their implementation.[47] The accent on human rights, then, falls squarely on the notion of responsibility or duty. As Hart noted, this involves the idea of sacrifice or renunciation:

> It seems clear that the sacrifice of personal interest which such rules demand is the price which must be paid in a world such as ours for living with others, and the protection they afford is the minimum which, for beings such as ourselves, makes living with others worthwhile.[48]

Rights and responsibilities are inseparable.

In this examination of human rights, no attempt has been made to provide a basic social, political, or legal theory of human rights. Rather in examining the rhetoric and the reality of human rights in Ireland and throughout the world, fundamental characteristics present themselves as the basis for theological reflection.

Theological reflection on human rights

In pursuing the 'theology of the wayfarers', then, what does the phenomenon of human rights disclose about the nature of God and the nature of humankind?

The very fact of human rights is indicative of the radical nature and scope of the alienation between human beings and groups of human beings. Even if all adequate human rights or guarantees were enunciated for individual, groups or societies, the very fact that they had to be enunciated in itself would be a pointer to the destructiveness of human beings. Sir Isaiah Berlin in his famous inaugural lecture as Chichele Professor of Social and Political Theory at Oxford University located his discipline within such a problematic:

> If men never disagreed about the ends of life, if our ancestors had remained undisturbed in the Garden of Eden, the studies to which the Chichele Chair of Social and Political Theory is dedicated could scarcely have been conceived.[49]

Similarly with human rights, if humankind was at one and able to assimilate differences between individuals and groups, there would be no need for the reality of human rights. But human rights are a reality, arising from alienation and sin.

Alienation involves the separation from something regarded as essential; something which is essential for wholeness.[50] For St. Paul, this alienation or sin is essentially a 'falling short of participation in the glory of God'.[51] It is not simply an absence of doing good, but an active force towards evil. It involves the abuse of power through the exploitation, manipulation or coercion of other human beings and groups. It is a failure to treat human beings seriously.

Other contributors in this volume deal with the notion of sin comprehensively, and therefore I will confine my self to stressing two or three points rather than giving a fuller and more systematic account.[52] First of all it must be stressed that in talking about the relationship between sin and human rights, the Christian has no vantage point to accuse others of sin, even if that was a possible Christian attitude, which it is not. In examining human rights I as an individual am pointed to my own sin. In his great Oratorio, *A Child of our Time,* Sir Michael Tippett exposes the treatment of the Jews by the Nazi regime. Sir Michael was greatly exercised by the problem of human rights, and out of his involvement he was to write as the climax of this work words, which seem to me to be an accurate reflection of the effect of involvement in human rights. He wrote: 'I would know my shadow and my light'.[53] Human rights show *me* the radical nature of *my* own alienation from God and other human beings. They are a radical judgment on me as an individual.

Secondly, human rights are a pointer to the sin and alienation in society. They point not just to individual sin, but also to what Reinhold Niebuhr termed, *Immoral Society,*[54] when he pointed to the reality of collective sin, in a way which had not been stressed previously. In his analysis he emphasised the inevitability of social conflict in society:

> What is lacking among all these moralists, whether religious or rational, is an understanding of the brutal character of the behaviour of all human collectives, and the power of self-interest and collective egoism in all inter-group relations. . . . They do not see that the limitations of the human imagination, the easy subservience of reason to prejudice and passion, and the consequent persistence of irrational egoism, particularly in group behaviour, make social conflict an inevitability in human history, probably to its very end.[55]

In the aftermath of the Second World War, the Holocaust and the U.N. Development Decades there is no need to argue the concept of social sin; it has been, and still is, a terrifying reality within and between every society. It is what the Minority Report in the Kilbrandon Commission on the Constitution in the United Kingdom called 'the we-they syndrome'.[56] Every group of human beings excludes. Every group tries to protect its self-interest through self-assertion, and if that does not work to its satisfaction, then the group turns to aggression or worse. It is so easy for a group to call for the 'common good' in its relations with other groups, where the common good is what 'we' have defined it to be.[57]

Thirdly, having seen the reality of my individual sin, and of collective sin in human rights, there is the fact that human rights are a judgement on the churches. I as a Christian am involved in individual sin and in collective sin. But the church is also involved. Human rights are a judgement on the church not because of sins of omission (the marginalised whom the church should have been supporting but did not) but because the church has also oppressed human beings and groups. This oppression has occurred in relation to groups in society, but also to human beings within the Churches. Why is it that human beings and groups within the Churches regard themselves as being oppressed or exploited? The reality of the exercise of power within each Church coincides all too closely with the reality as exercised outside the Churches. Power is used to help people affirm themselves and their convictions, but it is also used to enslave, coerce, manipulate, exploit. Canon David Jenkins in his book, *The Contradiction of Christianity,* phrases this well:

> The contradiction of Christianity is real. The phrase is not a manner of speaking. Our behaviour as Christians and the performance of the institutions of Christianity have been such as to deprive us of the right to be Christians or to expect credibility for what Christianity stands for. Further this is not a mere matter of definition (for example, some version of the argument that 'real' Christianity is the following of Jesus Christ and most 'Christians' do not 'really' follow him). Real Christianity is quite clearly what Christians actually do and are together with the institutions which they in fact have.[58]

This contradiction is arguably most apparent in the area of human rights. Canon Jenkins continues:

> There is a vital sense in which God, in and through Jesus, speaks and is active precisely in and through this contradiction'.[59]

If then in our analysis of human rights we come to a stronger awareness of the sin of man, and of the corporate reality of sin also, as one of the factors of the nature of man to which human rights points, what do we learn about God through this very contradiction?

In attempting to elicit from the phenomena of human rights, insights pertinent to our understanding of the nature of God a number of assumptions are operative about the relationship between God and history. It is important at this point to expose these presuppositions, and thus to come to a clearer understanding of a 'theology of the wayfarers'. In a paper of this nature it is not possible to enter the debate on the Christian understanding of history, which has been the subject of much thought by theologians particularly in this century.[60] It is important here, however, to elucidate the salient features of a Christian approach to history. The world view in which the Christian understanding of history is located is that of the Semitic tradition which sees history in linear terms, as against the classical Greek view of history as cyclic:

> Under no dimension does time go backward. Some qualities of a particular moment of time can repeat themselves, but only those qualities which are abstracted from a whole situation. Time, so to speak, runs ahead toward the new, the unique, even in repetitions. In this respect time has an identifying mark under all dimensions; the after-each-other-ness cannot be reversed.[61]

Such a Judaeo-Christian view of history derives both from the analysis of occurrences or happenings and their relation to each other in history, and from the appreciation of a sense of meaning arising out of the discernment of a pattern in the relation between occurrences. It is to convey this distinction that H. Richard Niebuhr has designated these 'external history' and 'internal history' respectively.[62] It is in 'internal history' that an occurrence in history is perceived primarily as an event. Thus Paul Tillich begins his exposition of 'History and the Kingdom of God' in his *Systematic Theology* with the following assertion:

> Historical consciousness expresses itself in a tradition, i.e. in a set of memories which are delivered from one generation to the other. Tradition is not a casual collection of remembered events but the recollection of those events which have gained significance for the bearers and receivers of the tradition. The significance which an occurrence has for a tradition-conscious group determines whether it will be considered as a historical event.[63]

For Tillich the designation of an occurrence in history as an event is a running together of fact and interpretation.[64] It is through the 'internal history' of the specific group that all historical occurrences are assessed. It is because events are apprehended within a more of less coherent pattern that the insights of 'internal history' are deemed to possess universal meaning or significance. Thus Wolfhart Pannenberg asserts from within the Christian tradition:

> All theological questions and answers are meaningful only within the framework of the history which God has with humanity and through humanity with his whole creation – the history moving toward a future still hidden from the world but already revealed in Jesus Christ.[65]

To declare that Christ is the centre of history as Pannenberg does, need not preclude other interpretations of the movement of history, nor of specific events in history. Rather the Christian makes this assertion from within that tradition in which Jesus is apprehended as the goal and fulfilment of history. When the Christian asserts that Jesus is the centre of history, what is being expressed is that Jesus is a moment in history for which everything before and after is both preparation and reception. In the New Testament, e.g. *II Corinthians* ch 6v2, such a moment is designated *kairos*. That is, such a moment is pregnant with a new understanding of the meaning of history and life. Such a moment is the fulfilment of time. To perceive Jesus as the 'kairos' is to declare him 'Lord and Saviour', since this event becomes decisive for the way in which all life is approached. Indeed the event of Jesus is experienced as having a liberating effect – liberating the community to be free in the present and to look for God's future. To perceive Jesus as 'kairos' is, in Ernst Fuchs' phrase, to 'stand in the event'.[66]

Because of Jesus the Christian community sees itself as living 'between the times', as looking for the disclosure of God and humankind. Jürgen Moltmann conveys well this character of living between the times:

> The man who is recipient of this revelation of God in promise is identified, as what he is – and at the same time differentiated, as what he will be. He comes 'to himself' – but in hope, for he is not yet freed from contradiction and death. He finds the way of life – but hidden in the promised future of Christ that has not yet appeared. Thus the believer becomes essentially one who hopes. He is still future to 'himself' and is promised to himself. His future depends utterly and entirely on the outcome of the risen Lord's course, for he has staked his future on the future of Christ. Thus he comes into harmony with himself *in spe*, but into disharmony with himself *in re*. The man who trusts himself to the promise is of all people one who finds himself a riddle and an open question, one who becomes in his own eyes a *homo absconditus*. In pursuit of the promise, he finds he is in search of himself and comes to regard himself as an open question addressed to the future of God.[67]

A 'theology of the wayfarers' therefore is making at least two important affirmations. The first is that all life and events of history are perceived through the event of Jesus of Nazareth, and the Christian life is an attempt to live that life which is perceived in Christ. Secondly, because of the fact that we in some sense 'see through a glass darkly' (*I Corinthians* ch 13v12) the Christian as he travels life 'in the event' looks for signs of God's activity in the world in the hope of coming to greater clarity in understanding himself and God.

In the Christian and Jewish traditions the revelation of God is primarily described in terms of specific acts in history – acts which were seen to disclose the nature of God. In the Old Testament one need only look at the development of confessions of faith, or confessional formula, to perceive that it is through activity in history that God's nature is revealed, and the identity of the individual and the community is disclosed. From the first faltering confessions, 'A wandering Aramean was my father' (*Deuteronomy* ch 26v5) and 'Yahweh, who brought Israel out of Egypt' (*Deut.* ch 6v21) to the larger and more strident confessions of *Joshua* (ch 24) and *Nehemiah* (ch 9) the focus is the activity of God as seen through the events of the community's history.[68] It is for this reason that God is often described in the Old Testament as *'dabar'*, that is the Word. As the Old Testament scholar, Edmund Jacob, reminds us:

> It is necessary to remember the common belief throughout antiquity in the value and efficacy of a word. A spoken word is never an empty sound but an operative reality whose action cannot be hindered once it has been pronounced . . . it is in history that the word is revealed and its action in nature is only a pale reflection of its work in history.[69]

For the Judaeo-Christian tradition, God's revelation is seen primarily as disclosure in history. The Word of God in Old Testament is primarily a 'word of power'.[70]

Similarly, in the New Testament, it is through the event of history, Jesus of Nazareth, that God discloses himself. This has been the pattern of the experience of the Christian community. Thus André Dumas writes:

> We have access to God primarily through historical events, through the message which they convey and which we recount

concerning them; through something which is temporal in character and not a lapse into meaninglessness but a revelation at specific times and places.[71]

In our examination of human rights, then, the theologian comes to the subject with certain expectations, of which the most important is that because of the experience of the Christian community, he expects to find a word of God. In our analysis of the human rights phenomena, certain features of the concept and reality of human rights were isolated as being important in the attempt to understand this contemporary movement. These features centred on 'conflict', 'protection', the 'developing understanding of man's nature', and 'power'. It is in precisely these features that I believe that we can as Christians discern 'a word of God'.

In his analysis of the Old and New Testaments, André Dumas in *Political Theology and the Life of the Church,*[72] sees a recurrent pattern of conflict in the events recorded – a conflict which arises primarily because of the differences between individuals and groups. Such conflict possessed then, as it does now, both destructive and creative elements. It is particularly in the creative element of conflict that God is seen to be active. In such conflicts, God appears as the 'Disturber'[73] or the 'praesentia explosiva'.[74] The more common term for such an activity of God in the Old Testament, though rarely there, and in the New Testament, is that of *skandalon.* The idea of 'skandalon' is a peculiarly Hebrew one.[75] It is only in the tradition of God's activity in history that the idea makes sense at all. As Enda MacDonagh notes:

> The reality is concerned primarily and predominantly with the strange ways of God with men. That his ways are not conventional human ways is revealed most strikingly and paradoxically in the climactic way of the incarnation, in the logos made flesh.[76]

Throughout his ministry, Jesus appeared to be a scandal to the Jewish people, and their religious leaders. He touched them at a very raw point. Over the centuries, elaborate traditions had emerged in response to the activity of God in relation to the community. Laws had emerged for every area of life in the attempt to regulate the way in which men and women had access to God. In the attempt to define the identity of the Jewish people, there had also been a tendency to define those who did not belong to the community of God's promise. It must have been galling to say the least to find a Samaritan women being regarded as a subject of God's grace (*John* ch 7 v53 – ch 8v11),[77] or a Roman soldier as a model of faith (*Matthew* ch 8 v5 – 10). While the Jewish people saw themselves primarily as a community, and had elaborate regulations to help the poor, the oppressed and the widows, the people in these groups were regarded as specific groups and classified according to their problem – as if 'they are not fully one with us', because they have characteristics that 'we' don't share.[78] It seems to have been primarily the marginalised in society with whom Jesus associated and conversed – fishermen, tax officials, women, the lame and maimed, and the possessed. Further, his message and teaching directed attention to the fact that God's gift of life transcended the ideas and divisions espoused by the 'religious' of the day. That such a message was provocative is seen early in Matthew's gospel where the mission of The Twelve is outlined, as is its manner of execution. Jesus warns the disciples that they must expect opposition, and that their message would be divisive. 'You must not think that I have come to bring peace to the earth; I have not come to bring peace, but a sword' (*Matthew* ch 10 v34).[79]

But why should a man talking about human wholeness provoke such a reaction? Jesus was perceived as a threat to the cherished traditions and values of his society. He questioned the neat pigeonholing of groups into this category or that group. His whole attitude was to treat everyone with whom he came into contact as a gift – to accept them as they were with all the unique potentialities they possessed. He did not expect everyone to fit into neat categories, he did not tell the Roman soldier mentioned above that he must become a Jew; he commended the gift of faith he perceived in him. He was able to accept the man as different, and not just in spite of the difference. This attitude was of course a source of scandal to the 'religious'. Enda MacDonagh has described well what I am trying to express:

> The world of the other with which one is confronted comes to one as gift in both senses of that expression. He is given: he is not in any sense one's own achievement but freely presented to one. He is present as *present* and in the second sense associated with gift he is present as *enriching* or at least potentially

> enriching one's own world. Any encounter with the world of another has this potential.[80]

When a person or a group are not accepted with their differences, and are not seen as helping the process of expanding the horizons of 'what it means to be human', then they appear as a threat. Certainly, any encounter with an individual or group different from 'us' forces us to revise our previously held convictions. It is to some extent destructive of our previous values and ideas. It forces us to be open to the fact that we must be open to the future, with all the dangers and pitfalls of that attitude.

> This hope of creative change through conflict and of discovering that threats to our present identities and self-understandings can become promises of something larger, deeper and more human is a hope derived from our Christian faith. For our faith and hope is in the God whose Spirit is at work after the pattern shown us in Jesus Christ. Thus we know that we can give what we have, that is ourselves however sinful and limited, to the task which is also a struggle and a conflict of helping one another to be more human in every and any area of human activity in which we are involved. For in every area of human life the Spirit of God is at work to use what we are and change what we are, through both our collaboration and our conflict with other human beings.[81]

In the attempt to help human beings be human, and thus also in the attempt to find our own humanity, the Christian is to see as paradigmatic the *way* in which Jesus helped people affirm their humanity. In the first place he did not use his power to assert himself, but 'emptied himself' – a facet of his being which has traditionally been described as *kenosis.* In other words he exercised his power in the manner which Rollo May described as *integrative.* He nourished people so that they might come to a greater appreciation of themselves. This use of 'power' has been called 'the counter-power' of Jesus Christ,[82] to emphasise precisely his rather uncharacteristic use of power. Indeed, this is the only really legitimate way in which power may be exercised at all. This power, and concern, is exercised for humankind in particular situations. It responds to the needs of men and women in particular situations as they confront us in their particularity, and as together the attempt is made to affirm a common humanity.

This of course is not the full story of the 'scandal of Jesus Christ'. He was crucified ignominiously precisely because he posed a threat to the current self-understanding and identity of the Jews. His cross is *the* scandal, pointing above all to the fact that the openness to what it means to be human, and to the future, is always going to be divisive, and decisive – in the sense of provoking a decision. It contradicts all the cherished notions held by men of the meaning of life, of the understanding of what it means to be human, and of our preconceptions of the nature of God.

Such a 'scandal' means for Christians that they are invited to follow this manner of living. What is called for is 'suffering imitation'.[83] It means that Christians should at least be open to the needs of humankind as presented through conflict situations – that is situations where claims are being made by individuals and groups to recognise their specific contributions and differences. In such situations they are to identify with Christ who identifies with the poor and the oppressed and enables them to become human. Jürgen Moltmann sums this up well:

> Thus the real presences (Trinity) of God acquire the character of a 'praesentia explosiva'. Brotherhood with Christ means the suffering and active participation in the history of this God. Its criterion is the history of the crucified and risen Christ. Its power is the sighing and liberating spirit of God.[84]

Conclusions

In this *theology of the wayfarers* then, we have not given a comprehensive Christian theology of human rights. What has been done is simply to examine the notion of human rights as presented to us through the literature of and on human rights, and by the concerns of contemporary human rights movements. In that analysis we have found a number of concepts and ideas which are of central importance – namely, conflict, power, protection and creativity. In the light of this analysis we have made an attempt to ask what is being said about our understanding of humankind and of God. We have been pointed to the sin of men and women in which we participate, and to 'a word of God'. Such an understanding of God as 'skandal' does not seem to be novel. It is clearly outlined in the Gospels. But the understanding of God as 'scandal' has not been a central theme in the theological traditions of Christianity. (In the past a few 'eccentric' theologians have pointed to this understanding of God – Søren Kierkegaard and Karl Barth with his *krisis* theology, for example; but in general the Christian traditions have ignored this.)

God continues to be a 'scandal' to us. He challenges us through the situations of conflict, which are presented to us as claims to human dignity, and for acceptance with the differences inherent in being human. The challenge to Christians is to respond to the 'word of God' as presented to us through human beings who have specific needs as they strive to affirm their humanity. It is in this way that a framework emerges, which helps us to face up to human rights issues. The activity of God points us to the necessity of continually seeking him in the conflicts of men and women. From the Gospels it is clear, as it is also from the experience of the Christian community, that he acts *enabling* people who are oppressed and marginalised to assert their sense of self-significance in even the most dire situations of life. The challenge to the Christian community is to participate in that 'enabling' activity.

Notes

1. In T. Crawford (ed.), *Love, Labour and Liberty:* the eighteenth-century Scottish lyric. Cheadle (Cheshire), Carcanet Press, 1976, p. 63 f. Poem: 'The Tree of Liberty'.
2. The 'Koran of Belfescu' is Wolfe Tone's phrase. see Mary McNeill, *The Life and Times of Mary Ann McCracken 1770-1866,* Dublin, Figgis, 1960, p. 65.
3. For a survey of this activity, and for the different theological approaches adopted, see my article 'The Churches and Human Rights' in *One in Christ* 13(4)77:321-350 – a shorter version of this in *Human Rights Review* 2(2)77:115-129.
4. For the background and approach to the Project and Consultation see 'Human Rights: a Dublin Project 'in *The Month* (new series) 10(11) 77:385-386 and *Journal of Ecumenical Studies* 15(2)78:402-403.
5. Johannes Wollebius *Compendium Theologiae Christianae,* Basel 1626, edited and trans. by John Beardslee III, *Reformed Dogmatics:* Seventeenth-Century Reformed Theology through the Writings of Wollebius, Voetius and Turretin, Grand Rapids, Baker Book House, 1977, p. 29. In adopting this terminology, I am not confining myself to Wollebius' understanding of it.

6. cf. Paul Lehmann's concept 'koinonia ethic' in *Ethics in a Christian Context,* New York, Harper & Row, 1963, p. 45 ff.
7. cf. Søren Kierkegaard *On Authority and Revelation,* trans. Walter Lowrie, New York, Harper Torchbooks, 1966.
8. cf. St. Gregory of Nazianzus *Oratio* XXVIII, 4 in A. J. Mason (ed.), *The Five Theological Orations of Gregory of Nazianzus,* Cambridge, 1899, p. 26; St. John of Damascus, *De Fide Orthodoxa* 1, 4 in P. Schaff and H. Wace, *A Select Library of Nicene and Post – Nicene Fathers* (second series), Vol. 9, Grand Rapids, Eerdmans 1963 (Therefore no Christian community possesses the truth, or God); for a contemporary expression of this, see Presbyterian Church in the U.S. 'A Declaration of Faith', ch. 1, 2 in *The Proposed Book of Confessions,* Atlanta, P.C.U.S., 1976, p. 149.
9. Faith and Order Report, 'God in Nature and History', §13, Lukas Vischer (ed.) *New Directions in Faith and Order:* Bristol 1967, Faith and Order Paper no. 80, Geneva, W.C.C., 1968, p. 30. See also Karl Barth, *The Epistle to the Romans,* trans. Edwyn Hoskyns, London, O.U.P., 1968, p. 425.
10. Jürgen Moltmann, *Theology of Hope,* trans. James Leitch, London, S.C.M., 1967, p. 286, talks of 'homo absconditus' who in the openness to the future continues to find himself or herself. See also H. Richard Niebuhr, *The Meaning of Revelation,* London & New York, Macmillan Paperbacks, 1960, p. 107.
11. cf. Søren Kierkegaard 'The Joy in the Thought that it is not the Way which is Narrow, but the Narrowness which is the Way' in *Edifying Discourses:* A Selection ed. Paul Homer trans. David and Lillian Swenson, Glasgow, Collins Fontana, 1958, p. 201 ff.
12. Jan Comenius, *De Rerum Humanarum Emendatione Consultatio Catholica,* (begun 1645) – General Consultation on the Reform of Human Affairs – Extract in Jeanne Hersch (ed.), *Birthright of Man,* Paris, U.N.E.S.C.O., 1969, p. 249 f.
13. Ibid., p. 250.
14. K. R. Minogue "Natural rights, ideology and the game of life" in Eugene Kamenka and Alice Erh – Soon Tay (eds.) *Human Rights,* London, Edward Arnold, 1978, p. 15.
15. John Kleinig "Human Rights, legal rights and social change" in *ibid.,* p. 46, argues that there is a need for human rights precisely because the moral values of love, care and concern have broken down. There is, however, nothing to suggest that such values have ever been dominant in any society. See Jeanne Hersch, *op.cit.,* for a comprehensive collection of writings and documents spanning the ages and world cultures, which demonstrates that the basic idea of human rights is universal, both geographically and historically.
16. Paul Tillich, *The Courage to Be,* Glasgow, Collins Fontana, 1962.

17. Rollo May, *Power and Innocence,* Glasgow, Collins Fontana, 1976. The author is a psychiatrist in New York.
18. Ibid., p. 20 f. For May, 'power' is to be seen as ethically neither 'good' nor 'evil'.
19. Ibid., pp. 40-45.
20. Cf. the case studies in Frantz Fanon, *The Wretched of the Earth,* trans. Constance Farrington Hammondsworth, Penguin, 1967, pp. 200-255.
21. May, *op. cit.,* pp. 105-110. In his analysis, May notes that competitive power can also be constructive power. The effects of continued repression are well described by Max Scheler, *Ressentiment,* ed. and intro. Lewis Caser, trans. William Holdheim, New York, Schocken Books, 1972, p. 69 f. even although his final conclusions are widely disputed.
22. Jan Comenius in Jeanne Hersch, *op. cit.,* p. 250.
23. e.g. Emile Durkheim, *The Division of Labour in Society,* trans. George Simpson, New York, Free Press, 1964, though his radical attack on the 'social contract' theory is open to dispute.
24. B. J. Diggs (ed.) in his Introduction to *The State, Justice and the Common Good:* An Introduction to Social and Political Philosophy, Brighton, Scott, Foresman & Co., 1974, p. 4, notes that because of the strength of selfishness and self-assertion at the expense of other people, a system of 'voluntary social control' is inadequate as protection.
25. Secretary of State for Northern Ireland, *The Protection of Human Rights by Law in Northern Ireland,* London, H.M.S.O., 1977, Cmnd. 7009.
26. Irish Council for Civil Liberties (I.C.C.L.), *Contempt of Court and the Law,* Report No. 1, Dublin, I.C.C.L., 1976, p. 18 f. On the value of Constitutions, see Christian Bay, *The Structure of Freedom,* Stanford, Stanford Univ. Press, 1958, p. 373.
27. I.C.C.L., *Children's Rights under the Constitution,* Report No. 2, Dublin, I.C.C.L., 1976. In the recent discussion of a Freedom of Information Bill, which is designed to ensure the preservation of an open society so that Government and local authorities are unable to take decisions arbitrarily which might affect individuals and groups in society, appeal is made to Article 40 of the Constitution of Ireland – see I.C.C.L., *An Act Requiring Open Meetings of Public Bodies and Freedom of Information Bill,* Dublin, I.C.C.L., 1978, p. 4.
28. *Constitution of Ireland,* Articles 40-44.
29. *Universal Declaration of Human Rights* Preamble in Ian Brownlie (ed.), *Basic Documents on Human Rights,* Oxford, Clarendon Press, 1971, p. 106.
30. It would be true to say that 'protection' as a concept is basic to any theory of law. For example, Henry Bredemeier in "Law as an Integrative Mechanism" in Vilhelm Aubert (ed.), *Sociology of Law,* Harmondsworth, Penguin, 1969, continually uses the terms 'protection' and 'con-

flict resolution' for the basic understanding of the purpose of law. Perhaps the distinction between law and human rights is that between rules and principles as H. L. A. Hart, *The Concept of Law* Oxford, Clarendon Press, 1961, argues, though R. M. Dworkin, *Taking Rights Seriously,* London, Duckworth, 1977, (and his *The Philosophy of Law,* London, O.U.P., 1977) points to the limitations of this distinction.

31. Richard Claude (ed.), *Comparative Human Rights,* Baltimore, John Hopkins Univ. Press, 1976, p. 16 f.
32. Zechariah Chafee Jr. (ed.), *Documents on Fundamental Human Rights,* New York, Atheneum, 1963, Vol. I, p. 25 f.
33. cf. *U.N. Declaration of Human Rights,* Articles 4; 9; 11. 2; 12; 15.2; 17.2; 20.2 in Brownlie (ed.) *op. cit.* Similarly, *European Convention on Human Rights,* Articles 3; 4; 5.1; 7 in ibid., p. 338 f. and the *Constitution of Ireland,* Articles 40.1, 4.5.
34. As James Fowler "Alienation as a Human Experience" in Francis Eigo (ed.), *From Alienation to At-One-Ness,* Villanova (Pennsylvania), Villanova Univ. Press, 1977 pp. 1-2, notes 'alienation' means separation from something deemed necessary for wholeness or completeness, with the implication that 'what it means to be complete' is known. In the conflict of human rights for which prospective protection is sought, there lies the presupposition that man and woman can be defined in a static way.
35. Jan Comenius in Jeanne Hersch, *op. cit.,* p. 250.
36. Karl Czernetz 'Discussion Paper on *The European Convention on Human Rights as European Law,* Vienna, Fourth Conference of Presidents of European Parliamentary Assemblies, 1977.
37. Ibid., Appendix p. 4. Such manipulation is as true when applied to men as it is in respect of women.
38. For the expansion of human rights through the Appeal to the Constitution see *Ryan v. Attorney General,* 1965, Irish Report 294. See John Kelly, *Fundamental Rights in the Irish Law and Constitution,* Dublin, Allen Figgis & Co., 1967 (2nd edn.), p. 36 ff. and McGee case 1974, Irish Reports 284.
39. See Kadar Asmal "Apartheid South Africa: The Illegitimate Regime" – Paper to the U.N. Lagos Conference, August 1977.
40. Maurice Cranston, *What are Human Rights?* London, Bodley Head, 1973, p. 81.
41. cf. Pius Msekwa "The doctrine of the one-party state in relation to human rights and the rule of law" in International Commission of Jurists, *Human Rights in a One-Party State,* London, Search Press, 1978.
42. cf. *U.N. International Covenant on Economic, Social and Cultural Rights,* 1966, in Brownlie (ed.), *op.cit.,* pp. 199-210.
43. Delhi Resolution 1959, in International Commission of Jurists, *The*

Rule of Law and Human Rights, Geneva, I.C.J., 1966, p. 9. A similar point is made by several contributors in K. Elliott and J. Knight (ed.), *Human Rights in Health:* Symposium held at Ciba Foundation, London, 1963, Ciba Foundation Symposium 23 (new series), Amsterdam and London, Associated Scientific Publishers, 1974.

44. H. L. A. Hart, *op. cit.,* p. 42 cf., J. E. S. Fawcett, "A Bill of Rights for the U.K." in *Human Rights Review,* 1 (1) 76:57-64. The notion of duties is emphasised in *Constitution of Ireland,* Article 9, 2; and in *Constitution (Fundamental Law) of the Union of Soviet Socialist Republics,* Moscow, 1977, Articles, 59-69.
45. e.g. Charles Elliott, "Financial resources: present and future" in K. Elliott and J. Knight, *op.cit.,* 3-18.
46. See e.g. Maurice Cranston, *op.cit.,* p. 21 f. cf. the U.N. Declaration which many lawyers regard as part of International Law, binding not only on relationships between societies but also within societies, e.g. W. P. Thompson at the World Alliance of Reformed Churches Centennial Assembly, 1977, 'The U.N. Declaration is an articulation of the law of the nations'. It was this universal character and application – and the binding of future generations – to which Edmund Burke objected in the French Declaration of the Rights of Man in his *Reflections on the Revolution in France,* 1790, (ed.) Conor Cruise O'Brien, Harmondsworth, Penguin, 1968.
47. Thus an organisation like Amnesty International may argue for its concern for human rights in every nation. The same principle seems to have guided the signatories to the Final Act of the Conference on Security and Co-operation in Europe. (the 'Helsinki Agreement'), even although the U.S.S.R. at times expresses its uneasiness over the implications of this. The U.S.S.R. has however fulfilled its obligation to publish the text of the Helsinki Agreement. Other signatory nations, including Ireland, have still not published the text. See Conference on Security and Co-operation in Europe, *Final Act,* Helsinki, 1975, p. 135: "The text of this Final Act will be published in each participatory State, which will disseminate it and make it known as widely as possible".
48. H. L. A. Hart, *op. cit.:* 176. It seems to me that this statement has validity even if one is not prepared to accept the author's 'legal positivism'.
49. Isaiah Berlin, "Two Concepts of Liberty", in *Four Essays on Liberty,* London, O.U.P., 1969: 118. It does not seem to me to be correct to link the concept of human rights with altruism as David Owen does in *Human Rights,* London, Cape, 1978, p. 2 f.
50. James Fowler, *op. cit.,* p. 1.
51. See W. D. Davies, "From Tyranny to Liberation": Pauline Experience of Alienation and Reconciliation in Francis Eigo, *op. cit.:* 93-131.
52. See the paper by Fr. Gabriel Daly, O.S.A. cf., my article "The Christian

and Human Rights" in *Doctrine and Life* 29 (2) 78:77-92, in which I treat the concept of sin among other topics. The reality of alienation or estrangement is called "the question which overshadows all" by F. W. Dillistone, *The Christian Understanding of Atonement,* London, Nisbet, 1968:2.

53. Michael Tippett, *A Child of our Time,* London, Schott & Co., 1944, cf. Dietrich Bonhoeffer's prayer in prison where in the midst of human misery and atrocity he prays with his fellow prisoners *"In me* there is darkness" – *In Letters and Papers from Prison* (ed.) Eberhard Bethge, New York, MacMillan, 1972 edn., p. 139.
54. Reinhold Niebuhr, *Moral Man and Immoral Society:* A study in Ethics and Politics, London, S.C.M., 1963.
55. Ibid., p. xx.
56. Lord Kilbrandon (chairman), *Report of the Royal Commission on the Constitution,* 1969–73, London, H.M.S.O., 1974, (Cmnd. 5960) Memorandum of Dissent by Lord Crowther-Hunt and Prof. Peacock.
57. Such an approach too often justifies 'the ideology of national security'. This is not to deny the importance of the need to phrase and re-phrase continually an idea of the 'common good'.
58. David Jenkins, *The Contradiction of Christianity:* The Edward Cadbury Lectures in the University of Birmingham, 1974. London, S.C.M., 1976, p. 9, also Nils Ehrenstrom and Walter Muelder (ed.), *Institutionalism and Christian Unity,* London, S.C.M., 1963. cf. Netherlands Council of Churches Faith and Order Report "Giving Account of the Hope in an Ambiguous Existence" in Faith and Order, *Giving Account of the Hope Today,* Geneva, W.C.C., 1976. It is imperative that the Churches match their ecclesiologies to the reality of the church and not to some idealised state.
59. David Jenkins, ibid.
60. See, for example, Reinhold Niebuhr, *The Nature and Destiny of Man,* (Gifford Lectures, 1939), 2 vols., London, Nisbet, 1941, 1943; Nicolas Berdyaev, *The Meaning of History,* London, Bles. 1936; John McIntyre, *Christian Doctrine of History,* Edinburgh, Oliver & Boyd, 1957; Oscar Cullmann, *Christ and Time,* London, S.C.M., 1957; Jürgen Moltmann, *op. cit.;* Paul Tillich, *Systematic Theology,* Vol. III, London, Nisbet, 1964: 315-452. see also R. G. Collingwood, *The Idea of History,* London, O.U.P., 1961.
61. Paul Tillich, ibid., p. 340.
62. H. Richard Niebuhr, *The Meaning of Revelation,* op. cit., p. 61.
63. Paul Tillich, *op. cit.,* p. 320.
64. Ibid., p. 332, cf. Gerhard Ebeling, *Word and Faith,* Philadelphia, Fortress, 1963 and *The Word of God and Tradition,* London, Collins, 1968, where 'word of God' is seen as interpreted event.

65. Wolfhart Pannenberg, *Basic Questions in Theology,* Vol. I, trans. George Kehm, 1970, p. 15.
66. Ernst Fuchs quoted by Ronald Gregor Smith, *The Doctrine of God,* Glasgow, Collins, 1970 p. 32.
67. Jürgen Moltmann, *op. cit.,* p. 91.
68. See particularly Gerhard von Rad, *Old Testament Theology,* trans. David Stalker Edinburgh, Oliver & Boyd, 1962, Vol. I and his *The Problem of the Hexateuch and Other Essays,* Edinburgh, Oliver & Boyd, 1966; Martin Noth, *The Laws in the Pentateuch and Other Studies,* Edinburgh, Oliver & Boyd, 1966.
69. Edmund Jacob, *Theolcgy of the Old Testament,* trans. A. W. Heathcote and P. Allcock, London, Hodder & Stoughton, 1958, p. 127 and 129.
70. cf. Rudolf Bultmann, *The Gospel of John,* trans. G. R. Beasley – Murray, Oxford, Blackwell, 1971, p. 20.
71. André Dumas, "A Society which creates Justice" in *Ecumenical Review* 30(3)78 p. 214. cf. Wolfhart Pannenberg (ed.), *Revelation as History,* trans. David Granskou, London, MacMillan, 1968 – particularly the editor's 'Dogmatic Theses on the Doctrine of Revelation', pp. 123-158.
72. André Dumas, *Political Theology and the Life of the Church,* trans. John Bowden, London, S.C.M., 1978 – particularly chs. 2 and 4.
73. David Jenkins points to this, without elucidating it, in *The Humanum Studies 1969-75:* A Collection of Documents, Geneva, W.C.C., 1975, p. 72.
74. Jürgen Moltmann, *The Crucified God,* trans. R. A. Wilson and John Bowden, London, S.C.M., 1974, p. 338.
75. For the Old Testament background, which I shall not examine here, see the relevant section of Gustav Stählin 'skandalon' in G. Kittel (ed.), *Theological Dictionary of the New Testament,* trans. G. W. Bromiley, Grand Rapids, Eerdmans, 1971, Vol. VII, pp. 339-358. Stählin notes that this is a particularly Hebraic idea which the Christians of Greek background found difficult to grasp.
76. Enda MacDonagh, "The Judgment of Scandal" in *Concilium* 7, 1977, (Canon Law), p. 89.
77. While this passage is regarded as a very late intrusion into the Gospel manuscript, it is not inconceivable that Jesus could have had such an encounter. Even if he did not, the scribe who included this incident obviously saw it as a logical extension of Jesus' dealings with people.
78. There is now a considerable literature pertaining to the 'group nature' of these categories in the life of Judaism. e.g. Julio de Santa Ana, *Good News to the Poor:* The Challenge of the Poor in the History of the Church, Geneva, W.C.C. – C.C.P.D., 1977.
79. For a fuller exegisis of this passage see Floyd Filson, *The Gospel according to St. Matthew,* London, A. & C. Black, 1971 (second edition), pp. 127-135.

80. Author's italics. Enda MacDonagh, *Gift and Call:* Towards a Christian Theology of Morality. Dublin, Gill and MacMillan, 1975, p. 34.
81. David Jenkins, *op. cit.,* p. 53.
82. Study Department of the Churches' Participation in Development, *Domination and Development:* the role of the Churches. Geneva, W.C.C., 1974, ch. 4.
83. Gerhard Barth, "Matthew's Understanding of the Law", in Bornkamm, Barth and Held, *Tradition and Interpretation in Matthew,* trans. Percy Scott, London, S.C.M., 1963, p. 101.
84. Jürgen Moltmann, *op. cit.,* p. 338.

CHAPTER 15

CHRISTIAN THEOLOGY OF HUMAN RIGHTS

ROSEMARY HAUGHTON

Handling theologically the issue of Human Rights is especially difficult because the area of human experience evoked by this phrase is highly charged emotionally, but is also recognised as a complex one, requiring legal finesse and careful reasoning. It is difficult to bridge this gap between the inevitability and propriety of strong feeling about human suffering and the necessity for cool, impartial, and highly technical formulation if people are to be protected from injustice, and it is in this gap that theological analysis has to take place. Theology is concerned with the total human situation designated; not just the suffering of the oppressed but the things that happen to the oppressor; not just the sense of outrage at the twisting of justice to the service of power and greed but the reason why people should feel outraged, and whether they are right to do so, and why some don't, and what this tells us about ourselves. And so, more deeply, we have to ask whence and why the power of humans to oppress each other, and where is the theological point of insertion of a demand that they should not? It is essential that theology should be able to justify its analysis not only as rational but as corresponding to that elusive but essential human sense of reality, of the inarticulate twinges of response or revolt by which people react to each others' experiences and behaviour, yet it must not accept these reactions as necessarily appropriate, since the cultural conditioning of conscience is a basic part of human development, but also it is never *totally* successful.

What I am attempting to do here is not to present a full theology of human rights. What I want to do is simply to suggest a framework within which we can begin to think as Christians about this subject. But, if my sketch of the theological terms of reference is right, this cannot mean a framework of thought only, it must mean a framework within which reflection can articulate itself in moral direction, and both can wrestle with the basic experiences in prayer.

As a matter of fact, this apparently formidable undertaking proves to be, if not easy, at least simple, for there is one place where we are quite accustomed to listen to, and join in, the human attempt to make sense theologically of agonising experience in precisely this way – not excluding either the emotional or the technical but emerging mostly from the gap between them, in which the really important human things are done and discovered. The place is the psalms, and it seems to me that I can't do better than try to feel my way into the mentality of *Psalm* 72(73), and uncover the theology on which it is based.

It is not a very comfortable analysis, but is is a very catholic one, in the sense that the psalmist is struggling with real experience at many levels, refusing to exclude any, or to ease the existential problem by narrowing the terms of reference, terms imposed by the desire to enquire fully into so crucial an area of human life as the one we sum up under the rather 'enlightenment' heading of human rights.

The first thing that strikes me about this psalm is that, as the psalmist views the way in which some human beings oppress others, he seems to be concerned first of all not with the suffering of the innocent and oppressed but with the malice of those who 'plan oppression'. He counts himself among those whose human rights are violated. Yet he spends no time either describing or lamenting his sufferings, nor is he demanding redress, as some of the psalms do. What he is wrestling with is precisely the theology of the thing.

The description of those who oppress is not denunciatory in tone, it is almost detached, it is a careful and really spine-chilling description of people who have successfully imposed their demands, and their self-assessment, on those over whom their wealth gives them power. It is not so much the wickedness of the oppressor which causes the anguished questioning of this psalm as his complete success, not only in getting what he wants but in getting even the oppressed to accept this as inevitable. This is so exactly true to our experience that it seems shocking. It takes us right to the heart of the matter for the real theological problem is not the actual suffering of the oppressed and exploited, however horrible this may be; after all, an equal degree of suffering might have come to them by natural causes. What shocks and revolts and causes such painful questioning in a theological context is that this suffering can so easily be acceptable even to the sufferers, so that in a sense the oppressors take over the role of God. 'They have set their mouths in the heavens and their tongues dictate to the earth'. The whole machinery of propaganda is evoked by that sentence, and reminds us not only of the more overtly oppressive dictatorships but of the low-profile but damnably effective methods by which the wretched and needy in our own countries are persuaded that what they 'really want', or must submit to, is whatever is likely to enrich and still more greatly empower those who already have power and wealth. 'Their minds seethe with plots, they scoff, they speak with malice, from on high they plan oppression'. It is a soberly factual description of the kind of conversations one might overhear in the consultations of big business, of government, of armed forces, of trades unions. It would not be true of every consultation and planning session, but the thing rings true even from the limited and toned-down evidence to be gained from discussion broadcast on television between men representing such powers. This is exactly the atmosphere the psalmist evoked – the undertone of bland viciousness, the basic assumption of the worthlessness of opponents and the gullibility of the poor, the barely concealed intention of dominating others 'for their own good', a good they must learn to recognise and accept. And the results are plain to see, in a system which ensures that 'for them there are no pains, their bodies are sound and sleek: They have no share in men's sorrows; they are not stricken like other men'.

What we are up against here is sin in a very fundamental Pauline sense. It is not sin as individually wicked acts, or even the living of a wicked life, but rather of life lived according to totally false values, so deeply assimilated, so well integrated into every aspect of life, that it becomes hard to discern what precisely is wrong. Those who have made this successful cultural adjustment to evil values have done so because they require a great deal of money in order to have the things which appear to them desirable, and because the power to command those things has itself become something necessary, to the point at which it becomes unimaginable to be deprived of them. But the 'internalising' of the process of getting and keeping power and money requires that those who do it *approve* what is done, including all that must be done to perpetuate the way of life which they have created and by which they can accept themselves. This need to approve what is done has to be very powerful if it is to make possible the complete ignoring of evil consequences for others from the pursuit of wealth, and this power is so great that it imposes itself not only on the small circle of the wealthy power-holders, but on all those on whom they depend for the continunace of their affluence – that is, on the oppressed themselves. So, 'untroubled, they grow in wealth'. They really *are* untroubled, their lives are comfortable and full of good things – really good things such as hospitality and patronage of the arts and of learning, and so on. All this depends on the denial to others of the possibilities they themselves enjoy, but this cannot be admitted, it would be morally intolerable to realise this, and so the necessary doctrinal adjustments are made, convincingly explaining how the situation is inevitable, or will in the end bring affluence to all, or is, somehow, actually beneficial to all even now. They really *believe* such things, and their belief is pressed upon all, so that it becomes almost impossible to question the propriety of what is being done.

Even those who suffer most, those whose lives are manifestly being ruined by the system, and know it, can find no way to express what is wrong because it seems there are no other criteria of judgment than these of the ones who have created and perpetuated the evil! They say, 'How can God know. Does the Most High take any notice?' For it is not clear to what extent God can be *separated* from the situation. We can only refer ourselves to God's judgment of the violation of human rights by a sinful elite when we can conceive of God's judgment as *over against* the situation which causes the suffering. 'Does the Most High take any notice?' implies that we aren't sure whether he can really be involved in our situation without being subsumed in it.

The only way in which it seems possible to hold on to a concept of God which might offer an alternative to capitulation to the oppressor's God is by reference to objective law. To 'keep one's heart pure' in this sense is to try to live according to the clear cut demands of religion and faith, no matter how futile and demanding they may seem. Yet the very effort to do so seems to be evacuated of power and meaning by the alternative, and much more evidently effective, moral and cultural categories of the 'wicked', since to 'wash my hands in innocence' in this sense produces nothing but 'punishment', and with it a sense of guilt. The use of the word 'punishment' itself implies that *wrong* has been done, and the whole difficulty of the situation lies in the fact that it is the 'innocent' who feel guilty and inadequate and morally distressed. It is all, it seems, 'useless'. The poor and suffering are driven to '*envy* of the proud', not so much because they are wealthy and successful as because they are 'untroubled'.

This is the context, the essential, sinful situation, in which the question of human rights has to be viewed theologically. It is indeed hard to make sense of it, how to condemn the oppressor who may be, for instance, a happy and generous family, full of good will and idealism, and how to articulate the rights of the oppressed who may be servile, passive, uninterested, or merely negatively vengeful and quite uninterested in any future possibility except that of equalling the life style of the powerful, whether by replacing them, or by being accepted by them. No wonder this problem seems 'too hard for my mind to understand', yet there remains the obstinate conviction that there *must* be a way to make sense of this, to assert a different set of criteria for goodness in human life. 'I strove to fathom this problem', a way must be found, and at present the struggle to fathom the problem is being carried on in many ways, notably in the development of a 'theology of liberation' which has itself been through an interesting evolution.

The theological insight which is at the heart of the psalmist's breakthrough to understanding is summed up in the word 'phantom', I think. A phantom is unreal, unsolid, at best an unbodied appearance, more probably sheer imagination. The idea is that the whole vast, apparently indestructible, cultural system which imposes oppression is as unstable as a dream, precisely because it is built on *unreal,* essentially contradictory, *untrue* philosophical and economic and political doctrines. The psalmist calls himself 'stupid' because he did not understand. We are concerned here with the ability to see facts clearly. The facts, as perceived when we 'pierce the mysteries of God' are not as the oppressor would have us think. The whole construction, impregnable as it seems, is nothing but a card-house. 'How slippery the paths on which you set them, you make them slide to destruction'; the whole set up is basically unstable because its foundations are falsehood – that is, unreality.

It is important to get this clear, because the actual political struggle to achieve recognition of basic human rights in many countries and in many different contexts presents itself to us, naturally enough, as a contest between two powers of the same kind, though it seems often enough as if they were unequally matched, for the forces of oppression can muster such tremendous strength, since they are, by definition, un-handicapped by considerations of justice or humanity in organising their power. But to accept this as an accurate picture of the nature of the struggle is, in a sense, to concede defeat. It is to enter the battle on the enemy's ground and on his terms, in which case the outcome is scarcely in doubt, however bravely and obstinately we may carry on the fight. 'They dictate to the earth' and when we think of the struggle for human rights in the terms offered us by the double-talk language of conscious or unconscious oppression we are allowing those tongues to dictate to us; we are, in fact, among those who 'turn to follow them and drink in all their words'.

To consider the struggle for human rights in terms of a political philosophy of whatever kind which has no reference to any absolute moral standards is, then, to say 'How can God know?' We are so conditioned by the influence of 'non-directive' counselling and 'value-free' education that we find it difficult to say in so many words that political and social questions can be related to a moral assertion which is final and truthful and to which all attempts at justice must relate themselves. We feel embarrassed and apologetic before the scornful gaze of those to whom the relativeness of moral judgment is axiomatic, and who are deeply convinced, of course, of the absolute moral rightness of this particular stance. Yes indeed, 'I was filled with envy of the proud, when I saw how the wicked prosper'. Unlike mine, it seems, their consciences are as 'sound and sleek' as their bodies. And since de facto power can and does create the conditions of everyday life for everybody, and since these conditions are also to a large extent the conditions of possible thought, the ability to resist the confident doctrine of oppression is rare, and easily undermined. 'My feet came close to stumbling, my steps had almost slipped'.

Why only 'almost'? Why, in fact, is it that a resistance *does* persist, that, historically, we always do find a measure, however small and politically ineffective, of resistance to oppression? I think it is useful to ask that question, because the answer must be the one the psalmist gives. It is not, primarily, an answer discovered by reasoning about the situation, because, as we have seen when the terms of the argument are set for us by those who create the situation reason is heavily handicapped. ('Reason, your viceroy in me, is captur'd and proves weak or untrue', said John Donne, with his usual staggering accuracy). Reasons and careful argument are needed, indeed, to support and explain what is discovered, but the discovery of the power to resist and the reasons, for resisting come first of all from a deeper level than that. They come from a kind of human commitment which we can name as 'fidelity'. Fidelity to some basic awareness of what it means to be human is what is required. It is to this obscure but very tough allegiance that the psalmist appeals in order to break free from the vicious circle of thought and action created by the oppressor. 'If I should speak like that I should betray the race of your sons'. It seems at first sight, a strange statement, because it has nothing to do with actually tackling the causes of suffering. This is a strong inner revulsion, an intuitive reaction to something which is obscurely perceived as wrong, in a basic and absolute way. To 'speak like that' means to surrender to the oppressor, and when this is perceived, then if there is any remaining core of fidelity which has not been corrupted by pervasive falsity it will revolt, and this revolt is so strong that it can, indeed, enable us to 'pierce the mysteries of God'.

It is interesting that the word used is 'mysteries'. This is not a matter of mustering better arguments, it is first of all a matter of being in touch with the basic relationship of humankind to God, expressed by the word fidelity – God's absolutely faithful love, to which the only possible response is, also, an unconditional fidelity. This is the ultimate stronghold of humanness, if this is betrayed there is nothing left, hence the absoluteness of the refusal to surrender, even when no words can be found to explain the refusal, when the appeal is inarticulate and appears purely obstinate and unreasonable.

It is only when this central assertion of fidelity has been made that it becomes possible to see how it is, in fact, justified by the facts. It is in the light of this act of faith and defiance that the unreality of the huge and menacing structures of injustice become apparent. It is clear, then, that they are indeed 'phantoms', that in the daylight of truth they are 'like a dream one wakes from'. But, in the psalm, it is only the Lord who can 'dismiss them as phantoms', and until his vision is fully shared these phantoms have a very real destructive power. We, sharing the world with the wicked, are not able to see so clearly all the time, but it is vitally important, if action is to be taken on behalf of justice, that we strive to see respect for human rights not as one political option open to the powerful, who must be persuaded, blackmailed or bribed to choose it, but as one aspect of the only true vision of what human beings actually are, and a condition of their becoming what they are intended to be.

It really matters to say, and believe (even if we don't actually feel it that way, and even if it is very hard) that the world's unjust power structures *are* phantoms, bad dreams, unreal and therefore finally *not there.* This is especially so because we know that we, all of us in the West, are not in the position of the psalmist, who 'washed his hands in innocence', but, at least partially, in that of the wicked. We are those whose 'bodies are sound and sleek', and whether we like it or not they are so because others are poor, underpaid, exploited and often politically oppressed. We cannot avoid profiting to some extent from the plots of the oppressors. Because of this inescapable fact it is important that we become as clear as possible in our minds about the moral status of our prosperity, and the things it does to our thinking and feeling unless we struggle, like the psalmist, to fathom the problem, which is our own problem from both ends: as those who oppress, and as those who are 'stumbling' in mind because of oppression. The unvengeful realism of the psalmist about the fate of oppressors is like a cold shower. He is saying that all the complex structures of prosperity built in disregard for the human rights of the poor are simply going to collapse, sooner or later. And we know, historically, that this has always eventually happened, and economically that it seems very likely to happen soon.

This is a mind-boggling thing to cope with. On the one hand our future well-being is threatened, and on the other hand we are clearly expected to feel satisfaction about this. This is right, the phantoms of night *must* vanish; and if we are, in fact, relying on them, willingly or not, we are in for a rude awakening.

It is at this point that we need to look at the last verses of the psalm, and see how the whole thing moves into a different key, one which at first seems to have nothing to do with the earlier parts. It is pure praise of God's love, utter abandonment to his will and his glory. It seems to have lost touch with the situation described before, and to have moved away from all concern with earthly things. 'To be near God is my happiness'. Yes, but this is not an evasion, this is a matter of being in the place where truth is to be perceived, where it is possible to be 'pure of heart', no matter what the circumstances, and therefore to know what is to be done in order to make the known truth live in daily fact.

The psalmist confesses that all the bewilderment, and bitterness, the temptation to feel that all effort to 'keep my heart pure' is futile and merely wishful thinking, was the result of being 'stupid'. To be stupid is to be unable to learn, to believe untrue things, to have, above all, a truly deceptive view of things, which are seen according to some simple but inaccurate model. It refers to an inability to perceive truth which should be obvious, and often the accusation of 'stupidity' carries an implication of culpability. 'Don't be so stupid' means, you don't *have* to be blind, unaware. 'I was stupid and did not understand, no better than a beast in your sight' certainly means this. We are not *willing* to see the truth, because it will deprive us of the comforting reasons for a situation of injustice from which we profit. Starkly, we are 'stupid' if we refuse to see that the deprivation of human rights is not a gratuitous crime committed by some perverse people and which they must be persuaded to end, but something necessarily imposed in order to maintain the system which keeps some of us so safe and comfortable, for a time at least.

But even the 'stupid' and embittered are, whether they know it or not, enmeshed not only in the network of injustice but also in the net of God's love, which is their being. 'Yet I was always in your presence, you were holding me by my right hand'. Even when I was 'filled with envy', even when I 'almost slipped' there was still, somewhere, that firm grip, that central contact with truth which ultimately forced a recognition, demanded a response. So, having acknowledged the ultimate fidelity, I accept the guidance which is always available. 'You will guide me by your counsel, and so you will lead me into glory'. To be led implies choice. The Lord was always there, but I have to choose – to be led, to be guided, he does not drag me. The lines of mystical love which follow are not meant to separate the seeker after truth from the anguish of human choice, but to put him in the only place where these choices can be made with freedom – freedom not only from corrupting arguments and sublimal influences but also from guilt over unavoidable complicity in the violation of the basic rights of others' It is only when 'God is my possession for ever' that I am able, as the prophet Micah puts it, to 'act justly, and to love tenderly and to walk humbly with your God'. To 'act justly' is what is needed, but we see, now, that true justice can only be perceived by those who are 'near God'. Only they can resist the falsity seeking to penetrate mind and heart; they have made the Lord God their refuge and *therefore* they can 'tell of all his work' at the gates of the city. They can communicate forcibly and accurately and in practical ways what is required to be done, under the counsel of God, so that the 'glory' in human society may be revealed.

It is in considering the nature of this glory that we have to shift into a more explicitly Christian theological awareness. To the psalmist, the solidarity of the people, and his own involvement in them which is the basis of his recovery of vision ('If I should speak like this I should betray the race of your sons') is implicit, so fundamental as to be scarcely noticed. And this implicit fact is the basis of concern for social justice from a theological point of view, because it is not just a question of saving the oppressed and punishing the wicked but of somehow restoring a truthful relationship between people. The violation of human rights springs, as we have seen, from a false vision of life and of society. The 'glory' to which the psalmist hopes to be led is not a private paradise but, in the light of the Incarnation, the revelation of the true nature of human society, in which all are involved in an exchange of divine life and love, because that is what constitutes them, that is their basic being. The theological assertion which underlies all protest, or endeavour, against the violation of human rights is that human beings (together with all creation) are, when viewed truthfully, involved in what Charles Williams called the 'web of glory'. Their exchanges of love are not accidental, moments of beauty when they reach out from their essential isolation to give something to each other, but rather a brief but genuine revelation of the underlying reality which is the work of the Church to announce, the reality of incorporation in Christ which is to be (by the power of the Spirit) entered into, celebrated and released from its unnatural restrictions of sin, until the final glory is revealed. When we consider the facts of oppression and injustice in the light of this, the implacable nature of the opposition required of Christians becomes apparent. There is absolutely no room for compromise, which is the reason for the 'malice' and 'plots' of those whose interests commit them to the perpetuation of the system of oppression, and also for the bitterness and bewilderment of the questioning heart. But it is, besides, the reason for the demand for holiness, the cry of utter love and surrender of the whole being to God, by which the glory is perceived and may then be shared.

The sharing springs from this. It is a sharing of vision but of a vision which is incarnate. It is a sharing by word and act, and 'act' includes political and social action, and *also* (not as an afterthought but integrally) personal response to the facts perceived, at the level of daily life and its exchanges, and at the level of faith and prayer also.

The crossing-over point, which is only implicit in the psalm, is explicit in the revelation of God's love in Christ. The place of exchange, where self-giving to God becomes translated into whatever action is appropriate, is the cross. The frustration and bitterness become a suffering love, the pain and and anger of the oppressed are taken to the point of redemption and at that point they are to be received – as a gift of love – by those who are called to share that death. It is from this point that the real nature of oppression can be perceived, the sheer reality of the nightmare world which opposes itself to the network of glory shared through the cross, and from which, also, we perceive the way – the only way – in which that hideous phantom can be exorcised. From one point of view, the temptations of Jesus are all a demand that the phantom structures of evil should be taken at their own valuation. They look so solid – but their insubstantiality is revealed when it is realised that they exclude the possibility of exchange, on which the whole economy of divine love is based. They all turn back on the individual, exercising and holding power, preserving and displaying a self whose only meaning is in that exercise. And, in order to continue to be, this power must increasingly isolate itself from challenge and reinforce its self-valuation in that isolation by the exercise of its power to control, appropriate and impress. It is therefore the exact opposite of the way of exchange of which the cross is both symbol and means.

It may be unexpected that the conclusion to which all this leads seems to situate itself in the area of mystical theology rather than in the area of the 'social Gospel'. But these divisions are both arbitrary and frequently misleading, and they are the reason why much social and missionary activity, and ecclesiastical politics, have been so easily and so frequently corrupted. The only possible way for a Christian to approach the subject of human rights, of justice and injustice, is to do so from the point of view which sees human beings as Jesus saw them, that is, as people to die for. It is only in the light of that vision that it becomes possible to talk about justice at all. Justice is *rightness,* that is, the awareness of how things basically are between people, an awareness which immediately shows up the places where the real state of affairs is being contradicted by false assumptions and the false actions consequent on them. Injustice is the acting out of untruth about human life, therefore the assertion of human rights is the attempt to recover truth and make it actual. And this can and must be done at all levels, since truth is incarnate. It is done at the level of diplomacy and political action, both official and unofficial; at the level of 'consciousness raising' and direct local action to relieve the results of injustice; at the level of radical re-assessment of personal life-style, as a form of political protest, as an attempt to reduce actual dependence on the fruits of oppression, and as an aspect of the identification with the oppressed, which must also be present in all other levels of involvement. The final level is that of prayer, of deliberate involvement in the exchange of love through the cross, 'dying each other's life, living each other's death'. And this is basic because it makes sense of all the others. Just as the Christian body exists not just for itself but for all humankind, acting as the 'medium of exchange' with Christ's cross as its centre, so in this particular area the work of the Christian may or may not be to be involved overtly in the struggle for human rights, and not all who are so involved are Christian. The essential Christian work is to be consciously involved in the exchange which the cross represents, in whatever way is given to the individual to pursue, which may appear to be nothing much at all, and that 'nothing' may be more powerful, in the network of glory, than the most high-powered diplomacy. The ultimate 'nothing' which can be done is, of course, martyrdom, and that is a good sign of the kind of thing we are really involved in once we start talking about human rights. Perhaps that is a good place to end. Martyrdom is the ultimate involvement, in any cause; it is the point at which the phantom structures have to suppress the challenge which threatens to expose them. It is also the point of 'uselessness', of being nothing. It is the point of exchange, the cross itself, where human endeavour and dedication hand over to the sheer glory.

> 'What else have I in heaven but you?
> Apart from you I want nothing on earth.
> My body and my heart faint for joy;
> God is my possession for ever.'

APPENDIX

STATEMENT OF THE CONSULTATION

At its concluding session, the International Consultation on Human Rights, sponsored by the Irish School of Ecumenics, issued the following statement:

We, the members of the International Consultation on Human Rights, sponsored by the Irish School of Ecumenics in Dublin, 30 November to 4 December 1978, urge the Pontifical Commission for Justice and Peace, the Churches' Commission on International Affairs of the World Council of Churches, national and local Justice and Peace Commissions and Councils and Federations of Churches, as well as other Institutions from which we come:

1. to reaffirm their support for the *Universal Declaration of Human Rights* and to press on Governments the incorporation into domestic law of the international instruments designed to protect these rights, such as the *European Convention on Human Rights* or the *International Covenants on Civil and Political Rights.*
2. to promote study and action on the following Human Rights issues which received particular attention from the Consultation:

   i. the interdependence and inseparability of civil, political, social, cultural and economic rights;
   ii. the right of women to equal participation and leadership in both the civil and religious structures of society;
   iii. the involvement of First World Christians and Churches in political and economic structures which oppress Third World peoples, e.g. investment policies;
   iv. the rights of prisoners and the treatment of prisoners throughout the world;
   v. the rights of minorities in an increasingly pluralistic world.

The Consultation, meeting on the Thirteenth Anniversary of the Universal Declaration of Human Rights, expressed the fervent hope that humankind would not have to wait much longer for the full implementation of the rights enunciated in that Declaration.

INDEX

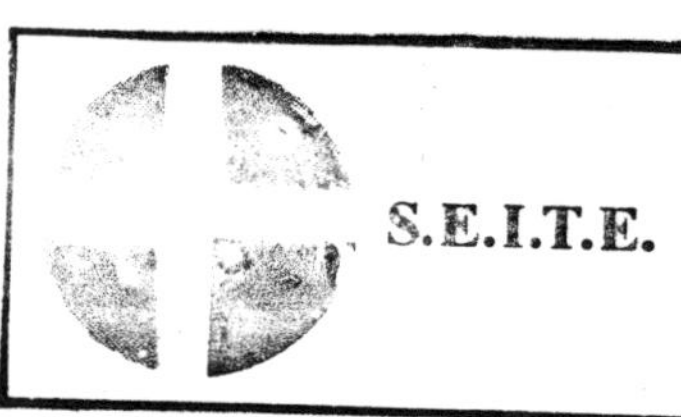
S.E.I.T.E.